CR ZYHORSE

Flying Apache Attack Helicopters with the
1st Cavalry Division in Iraq, 2006–2007

SCHIFFER MILITARY
4880 Lower Valley Road   Atglen, PA 19310

Daniel M. McClinton
CW4, US ARMY (RET.)

HORSE

TO CHUCK, SHANE, KEITH, AND JASON

Copyright © 2022 by Daniel M. McClinton

Library of Congress Control Number: 2022932095

Designed by Justin Watkinson
Type set in MicrogrammaDBolExt/Minion Pro/Univers LT Std

ISBN: 978-0-7643-6494-5
Printed in India

Published by Schiffer Publishing, Ltd.
4880 Lower Valley Road
Atglen, PA 19310
Phone: (610) 593-1777; Fax: (610) 593-2002
Email: Info@schifferbooks.com
Web: www.schifferbooks.com

For our complete selection of fine books on this and related subjects, please visit our website at www.schifferbooks.com. You may also write for a free catalog.

Schiffer Publishing's titles are available at special discounts for bulk purchases for sales promotions or premiums. Special editions, including personalized covers, corporate imprints, and excerpts, can be created in large quantities for special needs. For more information, contact the publisher.

We are always looking for people to write books on new and related subjects. If you have an idea for a book, please contact us at proposals@schifferbooks.com.

CONTENTS

INTRODUCTION

This is a story about my war experience in Iraq from September 2006 through December 2007, during a period that is commonly referred to by the military as Operation Iraqi Freedom 06-08 (also known as OIF 06-08).

I gratefully acknowledge all the help and suggestions that have been given me by friends and coworkers. All credit for readability and proper grammar goes to them, and any mistakes, misquotations, and misstatements are mine and mine alone. I have attempted to present the facts of what occurred to the best of my ability, and if I have left out something or misidentified a unit or person, it was purely unintentional on my part. I have purposely left out the names of some individuals.

First a little bit about me. I was born and raised in Waco, Texas, by my mom and dad, Marjorie and Jim McClinton. I had a normal childhood where I played Little League and Pee Wee Football. I rode my bike around the neighborhood and played "army," going on patrols with my toy M-1 rifle or machine gun, emulating such TV icons as the men on *Rat Patrol* and the soldiers on *Combat*.

My first exposure to Army helicopters was at the Heart of Texas Fair and Rodeo, which was held every year at the fairgrounds in Waco, located about four blocks away from my house. During the years of my youth the Army brought an incredible amount of hardware, including tanks, military vehicles, and even helicopters, to the fair, which ran for the first week in October. It was there that I first saw and sat in tanks, armored personnel carriers, and, most importantly to me, the OH-58 Kiowa scout, UH-1 Huey, and AH-1 Cobra attack helicopters. The bookshelves in my bedroom were always lined with anything I could find to read about military flying and with plastic models of aircraft past and present, which I spent many an hour building and painting. I also went through reams of paper drawing and sketching all manner of airplanes and helicopters over the years. One might say I was a bit obsessed.

As a teen I joined the Civil Air Patrol and entertained the desire to become a fighter pilot in the United States Air Force (USAF). I read everything I could get my hands on about the subject and knew every aircraft designation by heart. Unfortunately, for myself and the USAF, when I went to college I wasn't exactly focused on my studies, my grades suffered, and eventually that particular dream faded away.

Even though I graduated with a degree in drafting and design and had a job with a defense contractor as a mechanical designer in the Dallas–Fort Worth area, I never lost the desire to fly and serve the nation.

In 1985, I went down to the Army recruiter in Garland, Texas, and told them I'd like to enlist in the Army and go to flight school. In the spring of 1986, after being accepted as a warrant officer candidate, I went to basic training at Fort Sill, Oklahoma, and then to the Warrant Officer Entry Course at Fort Rucker, Alabama.

I graduated from flight school in October 1987 and was off to my first assignment as a WO1 to D Company, 4th Battalion, 3rd Aviation Regiment, in the 2nd Armored Division at Fort Hood, Texas, flying the Bell UH-1H helicopter, which is more commonly known as the "Huey." During my time flying the Huey, I had duties in addition to flying, which included performing as a company nuclear biological and chemical (NBC) officer, battalion aviation life support officer, the III Corps commander's primary pilot, maintenance platoon leader, battalion maintenance production control officer, and UH-1 maintenance test pilot. I flew all over the USA and visited the countries of Honduras, El Salvador, Germany, and Kuwait. Looking back on it now, flying the UH-1 and conducting the kinds of missions I did made me a more well-rounded aviator and exposed me to a lot of things that I never would have experienced if I had just been a gun pilot from day one. A reliable, simple, and sturdy aircraft, the Huey remains my favorite aircraft to fly to this day. If you could get a Huey started, you could pretty much count on going flying that day. Things change, and the Army eventually got rid of the mighty UH-1.

In 1998, I attended the AH-64A aviator qualification course and was assigned to B Company, 1st Battalion, 4th Aviation Regiment, in the 4th Infantry Division at Fort Hood, Texas. While assigned there, I became a pilot in command in the aircraft and eventually was assigned to 4th Aviation Brigade as the brigade tactical operations officer after I accepted promotion to chief warrant officer 3.

In 2002, I attended the AH-64D Longbow Apache transition course at Fort Rucker, Alabama, and after completion became the squadron tactical operations officer for the 3rd Squadron, 6th United States Cavalry, first at Fort Hood and then later at Camp Humphries, Korea.

In May 2004, I joined the 1st Battalion, 227th Aviation Regiment, of the 1st Cavalry Division at Camp Taji, Iraq, where they were deployed as task force attack in support of Operation Iraqi Freedom II, and I remained with the unit until my retirement from the Army as a chief warrant officer 4 in October 2011.

In September 2006, I and over four hundred other soldiers were deployed to Iraq as members of the 1st Battalion, 227th Aviation Regiment, 1st Air Cavalry Brigade, 1st Cavalry Division, United States Army, which is also known by its nickname, "First Attack." Others would come to know us from the call sign we used during this deployment: "Crazyhorse."

This was the battalion's third deployment to Iraq in support of Operation Iraqi Freedom, and its second trip to Camp Taji, an airstrip and camp located about 20 miles north of Baghdad. Originally, we expected to be in Iraq for a year, but our stay was extended to fifteen months when the troop buildup known as "the Surge" was announced about halfway through our tour. During those fifteen months the battalion was responsible for having at least two aircraft in the air twenty-four hours a day, seven days a week, weather permitting. During this deployment we engaged the enemy with direct fire in more than three hundred separate events. The unit's soldiers received the Distinguished Service Cross, thirteen Distinguished Flying Crosses, forty-one Bronze Stars, and more than fifteen Air Medals with Valor, and other awards for its actions during this time. We also suffered the loss of two great aviators and friends, CW4 Keith Yoakum and CW2 Jason Defrenn. The battalion returned to the United States in December 2007. Since September 11, 2001, 1-227 AVN has deployed in support of combat operations around the world.

The 1-227th has a great history in Army aviation, dating from when it was formed in the early 1960s. In February 1963, the Army began to gather helicopters into the 11th Air Assault Division at Fort Benning, Georgia, to test the airmobile concept. Originally known as the 31st Transportation Company, this unit was later enlarged and redesignated as the 227th Assault Helicopter Battalion on July 18, 1963. After expansion, the battalion underwent two years of intensified evaluation and training to develop and determine the capabilities of the airmobile concept.

In June 1965, the 11th Air Assault Division was joined with the 2nd Infantry Division for a short period of time to become an airmobile division. Then on July 1, 1965, the division exchanged colors again, relieving the 11th Air Assault Division from its assignment to become the 1st Cavalry Division. During that July change of colors, the 227th Assault Helicopter Battalion was redesignated the 227th Aviation Battalion.

On August 1, 1965, the 1st Cavalry Division was deployed to Vietnam. During its seven years of duty in Vietnam, the battalion participated in fourteen campaigns and received numerous decorations, including the first Congressional Medal of Honor ever awarded to an Army aviator, CW2 Frederick E. Ferguson.

During Operation Desert Shield / Desert Storm, the battalion successfully completed numerous day and night missions, flying hundreds of accident-free hours while losing only one AH-64A to enemy fire.

After completing training in the Unit Fielding Training Program (UFTP) in November 1998, First Attack became the first AH-64D Longbow attack helicopter battalion in the world.

In January 2003, 1-227th Aviation Regiment deployed in support of Operation Iraqi Freedom I. Attached to the 11th Aviation Regiment, the battalion planned and executed a deep attack in order to destroy the Medina Division of the Republican Guard and enable the 3rd Infantry Division freedom to maneuver north and seize Baghdad. On the night of March 23, 2003, First Attack launched north. Flying through hails of enemy gunfire and antiaircraft artillery (AAA), most of the battalion's aircraft were rendered combat ineffective. During the fight, one aircraft was shot down and its crew was captured by Iraqi forces. The battalion's aircraft limped back to their advanced location, known as Tactical Assembly Area (TAA) Rams, to refit for future combat operations. Eighteen days after the initial strike, both 1-227th pilots were rescued by ground elements closing in on Baghdad. The unit redeployed to Fort Hood in June 2003.

In February 2004, the task force once again deployed to Iraq in order to conduct combat operations in support of the Multinational Corps–Iraq and the 1st Cavalry Division in order to complete the transition of sovereignty to the Iraqi people. Flying over ten thousand AH-64D and nine thousand OH-58D Kiowa Warrior hours in theater, the task force answered every call, maintained a phenomenal operational tempo, and supported operations throughout the theater, from Baghdad to An Najaf to Al Kut. As part of those operations the task force was awarded the Navy Unit Commendation for its role in the second battle of Fallujah in November 2004. The task force redeployed to Fort Hood in March 2005.

In September 2006, First Attack deployed for the third time to Iraq in support of Operation Iraqi Freedom 06-08. Based once again out of Camp Taji, the unit supported up to eight separate combat brigades daily. The commander of 1st BCT, 1CD, summed up the battalion's support of his brigade with these words: "When we need security, First Attack is there. The pilots of 1-227th Aviation Regiment are totally fearless and have never failed to support us, no matter what the conditions."

First Attack is the unit I served in the longest, and the unit I served in combat the most with. It is and always will be my battalion.

As much as this is a story about people, it is also about an aircraft, the Boeing AH-64D Longbow Apache. The capabilities of the Apache allowed us to do things that were unheard of in previous wars. As much as the Huey is my favorite aircraft to fly, if I ever had to go to war again, I would want to do it in an Apache.

The AH-64 is a four-blade, twin-engine attack helicopter with a tailwheel-type landing-gear arrangement, and a tandem cockpit for a two-man crew. The Apache was developed as Model 77 by Hughes Helicopters for the US Army's Advanced Attack Helicopter program to replace the AH-1 Cobra and was first flown on September 30, 1975. The US Army selected the AH-64, by Hughes Helicopters, over the Bell YAH-63 in 1976 and later approved full production in 1982. McDonnell Douglas continued production and development after purchasing Hughes Helicopters from Summa Corporation in 1984. The AH-64 was introduced to US Army service in April 1986. The first production AH-64D Apache Longbow, an upgraded version of the original Apache, was delivered to the Army in March 1997. Production has been continued by Boeing Defense, Space & Security; over one thousand AH-64s have been produced to date. Today, the latest version of the AH-64 is the AH-64E Guardian. This aircraft was not fielded during the time frame discussed in this book, so I won't go into it any further.

The AH-64 Apache features a nose-mounted sensor suite for target acquisition and night vision systems called the TADS (Target Acquisition and Designation System). It is armed with a 30-millimeter (1.2-inch) M230 chain gun carried between the main landing gear, under the aircraft's forward fuselage. It has four hardpoints mounted on stub-wing pylons, typically carrying a mixture of AGM-114 Hellfire missiles and Hydra 70, 2.75-inch rocket pods. The AH-64 also has a large amount of systems redundancy to improve combat survivability.

A tribute to the aircraft's rugged design and construction is its ability to take a lot of abuse and still perform its mission of supporting troops on the ground. Our number one priority was to respond to those on the ground in need of help. It made my job worthwhile to hear a word of thanks from those guys when we were able to help. Conversely, it was the most helpless feeling in the world when you were flying overhead, seeing a detonation of an IED or talking to wounded soldiers, and being unable find the people responsible or to bring assistance as fast as you would like. Fortunately, the days we were able to help vastly outnumbered the others. I am proud to say that I'm an Army aviator and a gun pilot who flew the best attack helicopter in the world, the AH-64 Apache.

I would be remiss if I didn't mention the men who came before us: the gentlemen who made Army aviation what it is, and set the standard by which we judge ourselves today, the Army aviators of the Vietnam era.

When I first entered the Army, there were a great many Vietnam vets still in the ranks, and it was their teaching and guidance that enabled me and others of my era to be the aviators that we became. Without them and the sterling example they set by word and action on the field of battle, the fantastic performance of your Army aviation troopers on the battlefield today would not be possible.

I was a Texan serving in the US Army in the early twenty-first century. As such, we used a mix of metric and imperial measurements and notations. So, if I veer rapidly from meters to knots, then statute miles to inches and back to kilometers again, I apologize, but that's the world I lived in. If you insist on knowing the actual distances and measures involved in your preferred system of measurement, then get a calculator.

Finally, the modern military vocabulary is rife with profanity. As such, some of the language I have used herein is not what most of our mothers would approve of. It is authentic, however, and I would beg your forgiveness if the language I have used here is sometimes rather salty.

Here's to those and those like us . . . damn few left.

I am an American Soldier.
I am a Warrior and a member of a team.
I serve the people of the United States and live the Army Values.
I will always place the mission first.
I will never accept defeat.
I will never quit.
I will never leave a fallen comrade.
I am disciplined, physically and mentally tough, trained and proficient in my warrior tasks and drills.
I always maintain my arms, my equipment, and myself.
I am an expert and I am a professional.
I stand ready to deploy, engage, and destroy the enemies of the United States of America in close combat.
I am a guardian of freedom and the American way of life.
I am an American Soldier.

CHAPTER 1

CAMP DOHA, KUWAIT: FEBRUARY 2005

The colonel is late.

After a year in Iraq, Task Force Attack is undergoing what is referred to by the Army as "reintegration." We are over four hundred soldiers living packed into a couple of warehouses in Kuwait for a week or so until we return home to Texas. In the meantime, we wash our equipment, helicopters, other units' vehicles; walk around the compound; visit the PX; do laundry; catch each other's respiratory infections; and try not to count the time until we get on the plane for the twenty-plus-hour ride back to Fort Hood.

Task Force Attack was composed of members of 1st Battalion, 227th Aviation Regiment (First Attack), an AH-64D attack helicopter battalion plus the two aviation troops of the 1st Squadron, 7th Cavalry Regiment (Garryowen), that were equipped with the OH-58D Kiowa Warrior, a light attack / scout helicopter. The task force had just completed a yearlong deployment to Iraq in support of Operation Iraqi Freedom 2 (OIF2). It had fought with valor in such places as An Najaf, Fallujah, and Sadr City. We flew missions from Kuwait all the way north to the Turkish border with Iraq. The unit was awarded the Naval Unit Citation for its efforts in support of operations in Fallujah in November and had won the Ellis D Parker award for the Combat Aviation Unit of the Year for 2004. We were going home; we had done a good job, and everyone was feeling their oats a bit.

Today we are standing in the hot sun, in a parking lot near the metal warehouse buildings we call home. Rumor has it a VIP is coming to say hello. We were told to be in formation at 1500 hrs. (3:00 p.m. to those unfamiliar with the twenty-four-hour clock). Naturally, this being the Army, someone has us there fifteen minutes early. It is now 1520, and some smart-ass in the ranks is heard saying, "What time is the 1500 formation?" It is not like we were not all thinking it. The battalion command sergeant major (CSM) has already called the formation to attention a couple of times to practice "sounding off." He's concerned that we won't yell our unit motto loudly enough to impress those within range of hearing. The chances of us underperforming increase by every minute we stand in the hot Kuwaiti sun. The longer we stand there, the more horseplay and griping take place. Sweat runs down my back. The minutes tick by, and forty minutes after we were told to be there, a couple of SUVs pull up.

They could be on time, they could be late, we'll never know. All we do know is the fact that we've been standing here sweating for almost an hour, and whatever it is we are waiting on had better be good. I mean this had better be the Dallas Cowboys Cheerleaders or the Playboy Playmate of the Year kind of good. Of course, we think it had better be good, or what? What would we do? Go back to the warehouse, wipe the sweat off, and sulk? Yeah, that's pretty much it.

It was not, in fact, good. The girls from the Salt Lake City Hooters would have been better. Even a visit from the surviving cast members of the early 1960s TV show *Leave It to Beaver* would probably have been better.

While we stand, slowly dying from heat exhaustion, people eventually get out of the vehicles. We are arrayed across the parking lot in a task force formation by company; with the commander and his staff out front and companies in the back, I am so far away from whoever it is that I can tell only that there is a gentleman of rather large stature talking with the task force commander. He hands the CO what appears to be a football. We are called to attention. We numbly yell, "Task Force Attack!" (I will say whatever you want; just let me go back to my cot), while the malcontents from 1-7 CAV who were never really happy being assigned to an attack battalion bellow their own motto, "Garryowen." The combination of the two groups of people sounding off with different things results in an unintelligible mass of people yelling. I can only imagine how impressed people who heard this verbal display might have been.

"At ease!" is then the command. The speechifying then commences. First up is Attack 6 (the commander) telling us stuff we already know, which is mostly for the visitor (who has now been identified as former sports star Bo Jackson), but we get to listen anyway. After the commander is done, Bo says something that none of us can hear. The colonel holds up a football, and the task force staff, who are standing in front of the formation, start to clap and cheer like a bunch of trained seals about something that we cannot hear. After that performance, Bo and the colonel proceed to walk around the formation, taking a few pictures in front of the troops. Wiseasses in the ranks start muttering under their breath things like "Bo don't know shit" or "Does Bo know fucking Sadr City?," referring to his Nike commercials from when he still played professional sports, and one of the rougher places we operated over in Iraq. It soon becomes apparent that we are not here to meet with Bo (Mister Jackson if you're nasty) as the group heads for the waiting cars. Bo gets back in the SUV and leaves; we are dismissed and nobody in the task force ever sees that football again.

"What the hell was that all about?" somebody asks as we walk back to the warehouse. Another voice cynically says our battalion motto, "ATTACK!"

"The war must be over if we have time for dog-and-pony shows." But most of us know the war isn't anywhere close to being over. Even as we were sitting in a warehouse in Kuwait waiting to get on the plane to go back to Texas, those of us who were staying in the Army for a while knew that we would be coming back to Iraq. It was just a matter of time.

"ATTACK!"

SUMMER 2005:
FORT HOOD, TEXAS

There was a new sheriff in town. One of the good things and bad things about the Army is that your boss will change every couple of years. It is a good thing if you do not like your current boss. It is a bad thing those times when you realize that the outgoing commander, whom you did not care for all that much, suddenly seems to be not that bad of a guy when compared to who just took over. The Army makes a big deal trying to convince everyone that a person given a "command" is someone handpicked, special, a direct descendant of all our great combat leaders. The truth of the matter is that often a commander is someone who was at the right place at the right time or, in the worst case, a person who is ill suited for the job but got it because they "knew someone." So as much as the Army touts the fact that people get promoted on merit and merit alone, just like a large civilian corporation or business it often helps to know people.

In the summer of 2005, First Attack got a new commander. This person would lead us from then until we returned from the next deployment to Iraq. We all gathered in the West Fort Hood Dining Facility (DFAC) the day of the change of command to hear the new commander's initial thoughts on taking over our unit. For those of us who had been in the Army for a while, we waited, hoping for the best but prepared for the worst. A new commander was like that proverbial box of chocolates; you never knew what you were going to get. His speech that day was not that much different than any other new commander's welcome speech—we're going to work hard, enforce standards, discipline—and was wrapped up with a quote from the film *We Were Soldiers* . . . well, the movie quote was different, but we would hear more of those as time went on. One thing we knew for sure: for better or worse, he is the new Attack 6.

I also had a new job. Upon our return from Iraq, I took over the position as the battalion tactical operations officer (TACOPS). It was a position I had held in my previous unit, 3rd Squadron, 6th Cavalry (Heavy Cav!), at Camp Humphries, Korea. Prior to that posting, I had served as the brigade TACOPS officer for the Aviation Brigade, 4th Infantry Division, as well as the 1st Battalion, 4th AVN, before that, also at Fort Hood. So, it was a job I had plenty of experience in, and was well within my capabilities to perform, and I was looking forward to doing it since it was something I enjoyed doing.

The battalion TACOPS officer works directly for the BN operations officer (S3) and is the primary advisor to the BN commander for the programming and use of aircraft survivability equipment, airspace management, joint forces coordination, and tactical mission planning. In Iraq, I was responsible for the daily posting of airspace information, which was vital for the avoidance of restricted operations zones (ROZ) used for unmanned aerial vehicles (UAV), artillery, and other things such as Special Operations Forces (SOF) raids. Additionally, I was solely responsible for maintaining the automated flight-planning information that we carried on board the aircraft, using the Aviation Mission Planning System (AMPS), plus the distribution of the Special Instructions (SPINS), which gave us, among other things, information about combat search and rescue (CSAR) and escape and evasion procedures in theater. Finally, I was the person tasked with tracking enemy threats to aviation, looking for threat patterns, enemy techniques, and trends and advising aircrews on how to best avoid the surface-to-air threat. It was going to be a busy deployment for me, of that there was no doubt.

For the next year we trained for the coming deployment. Slowly, replacements arrived to replace people we had lost either to transfer to another unit or just getting out of the Army altogether. We were lucky in one respect, in that the bulk of the pilots who were deployed for OIF 2 had stayed with the unit. That left us with a seasoned core that included some of the most experienced AH-64D pilots in the US Army. Additionally, many of the replacements we received had combat flight experience with other units. So, from a position of combat-proven aviator competence, we were truly fortunate, and it showed during our training. It also enabled the aviator training to progress through basic maneuvers to team drills quickly. Being proficient in the process of working as an attack weapons team (AWT) is necessary for aircraft employment downrange to occur quickly and precisely. Looking back now, I am certain this experience shallowed out the learning curve and helped lead to our considerable success on the battlefield during the deployment.

WINTER–SPRING, 2006: FORT HOOD, TEXAS

In January 2006, B Company, 1-227th AVN (Reapers), was tasked to conduct training at the Army's National Training Center (NTC), near Barstow, California, along with naval special operators, USAF combat search-and-rescue HH-60 helicopters (the HH-60 is a version of the Black Hawk helicopter, also used by the Army), and AC-130s (the gunship version of the venerable C-130 Hercules transport aircraft) from the Air Force Special Operations Command (AFSOC). It was rare for the NTC at that time, because in the past the focus at the center was one of massive force-on-force pitched battles featuring tanks rolling across the desert in preparation for Cold War–style conflict. It was an excellent training opportunity, and it allowed our pilots to interact with units we had worked for in the past and would again in the future. Simultaneously, most of the battalion's instructor pilots were undergoing forward air controller–airborne (FAC-A) training with the Marines in Yuma, Arizona. Conducting this training would not be without challenges, however.

It started with the logistics and maintenance nightmare of having two aviation operations away from home station, at remote sites far apart and with no external maintenance support. It was a disaster waiting to happen. Looking back on this now, whoever signed off on this operation was definitely an optimist . . . and yet, somehow the BN pulled it off with no significant issues.

One of the S3 battle captains (Capt. Chris Morton) and I flew one of the aircraft to be used for scheduled FAC-A training out to Yuma, where we dropped off the aircraft. Not knowing when we'd get the chance anytime soon, we had a steak that evening, and after spending the night in a hotel, we picked up a rental car and drove what was probably one of the most scenic routes I've ever been on to Las Vegas. Paralleling the Colorado River, the road ran past the popular spring break destination of Lake Havasu, Arizona, through the desert, and eventually over the Hoover Dam and into Vegas, where we spent the next night. The next morning, we went to McCarran Airport (now Harry Reid International Airport), where we picked up another soldier who had flown in commercial from Fort Hood. We then continued to NTC to begin coordination with the various agencies required to accomplish the training, which would happen concurrently with the FAC-A training in Arizona.

An AH-64 from B Company, 1-227th AVN, 1CD, over West Texas. *Photo by author*

We had been in contact with the Navy unit we were going to train with for a while. The link-up and getting our equipment set up in the Joint Operations Center (JOC) was smooth and seamless. Our Army friends who worked at the NTC were another matter entirely. Our chief problem, at least at first, was finding a place for our forward arming and refueling point (FARP). We had located a place near the post ammo storage facility that had hard ground and was unlikely to cause the pilots to "brown out" (lose sight of the ground in a dust cloud) when landing. This was vetoed by the Eagle Team (the Army aviation evaluators and trainers at NTC) because according to them, the aircraft taking off or landing at the FARP with live ammo might point their weapons at the base housing area approximately 6–7 kilometers away. While I wasn't aware that accidental discharge of weapons from AH-64s was an issue (I know that during our time in Iraq flying over Baghdad, it NEVER occurred), it's possible it could happen. It's also possible that rabid badgers could kill me while I fill my car with gas at the Stop-n-Go. I wanted to ask them how USAF aircraft regularly took off from Nellis AFB (near Las Vegas, 100 miles to the north) with live weapons, flew to NTC, dropped their bombs, and then went home without ever accidentally dropping their weapons on the people they flew over on the way to the NTC. But since they would have just thought me a smart-ass and miss the point entirely, I just sat there in silence . . . stewing. In the end, it was just easier to find another place to put the FARP or, better yet, ask them where they wanted us to put it.

So, we asked them.

And for our sins they gave us a place. Located in a place called "the Valley of Death" was the site that came to be known as FARP Daigle (named after the FARP officer in charge [OIC], Capt. Paul Daigle). Given the crappy-accident-waiting-to-happen kind of place that it was, I am not sure if I were Capt. Daigle that I would have been down with that. The Valley of Death was so named because it was a narrow valley (about 1 kilometer across) with a 9,000-foot mountain on one side and an incline to a ridgeline about 200–300 feet above the valley floor on the other side. When the NTC was doing full-on, force-on-force, Red vs. Blue, Cold War–style maneuvers, this was the valley where tanks went to die. On the plus side, it was fairly sheltered from the high winds that plagued certain parts of the NTC. It was also within a couple of kilometers from the dry lake bed where we were going to stage our aircraft (Bicycle Lake Army Airfield). On the bad side, since a lot of vehicles have traveled through that valley, the soil is fine, which lends itself to brownouts. Unfortunately, this was a feature we were soon to learn more about.

Once the location of the FARP and other arrangements were finally sorted out, it was time to get down to business and start training. B Company had arrived and had their aircraft parked out at Bike Lake, which was located about a mile from main post, where the Army had established a primitive airfield to support the NTC. The JOC was in a large, prefabricated metal building back on post. Inside the JOC, Capt. Morton and I set up a BN S3 plans-and-operations cell that consisted of a couple of computers, a printer, and a telephone. Across the aisle from us was the AC-130 representative, and at the end of our row were the HH-60 dudes. In front of us was the Navy battle staff, the intel folks, and other people necessary to conduct operations. Behind us, in the back of the building, were the Navy staff spaces, which included a cubicle for their commander. Just outside the JOC there were several tents erected for mission planning, rehearsals, and other things. B Company had a tent available for its use, and next door the Navy had an area where they carried out their planning.

In another arrangement that was nonstandard to those who had participated in NTC rotations before, we were staying in a barracks on post rather than living in a

Capt. Paul Daigle (*left*) and an unidentified pilot prepare to load an AGM-114 Hellfire missile at FARP Daigle. *Photo by author*

An AH-64 from B Company, 1-227th AVN, 1 CD, fires an AGM-114 at NTC. *Photo by author*

collection of tents out in the desert. Next door to us were the USAF HH-60 pilots and crew. It was quite the contrast seeing the way they carried themselves and the things they thought acceptable versus what we endured as a matter of course as Army aviators. It was not unusual for us to return from mission planning or after a flight to see the Air Force guys with the grill fired up, beers in hand, wearing civilian clothes and having a grand old time. We, on the other hand, while we were on this trip, were subject to General Order #1, the infamous order that forbade, among other things, the ingestion of "adult beverages" while we were at NTC. While most of us who had been in the Army for a while understood what was going on and accepted the situation as "par for the course," it couldn't have made things very easy for Capt. Welch, the B Company commander, to justify to his younger troops how "they" could do something "we" weren't allowed to do.

Even with these challenges, we completed the orientation and coordination phase and prepared to begin our training. Our initial mission was to support a raid on an enemy safe house. We were requested to cover and clear the ground infiltration (INFIL) and exfiltration (EXFIL) as well as to provide support for the raid itself by providing deception and covering fires and providing close observation of the objective once the team was on target. Among the things we were looking for were people fleeing from the target house (who were commonly called "squirters"). It was during this planning process that we encountered one of the observer/controllers (O/C) assigned to the NTC, who were there ostensibly to "observe and mentor" us. He was insistent that we provide him with the mission graphics. Graphics usually consist of a map with such things as routes, areas of responsibility, phase lines, and assorted other military graphical type stuff drawn on it. He initially came to me, and I informed him that there weren't any graphics at the moment and there were unlikely to be any until just before mission launch, because that was something the USN team conducting the raid would produce. Not liking my answer, he turned to Capt. Morton, seated next to me, who essentially told him the same thing. I found that sort of insulting, but whatever floats your boat, I guess. On the basis of my previous experience supporting these kinds of operations during the previous deployment, not having graphics was not that unusual and was something we could work through.

Our O/C didn't have any experience in supporting this kind of operation or any other kind of combat operation, for that matter. He had never been deployed to a combat zone. He was nonetheless going to tell us how we should do the mission better at the mission debrief. In retrospect, it was possible that he may have been able to provide some helpful advice or insight into the process, but as far as I was concerned, he burned so many bridges at the jump that he could have given me directions to Coronado's lost gold, and I wouldn't have listened. I viewed it as just another indignity we had to put up with so we could enjoy the privilege of serving this great nation of ours.

He was also quite antsy, since his boss (a real screamer of a lieutenant colonel) was demanding to see the mission graphics that didn't yet exist. He was either unwilling to believe us or to tell his boss that there were, in fact, no graphics yet, so he set off to ask the Navy guys about the nonexistent graphics. About five minutes later we heard yelling coming from the direction of the team commander's cubical at the back of the JOC. It appeared our O/C had wandered around looking for the phantom graphics until he ran into the head honcho of the operation—a Navy SEAL lieutenant commander. I looked up in time to see a green camo blur headed for the front door of the JOC, being followed by the muscular figure of the team commander, who was yelling at him to "get [his] ass out of the JOC and never come back."

On his way back to his cube, the commander saw us looking over. He came over, smiled, and asked us, "Was that guy bothering you?"

Capt. Morton diplomatically said, "No sir; he was just trying to do his job."

Not being in such a diplomatic mood, I said, "Yes sir; he was."

The commander then said, "Don't worry; you won't see him again."

We never did. I was starting to like working with these guys.

With the graphics issue out of the way, we settled into a battle rhythm where we planned a mission one day and flew the next. Additionally, we had opportunities to do joint live-fire training with Navy close air support (CAS) F-18s and the HH-60s during nonmission days. We kept busy during our time at NTC, and all the rated aviators got a chance to fly at least a few times.

The NTC is a challenge even to experienced aviators due to the rapidly changing weather conditions and extreme terrain. High winds were especially common during the time we were training there. On one night I was flying with an AWT in support of a mission to capture or kill a high-value target (HVT) located in a village the Army had thoughtfully built in a valley near a terrain feature known as "the Peanut." The Peanut was a small hill mass north of the village that was shaped like (you guessed it) a peanut. The plan was for us (the AH-64s) to utilize 30 mm cannon and 2.75-inch rocket fire as a diversion between the village and the Peanut to draw the enemy's attention just prior to the main attack from the south. We intended to mask our approach by using the Peanut and then to use the hill as a rally point if we became separated once the shooting began. Even though it was night, we always assumed that the enemy could see us (using night vision devices), and operated accordingly by using available terrain to mask our approach.

To start the mission, we repositioned our aircraft from Bike Lake, flying about 2 miles east down the Valley of Death to beautiful, exotic FARP Daigle. It was my first time landing there, and it easily lived up to its already poor reputation. We landed at last light, coming to a bone-rattling, bouncy stop as we rolled over the rutted ground. At touchdown, the aircraft was quickly enveloped with a dust cloud, obscuring all but the grounding stake (a metal rod pounded into the ground, used for static grounding), which ended up being about a foot in front of my right rocket pod, located about 6 feet away from where I sat. This was more by some stroke of luck than my superior flying skills, since the ghosts of Igor Sikorsky, Audie Murphy, and John B. Stockton were obviously watching over my dumb warrant officer ass. Yeah, this was going to be fun when we came back later tonight.

We took our load of rockets and departed the FARP on time for the mission. We traveled north past Red Pass Dry Lake, going the long way around the reservation and up toward the East Gate, eventually arriving around 20 kilometers north of the target, where we turned back toward the Peanut. We did this to give us time and a pace to allow precise timing. It was critical to the operation that we arrive at our predetermined time on target (TOT), because if we arrived on station too early, we could give away the operation to the enemy. The result of arriving too late was something we didn't even want to consider. It was evident as soon as we passed "the Whale" (a hill at the east end of the Valley of Death that resembles the back of a whale coming out of the water) that the wind was howling that night. With about 90 knots true airspeed indicated, I looked down at my tactical situation display (TSD). A quick glance told me our ground speed (the rate the aircraft was traveling over the surface of the earth) was a shade over 40 knots. I did a little math in my head (crazy, but true) that told me we had a 50-knot headwind. The good news was that at least the wind was steady, and the turbulence was fairly light, all things considered. We were going to get some help with a tailwind when we turned toward the target, but we still needed to bust ass so we wouldn't be late.

The real fun began as we arrived on station and established a racetrack pattern north of the village, in preparation for firing on the diversionary target to initiate the operation. The approved target was located near a large hill that was being used as a backstop in case our rockets went long. This situation forced us into a pattern where our inbound pass was being made with the 50-knot tailwind. I found myself with the almost impossible task of trying to slow the aircraft down enough to give my copilot/gunner (CPG) the time to acquire the target, fire the laser to determine range, send data to the fire control computer, and adjust the rocket pods as necessary. This was immediately followed by shooting the rockets, when he finally said the magic words: "Match and shoot!" I ended up with the cyclic almost in my lap as I tried to slow the aircraft down enough to get the shot off. The result of this process was that when we broke off the attack and turned out into the hellacious headwind, our ground speed almost immediately dropped to zero. To correct, I had to push the nose of the aircraft down to accelerate. I put the spurs to her to attempt to get some ground speed in order to get out of my wingman's way so he could fire. Then we had to race down the outbound leg to get into a good position so I could turn back around to cover my wingman's break after he finished shooting. It was also a challenge to fight the common trend to make the orbit tighter and tighter as each pass was made. This task was made more difficult by the fact that you were constrained by the field of view of our night vision systems and couldn't look over your shoulder to acquire the other aircraft like you can during the day. Once we made the turn and came inbound toward the target, there was no problem finding our wingman, since the whole world lit up as he fired his rockets. Due to the constraints of the range we were using, we had only this one authorized live target, so we shot everything we had on the diversionary target. Finishing up our engagements, we then established an orbit in the vicinity of the mission objective and began looking for squirters. Due to the presence of high ground to our east, we couldn't establish an orbit around the target that allowed us to maintain constant observation, or we had to establish a holding pattern to one side and stagger the flight, which allowed one aircraft to always have eyes on the target. It was tough, challenging training.

After about an hour the HVT was captured and the team began its exfil from the target. We were released as the convoy passed our coverage boundary, and with that, we relayed the appropriate code words and headed home. The biggest challenge of the night loomed ahead—getting back into FARP Daigle. The challenge was threefold: First we had to find the stupid thing using our first-generation forward-looking-in-frared-derived (FLIR) imagery, called the Pilot Night Vision System (PNVS), which most of us thought should be called the POS (piece of shit). Second, since we had already established that the landing area wasn't exactly billiard table smooth, and seeing the obstacles we already knew were there with the Mark 1 POS FLIR, was kind of problematic at best. Finally, it was so dusty that if you attempted to land by slowly hovering the aircraft into the landing area, you would brown out. So, what to do?

There are a couple of options when landing a helicopter in a dusty environment. First, you can shoot a shallow approach, gradually slowing down until just above effective translational lift (also known as ETL) airspeed (16–20 knots) and then landing with the aircraft rolling forward, keeping the dust cloud behind you. This was the technique I used at last light because we could still make out the terrain well enough to be able to pick a good path to navigate our way around some bushes and rocks. Now, however, in the pitch-black darkness of the Mojave Desert, this technique was a bit more difficult given the poor FLIR conditions we had. The other option was to use a steeper approach angle and attempt a landing with little to no forward movement when we touched down. At the last moment you bring the nose of the aircraft up into a decelerative attitude called a flare. The redirected rotor wash then clears the landing area of dust momentarily, and then you attempt to touch down before you brown out. This was the technique I eventually used. However, for that technique to be effective, you had to be able to tell where you are supposed to land in the first place, which was a challenge with the conditions we faced.

The pilot of an Apache also has help from the symbology shown in his helmet display unit (HDU) over his right eye, which shows you FLIR imagery as well as your airspeed, altitude, true ground track, drift rate, and a bunch of other stuff, all designed to help you fly the beast and not break it when landing in a desert shithole like FARP Daigle.

After we circled the location a few times, we had a fairly good idea where everything was at on the ground. I started to make the steep approach, wanting to reach zero airspeed with about a 100-to-200-foot-per-minute rate of descent at touchdown. The first time in, everything was looking fairly good till we got to the bottom of the approach, where I managed to misjudge the landing spot. When we touched down, I felt and saw the HDU symbology showing the aircraft tilt to one side, as if we were going to roll over. As we were being enveloped in a cloud of dirt, I leveled the aircraft and applied power, initiating what is called a go-around.

The second time around I really planted it, and my CPG stood on the brakes for me, stopping the aircraft right on top of the panel they marked the arming position with. It ended up being a nice aerobic workout for me, since my heart was beating like a rabbit the entire time the armament dawgs were "safeing" the aircraft. This is a procedure done after firing to make sure the aircraft has no live rounds left on board.

My wingman had an even worse time as they made four attempts to get their aircraft into the FARP. It was almost worse watching them try to get the aircraft down than it was to fly it myself. We watched on the FLIR as they were coming down, aircraft slowing, dust cloud growing, with the helicopter finally disappearing into the cloud. Then you would see the tail tilt up and out of the cloud like a shark's fin, and hear them call for a go-around. Each time it looked like they had it made, and then at the last moment we would see a boiling cloud of dirt and hear an exasperated call of go-around on the radio. Finally, in the name of safety, they recovered to the hot pad at Bike Lake. Departures from the FARP to head back to Bike Lake were not even anywhere near the gut-wrenching experience that landings were, especially since we weren't full of fuel and ammo. Once we were declared empty of ordnance (safe), we took off and flew the 2 or 3 miles to our airfield home du jour. Fortunately for us, the rest of our encounters with FARP Daigle were during the hours of daylight, and we escaped the NTC without incident.

Meanwhile at MAWTS-1 in Yuma, Arizona, our IPs trained with the Marines to create the first conventional Army aviators qualified to be a forward air controller–airborne (FAC-A). This training culminated with our IPs controlling airstrikes conducted by jet fighter aircraft at night while using NVG and FLIR. In previous discussions downrange and after we returned in 2005, several experienced aviators remarked about the need for this type of training, on the basis of our experiences during previous deployment(s). For me the need for this capability was never more apparent than when I found myself the air mission commander of a flight attempting to coordinate the recovery of the crew of an RAF C-130 cargo aircraft that had been shot down near Camp Taji, Iraq, during OIF2.

On January 30, 2005, I was conducting reconnaissance as a member of an AWT, call sign Vampire 17 (C Company, 1-227). We were west of Camp Taji, near an area where one of the Reapers aircraft had been shot up badly earlier that day. The sun was out, with a few clouds in the late afternoon sky. Back in the States this would be considered a great day. Flying over a farmer's field near a canal where the earlier attack took place, my back-seater, CW4 Bill Ham, noticed something odd in the middle of the plowed field. Upon further investigation it appeared to be part of a plastic sheet partially covered by loose earth. We called our wingmen (CW4 Larry Harper and CW2 Shaun Miller) and had them look at it as well. Between the four of us we couldn't really come up with an explanation for it. Given its proximity to the attack site and the fact that Anti-Iraq Forces (AIF) regularly buried weapons in the ground, we called in the location and what we were seeing to the battle captain in the TOC.

The TOC was the nerve center of the task force. Stationed in the TOC, an officer referred to as the battle captain functioned as the commander's representative and made decisions on the movements and employment of the task force's assets (in this case primarily aircraft) in accordance with the task force commander's guidance. The commander and the battalion S3 had an office in the TOC, and one or the other was available if needed. Equipped with an array of radios, computers, and other communications equipment, the TOC is the place to be if you want to know or control what is going on within the unit. Sometimes the TOC was the source of good news, sometimes bad. Today they would end up being a source of utter frustration.

After some discussion about site, in question, we decided to call the location a possible weapons cache and were eventually cleared by the TOC to fire some 30 mm rounds into it just to see if we could get some secondaries. Given that the only structures around were a farmhouse and associated buildings about 100 meters away, there was little danger to any innocents. We set up an attack pattern and fired a few bursts, which really got no secondary effects. Personally, I was ready to give up on it as just another weird thing that Iraqis do that we can't figure out. Then, the F-16s showed up.

I guess word travels fast when there's stuff to be blown up. The TF Attack TOC (which was also known as Attack Mike) gave us a frequency and a call sign for a flight of US Air Force F-16 fighter aircraft that were coming to help. After working through a bunch of communication issues, including not being able to understand the F-16 flight lead's radio, the fighter dudes tell us they want to drop a bomb on the cache site. I didn't really think that was a good idea, given the proximity of the farmhouse to the site, and we proceeded to have a bit of internal debate on the subject. The minimum safe distance for the ordnance they were trying to use was "a bit" over 100 meters . . . and by "a bit," I mean a lot. We are in the midst of this discussion in an orbit around the site when back to the east, toward Camp Taji, we see a sheet of flame in the sky. Actually, it appeared as two sheets of flame, each traveling in opposite directions at a low altitude.

Aircraft regularly skirted to the west of Camp Taji airspace, going from Balad Airbase to the north and Baghdad International Airport (also known as BIAP) to the south. Upon seeing the flames and their location, my first thought was that there had been a midair collision. The reality was that a UK Royal Air Force C-130 had been shot down by the AIF. The second sheet of flame was caused by one of its wings tearing off and falling to earth while the rest of the aircraft continued forward.

I queried the flight about what I had seen. While Bill had seen it, Larry and Shaun did not, since they were on the opposite side of the orbit from us and had their backs to the shoot-down. Then I asked the F-16s if they could see anything in that direction with their targeting pod, and was told that they could see what they thought was a pipeline fire but nothing that looked like an aircraft. Having seen plenty of pipeline fires, I knew that wasn't what I had seen. We asked permission from Attack Mike to break station on this "suspected cache" and go over and look where I suspected a midair collision had taken place. We were told to maintain our position, since the powers that be were still interested in dropping a bomb on this thing. I wish I had objected more, because we might have been able to catch and kill the people who shot this aircraft down if we had gotten there sooner, but I didn't and we stayed near the cache site, continuing to look for AIF activity. We continued to ask the TOC for permission to break station and were denied every time. I was beginning to get very frustrated and angry that we couldn't get them to understand what we had seen and to forget about this stupid piece of plastic sticking out of the ground. In retrospect I place some blame on myself in the choice of words I used when describing the original situation to the TOC. I think they thought we had located something significant, when in fact we were just reporting our suspicions. All in all, this is a good example of what is sometimes referred to as the "fog of war."

In the meantime, word was working its way up the chain of command about a missing C-130. Someone eventually redirected a UAV over the area to the east of us, which spotted the wreckage of the C-130. About ten minutes after we were told to stay put for the third or fourth time, we got a call from Attack Mike, which gave us a grid coordinate and directed us to fly over and investigate the crash site.

We sped toward the grid as fast as the aircraft would go, but when we arrived at the location, all we could see were parts and pieces strewn everywhere. The only thing I recognized as belonging to an aircraft was one of the main landing gear, which I identified as possibly belonging to a C-130. There were a couple of locals sifting through the wreckage, who scurried away as soon as we arrived overhead. They went to homes nearby, so we made a note of their location and reported that information to "higher," so follow-on forces could investigate if necessary. Larry and Shaun landed and made a more complete assessment of the situation while we climbed out of small-arms range and picked up an orbit to maintain security for our wingman. It was immediately obvious to us that nobody survived this incident. We made a complete situation report to Attack Mike and set up security for the site until ground forces arrived to begin a recovery operation. During the rest of the seven-hour mission, we took charge of the airspace over the crash site by sorting out and assigning tasks to and deconflicting CAS, Marine helicopters, USAF HH-60s, and an AC-130, while simultaneously directing and providing security for ground forces moving to the area of the crash site. An added challenge was that the maps of the area weren't entirely accurate. Because of various canals that were in the area, we had to walk the arriving ground unit several miles, monitoring every turn to ensure they got to the crash site. The last several hours of the mission were conducted at night, blacked out with the aid of NVGs and FLIR. While we were able to successfully conduct these operations without a FAC-A qualification, it should be noted that my flight was not typical, in that three of the pilots were CW4s and we, as a flight, had in excess of sixty years of combined aviation experience. In retrospect, even with that amount of experience, had we been taught airspace coordination, deconfliction, and other techniques that are part of FAC-A instruction/qualification, our mission, that day and night, would have been made much simpler, safer, and more efficient.

Upon our return to Texas, it was this situation and a couple of other similar events that caused me to write a decision paper advocating sending selected IPs through the FAC-A qualification process. I did the legwork and made numerous phone calls and sent emails to the USMC FAC-A instructors at Yuma and USN/

USMC instructors at the FAC-A ground school in Coronado, California, to assess the possibility of getting some of our IPs trained, with the intent that they would return to the unit and spread their newly gained knowledge to the rest of the battalion. My intent was never to make the entire battalion forward air controllers, but to make them familiar with the techniques and control measures used for CAS and airspace deconfliction and to use those tools to better leverage the assets already available on the battlefield to our advantage.

Eventually, after a lot of emails, phone calls, briefings, and meetings, our brigade (1st Air Cavalry Brigade) and our division (1st Cavalry Division) signed off on this plan. Money and time on the event calendar were then made available for training. The training itself went off without a hitch, and the pilots we sent received valuable exposure to tactics, techniques, and procedures that were applicable to the tasks we performed daily downrange.

Unfortunately, there were those who couldn't (or didn't want to) see the value in the training and actively worked to see that nobody in the conventional Army would do this in the future. Most notable would be an Air Force colonel who apparently thought that Army aviators, or maybe just helicopter pilots in general, were incapable of handling the complex task of being a FAC-A. There were also people at the sometimes ironically named Army Aviation Center of Excellence who spoke vigorously against the training concept, even though they knew little, if anything, about it.

Ultimately, even though we never cleared a single jet "hot" on a target in anger, the training First Attack received in FAC-A techniques and procedures paid dividends downrange in the amount of coordination and cooperation achieved with our fixed-wing brothers . . . much more than units that never trained in those procedures accomplished. It reduced our risk because we utilized the fixed wing's sensors and gave us less exposure and more situational awareness. It's sad to me that this initial effort has gone by the wayside. This was a definite opportunity lost due to a failure of imagination as well as interservice rivalry and internal politics.

What followed after we returned from out west was the final training push before deployment overseas. We completed helicopter gunnery tables, convoy live fire, and all manner of common skills training that the Army requires for a unit to be certified combat ready. This was immediately followed by a trip to the Joint Readiness Training Center (JRTC), located at Fort Polk, Louisiana.

When you tell people you are preparing to deploy to Iraq by training in central Louisiana, a lot of people might scratch their heads and say, "Yeah, that sounds like something the Army would do." Actually, when considering where we were going to deploy in Iraq (Baghdad, a city of approximately 7.5 million people), it didn't make much difference where we trained as long as we got the opportunity to practice the tactics, techniques, and procedures involved in supporting ground operations. Not that the "Big Army" put much thought into that anyway. Rotations at combat training centers (CTCs) are organized mainly for the ground brigade that is there training; aviation is a supporting effort in that training. Aviation units do get trained and receive training, but we are not the main effort. As a result, there are some artificialities and constructs that inevitably lead to frustration and a lack of realism for the supporting elements from time to time.

Since the 1980s, the Army has had two major CTCs in the United States: NTC at Fort Irwin, California, and JRTC, which was first located at Fort Chaffee, Arkansas, and later moved to Fort Polk (in 1993). Historically JRTC was used for training "light" units such as the 82nd Airborne, 101st Air Assault, and Special Operations Forces (SOF), but now, given the expanding need of combat in Iraq and Afghanistan, units from all over the Army were going to both centers to train before deployment. I had always been assigned to "heavy" units at Fort Hood, so I had ten-plus visits to NTC under my belt, I had visited Fort Polk for only one miserable JRTC rotation in the 1990s with the 6th Cavalry Brigade, and I was hoping and praying that this wasn't going to be a repeat of that experience.

So off we went to the bogs and pine forests of central Louisiana to train for a war being conducted in the middle of the second-largest urban area in the Middle East.

MAY 2006:
FORT POLK, LOUISIANA

Leading hand sanitizers claim they can kill 99.9 percent of germs. Chuck Norris can kill 100 percent of whatever the fuck he wants.

—Posted on the wall of the First Attack TOC at JRTC

Stress does strange things to people, and the CTCs were all about producing stress. To be honest, most of what occurs on a day-to-day basis in a combat zone is pure dull, boring common stuff. Almost anyone with rudimentary training can pretty much handle most if not all of that. In order to get people ready for what could be the worst day in their lives, the CTCs produce stress on a grand scale. Most of these events are scripted and involve unexpected things such as aircraft being shot down, convoys ambushed, and commanders killed (so subordinates must take over), all designed to put stress on the units involved to test if their organization is trained and works as it is supposed to. Some of the stress is self-generated, but it all serves to prepare the unit for what is to come.

The CTCs also give rise to poor habits and techniques that don't work well over the long haul. A CTC rotation has a definite schedule; you know going in that the "war" is going to last only so long, and as a result, more than a few staff officers choose to "power through" by pulling all-nighters, some staying up days at a time. This behavior is encouraged and even rewarded by many in the Army. Unfortunately, when they do that, they don't train the staff as they should. There is no way you can "power through" an entire year or fifteen months' worth of a deployment. There's a saying, "Train like you fight," that can be applied here, but often it isn't.

A line of AH-64s belonging to 1-227th AVN sit and wait at JRTC at Ft. Polk, Louisiana. *Photo by author*

I have learned recently that a study commissioned by the FAA regarding crew rest and pilot fatigue found that if you are awake for more than sixteen hours straight, it is the equivalent of having a blood alcohol level of 0.05% without all the fun of boozing it up . . . a fact that explains many of the things I have read that came from tired staff officers over the years.

Whether it was from stress, lack of sleep, germophobia, or just plain weirdness, I don't know, but Attack 6 had a tent inside a room inside a building on the forward operating base (FOB) at JRTC.

You couldn't miss it. When you entered the BN headquarters on the ground floor, there it was, first door on the right: a two-person pop-up tent erected in the middle of the room. Every pilot coming in for the first time to get a mission briefing came past my desk and asked, "Why does the colonel have a tent in his room?" Before long, soldiers who wouldn't otherwise even get anywhere near the TOC were coming to see the tent inside the room inside the building on the FOB. Eventually you just began to accept that there were some things that there was just no answer for. Such as why isn't there hand sanitizer that kills 100% of the germs? Why just 99.9%? You may think this is a silly notion, and why would someone ask or even think about such a thing. I can assure you, however, that this is not silly, and an Army flight surgeon was sent on a mission to find hand sanitizer that would, in fact, kill 100% of the germs. I know this is true because I was there.

Every day at 1600 hrs we had a battle update briefing (BUB). In theory it was a chance for the staff and subordinate commanders (or their designated representative) to brief the battalion commander on the previous twenty-four hours and what challenges they expected to face in the coming twenty-four. It was also where the commander gave guidance and expressed his intent. In practice, at JRTC it was—at the least—a two-hour beatdown where even if the slide for a section had no changes from the previous day, it was still shown and briefed in detail. It was during one of these "festivals of suck" that Attack 6 asked the BN flight surgeon, during his presentation, if he could find some proper hand sanitizer for the handwashing stations at the port-a-potties. Doc replied that there already was hand sanitizer at all the port-a-potty locations. The colonel then said, "No, you don't understand; I don't want that stuff that kills only 99% of the germs. I want something that kills everything." He paused in thought and then said, "Doctor, have you ever heard of the Super Germ?" Of course, this was before the age of COVID-19 and all the associated paranoia, so the room became really quiet; the people who were dozing woke up and shifted nervously in their seats, waiting to see what was coming next. The commander was still kind of an unknown quantity to us at that point, and I don't believe any of us knew for sure what was going to happen next. Nobody really likes to witness an ass-chewing, especially because you never know if you might become a victim of collateral damage. In my experience, once the dogs are off the leash, they are seldom satisfied by getting just one person. Today, we all survived thanks to the doc's quick thinking.

You could tell that the good doctor was taken aback by the look on his face, but he recovered nicely and simply said, "Yes sir; I'll see what I can do." And with that, the crisis was averted for the moment, and we were all spared. A collective sigh was let out, and we continued with the briefing, with everyone hoping that this marked the conclusion of the "crazy" for the evening.

I don't think Doc ever found that hand sanitizer, and as far as I know, the colonel never brought it up again. At least he didn't bring it up during the BUB. However, he did get reminded about the "Super Germ" constantly for the remainder of his time with us.

The one good thing about the "Super Germ" fiasco was that it got someone out of our little prison of a FOB, allowing them to eat some actual "edible" food while they were searching for the hand sanitizer at the PX and, later, the Walmart in Leesville, Louisiana. I suppose it all depends on how you define edible, but I would have taken a hot dog that had been stuck in the movie theater cooker for a week over the swill they were giving us at the DFAC on the FOB. It was BY

The master gunner of 1-227th AVN, CW4 Jim Massey, has a moment at JRTC. *Photo by author*

FAR the worst food I attempted to eat in the twenty-plus years I served in the United States Army. It even beat out an exercise called REFORGER '90, where the unit I was in had nothing to eat but mac and cheese and beef and carrots for two weeks straight, because at least that stuff passed as food.

The "food" at JRTC was being served up by local vendors contracted by the Army. Part of me wanted to say they were serving food left over from Hurricane Katrina, from almost a year before, and this was their vengeance on the federal government for some perceived injustice. Another part thought that whatever the taxpayer was giving these people for this slop, it was entirely too much.

Normally I would really be upset about being kept in meetings that threatened to cause me to miss one of the two hot meals served per day, but in this case, it was truly a blessing. On the bright side, not only did I miss the horrible food, but I also lost some needed weight as a result. Win, win! If I had been thinking straight, I would have slipped a few bucks to the doc and had him bring back a pizza. I was quite likely delirious from the onset of starvation (part of the training, no doubt). When I did venture to the chow tent, it was more for a change in scenery than sustenance. Part of that scenery on one day was a guy I came to jokingly call the "Law Dawg."

Joe Belsha was a warrant officer who came to our unit right out of flight school. He was what is cleverly called "high school to flight school," which is another way to describe a person with no previous military experience who joins the Army through a program called Warrant Officer Flight Training (WOFT). It was a program that was popular during the Vietnam War, when the Army needed a lot of pilots really fast and cheap. These days, however, it's almost as if you have to know the secret handshake to apply. It's a challenge because not only do you have to meet the qualifications to attend flight school, but you also have to fight the recruiter, mostly because it means more work for them. They usually try to convince the person that it's easier to get into flight school once you are in the Army. A lot of people fall for it, and if you aren't insistent, they will steer you toward something other than what you came there for. I know, because they tried it with me when I joined the Army, because in the strictest sense I was high school to flight school or street to seat as well.

Initially, when Joe was finishing up his training at Fort Rucker, Alabama, Joe had orders assigning him to the 4th Infantry Division (the other division on Fort Hood, which was about to deploy), but he so wanted to be in the 1st Cav that he sought out our soon-to-be commander while he was in the AH-64D transition course and petitioned him to become a member of our unit. The colonel, one way or another, made it happen. As a result, Joe was persona non grata with the folks over in 4ID land. The Apache world is kind of small. Everyone knows everyone else, so many of us had heard about Joe from our friends in 4ID before he ever arrived at Fort Hood. Then, when he arrived at First Attack, the colonel introduced him to us at the weekly pilots' brief like they were best buddies. The colonel gushed about how Joe wanted to be with us and what a great guy Joe was. This was greeted by someone in the crowd blurting out, "That's nice; get your ass up here to the computer and flip the [PowerPoint] slides, bitch." Welcome to the CAV, Mister Belsha.

This is not the way a new warrant officer wants to begin his career. I had gotten an email asking me about Joe from one of my friends who was the standardization instructor pilot (SIP) for a company in 4ID, and he was rather upset that Joe wasn't going with them, because his unit was shorthanded. It's not that Joe is a bad guy, because he is not. He obviously wanted to be here and was enthusiastic about his job; he just needed some guidance. He was what we might call all velocity and no vector.

So I'm sitting in the chow tent at JRTC one evening, picking at my "food" and commiserating with Jim Massey, our master gunner, about such things as hand sanitizer, when into the tent comes something the sight of which I had never seen before or since. Backlit by the late-afternoon sun, striding purposefully and carrying his dinner tray, wearing a nonstandard leather holster with an old US cavalry belt buckle, his 9 mm pistol on his hip slung low like the gunfighters of old, was Joe Belsha. All that was missing was the soundtrack from *The Good, The Bad and the Ugly*. It was quite the sight, let me tell you. I let him sit down, and excused myself from the table and headed over to where he was sitting. "Hey, Law Dawg . . . ," I said. "You know your kind don't go around here, Law Dawg." Before he could reply, I turned around and walked away. While I was busting his chops with a line ripped off from the movie *Tombstone*, the message was intended to be this: new guys shouldn't stand out; they need to blend in. Now, I could have taken him aside and told him the same thing in a nice brotherly fashion, but what's the fun in that? Never saw that holster again though . . . He's a smart guy, that Belsha fella.

One thing they are big on in the Army is a process called a rock drill. A rock drill is basically a rehearsal, but we can't say rehearsal because either it recalls the movies, show business, or somebody at West Point who got his girlfriend stolen by a theater major from some East Coast college one time. I don't know, but it's the same damn thing as a rehearsal with rocks and string and toy army men. As big a deal as the Army makes of rock drills, it's an even bigger thing at CTC rotations. Essentially, because you can't quantify success at a rock drill, the O/Cs can shoot holes in your rock drill and feel superior to you without fear of contradiction, because it's all subjective. Besides, in the end, they must have something to critique you about. Because if they didn't have anything to say at the debrief, why were you even at the CTC in the first place?

There's no rock drill like a First Attack rock drill. We were told we had to take our muddy boots off prior to entering the building. Unbeknown to most of us, the colonel had contracted someone to make a giant vinyl map of the JRTC maneuver box, and they didn't want the map to get dirty. The map was spread on the floor in a building, and now the pilots and staff were gathered around it like we were going to participate in a giant game of Twister. In the good old days of the Cold War, a rock drill for conducting a major operation made a lot of sense. Even today, if we were going to attack a known objective at a set time and place, a rock drill made sense. But the problem in conducting a rock drill for doing what amounted to area recon was branches and sequels. It was like trying to do a rehearsal for a dogfight. You can't really rehearse something that is fluid and reactive. In reality there could be a thousand different outcomes because there were so many variables involved. If there was something, a procedure or technique the colonel or the staff wanted to reinforce or go over during this rock drill, it was not easily discernible, nor was it expressed to those of us who were there.

So, the four members of the first AWT step forward onto the game board. The spinner goes around and the call goes out: "Right foot green, left hand yellow!" It wasn't Twister they were playing, but in some ways that game would have made more sense than what they ended up doing. They were told, "Stand on the map in your flight formation; now take off and fly to your patrol area." The colonel sits in the middle of the map in a chair, clearly enjoying this. The air mission commander (AMC) is told to check in with the owning ground unit, and the fun soon begins.

The AMC uses the standard fighter check-in that we had used in Iraq previously: AMC; "Ironhorse Mike, this is Vampire 10; a flight of two AH-64 deltas carrying three Hellfires, thirty-six rockets, and two hundred rounds of 30 mm each. I have two hours of playtime, and I am requesting a task and purpose; over."

Then the real show began, the man of a thousand voices—you like him, you love him, you can't live without him; ladies and gentlemen, I present Attack 6 starring in the one-man presentation "The Nutty Commander."

For the next hour or so, the commander proceeded to act the part of ground BDE TOCs, company commanders, CAS, artillery, and individual soldiers on the ground, changing his voice for each different persona. Purposely screwing up radio calls, making the aircraft repeat transmissions, asking them to do things we aren't allowed to; it was all there. It was a real tour de force of that, there is no doubt. The imaginary critics raved. The *Houston Chronicle* could have written: "In his one-man show, "The Nutty Commander," Attack 6 is nuts!" The *Austin American Statesman* could have said, "Just call him Commander Peanut Butter, because in 'The Nutty Commander,' Attack 6 is as smooth as a jar of Skippy."

To be fair, there was some goodness in all of that, but after the first twenty minutes or so, any value was rapidly being lost from repetition and the exhaustion of the audience. I looked around the room, and the O/Cs had disappeared . . . even they didn't care anymore.

So as not to give you, dear reader, the impression that this adventure was solely without merit, there was value to be had in many of the training events we participated in during our stay in fabulous central Louisiana. To me, the best thing we did there, by far, involved a live-fire convoy-training lane that the JRTC had set up on a range north of the box. Capt. Paul Daigle (now an S3 battle captain) and I flew up with a wingman to the range, spending two nights and one glorious day in the deluxe accommodations afforded us in a GP medium tent, while sleeping on a standard canvas cot. But it was the flying that made it all worthwhile. It was perhaps one of the best live-fire training events I ever participated in.

Honestly, whoever came up with this idea should be congratulated. I'm pretty much certain, however, that this person isn't in the military anymore, because anyone with that kind of common sense and imagination would have left the service or would certainly be confined to a facility somewhere by now. The event began with aircrews meeting the members of a ground convoy who would traverse the range, while the Apache would provide overhead security. They would give us the route they were going to use, and we would brief them on TTPs for utilizing attack helicopter assets in the event they were being attacked. After finding out what time they intended to cross the line of departure (LD) and making sure we had the right call signs, radio frequencies, and codes, we departed to our aircraft to run up and do all the assorted checks involved with getting an Apache ready to fire live rounds.

The JRTC was nice enough to give us twenty practice rockets for this go. Rockets are always fun to shoot, and this time was no exception. So as the time for our link-up approached, Capt. Daigle and I went through our preflight checks and run-up procedures. We then took off (with our O/C in an OH-58 scout helicopter in tow) and headed for the LD, called, coincidentally, the El Dee. The link-up with the convoy was painless, and then the fun began. The vehicles were about 100 meters down the winding road when they began taking simulated fire out of the wood line to their immediate right side, about 75 meters away. We knew this without being told because we could see the actual "muzzle flashes" (caused by pyrotechnics set off by O/Cs), but the best was yet to come. The convoy commander quickly came up with an abbreviated "9 line" CAS request, which Capt. Daigle read back, and the flight was soon cleared, hot on the source of the fire. After coming up with a line of attack that ran parallel to the convoy, to ensure they would not be struck if rounds fell short or went long, we popped up and began several rocket passes. I was firing singles to give us more passes, and the rust from not having shot in several months showed on my first shot, as the rocket landed short. I adjusted and fired two more in quick succession, since we were closing on the target fast. I broke off the pass as the second rocket hit the target, and we were rewarded with some rather glorious secondaries (also pyrotechnics). As the exercise progressed, our AWT was vectored over to a target set farther away from the convoy that was a notional mortar team engaging friendly forces with indirect fire. We were given a grid coordinate that Paul plugged into the GPS and saved as a target into the aircraft database. He then directed the TADS to the grid, and we could see that our target was a white Toyota pickup truck (just like the ones the bad guys used in Iraq). We quickly came up with a plan of attack and began to engage the enemy position with our blue spears (a nickname for training rockets, because they are painted blue and don't explode like "real" rockets do). My first pass was kind of flat, and the rockets skimmed over the top of the pickup and hit on the other side.

Our O/C came over the radio and suggested that we bump a little higher, thus increasing our angle of dive and reducing what is referred to as the beaten zone (the area where the rockets can hit). The next pass I bumped higher and turned off to the side so I could pick up the target a little quicker as we came down. I put the crosshairs on the truck, and just before I pulled the trigger I checked my aircraft trim.

Everything looks good.

I announce, "Firing."

Since I am set up to fire single rockets, I squeeze the trigger twice. WHOOSH, WHOOSH. Two rockets appear on either side of me, streaking ahead of the aircraft and toward the target as they exit the rocket pods; one of them goes right through the passenger side window and strikes the driver's seat. I'm off to the left, pulling the aircraft around hard, looking for trail to get into position to cover his pass. I'm thinking, "Damn, that's the best rocket pass I've ever made." Turns out that it's easy to fire rockets when nobody is shooting back at you.

Rockets are unguided, and while we are in the US we do not get much practice firing them. The fire control computer of the aircraft helps quite a bit, and if you do everything correctly you can pretty much get target effect almost every time, but that was pretty good . . . luck.

We expended the rest of our rockets and then rejoined the convoy for the rest of the exercise. Time flew by. When things go well, it is a joy to fly, and today was awesome. The mission debrief is constructive, and we prepare to return to the FOB and our real jobs.

Finally, JRTC is coming to an end. The BN executive officer (XO), who is from Louisiana, comes up with an idea and suggests to the commander that in honor of the rotation coming to end, we have a crawfish boil for the troops. I was in the area while this was being discussed, and I decided to interject and ask, "Are you going to have an alternative for those who might not care for mud bugs?" I'm sure I wasn't the first person to ask that, but they gave me a look as if I were insane to suggest that someone might not appreciate the southern delicacy. Leaving nothing to chance the night of the big crawdad fest, I and several others appropriated a vehicle and drove to main post, where we dined at the Fort Polk Burger King. It was the best hamburger I ever ate.

AUGUST 2006:
TENROC RANCH,
NEAR SALADO, TEXAS

Our training is complete, and the only thing we have left to do is pack our bags and get onto an airplane operated by an airline nobody has heard of, full of sullen flight attendants who, in a monotone, read the FAA warning about no weapons while each of us, armed to the teeth, looks at each other and laughs. But before we can do that, there is mandatory fun to be had. Attack 6 wants a going-away party, and to be honest, the party planners have done a great job. This shindig is by no means cheap. I do not even want to think about how much money the rental of a fancy-ass ranch like this runs. Much less how much the kegs of Shiner Bock ale and catered BBQ and fajitas cost. Finally, let's not even think about where the money is coming from to pay for all of this. It was nothing if not nice. Nice right up to the part where the commander got up to speak.

Now anyone who has been in the Army for more than a day knows that if we are at a military soirée of any kind, at some point the highest-ranking person in the room is going to get up and tell everyone how much they appreciate our hard work, don't drink and drive, have safe sex, and wear your seat belt, and that we need to give 100% for the next however long that person is in command. That is a given. What we don't expect, however, is a long-winded speech peppered with unattributed quotes from various war films and the distribution of classified information to everyone in attendance in the form of air tasking order (ATO) call signs, followed by an uncomfortable explanation of Native American culture, culminating with the description of the baby Chief Crazy Horse suckling at the teat of the collective "Crazy Horse tribe" (I could have sworn he was a Sioux). But that is what we got.

The most troubling part of the speech, aside from the teeth-grinding *We Were Solders Once* quotes and descriptions of Native American wet nurses, was the fact that Attack 6 insisted on telling everyone—families, girlfriends, caterers, DJs, and, as far as I know, the guy down at the 7/11—that our unit call sign downrange was to be Crazyhorse. The ATO (where the call sign comes from) was a document produced for aircraft operating in Iraq and Afghanistan that was posted by the Combined Air Operations Center (CAOC; pronounced "KAY-ock") located in Qatar. Issued daily, it gave things such as radio call signs, mission weapon loads, and transponder and laser codes for every aircraft operating in theater. It is, as you might imagine, a document that was classified SECRET. The whole purpose of the ATO is that units will have nondescript call signs that don't describe their task or purpose and to the casual observer will be just message traffic from random aircraft when heard on an open network. Call signs are not individual and are to be assigned according to a time frame that is counter to the normal Army way of doing things, where a call sign has more meaning. For example, in the Army, if a person on the radio identified themselves as Attack 06, they have just told everyone on that net that they are talking to the commander of whatever unit that had the call sign Attack (in this case, 1-227th AVN). In fact, in our SOP, there was a long list of number identifiers for specific positions within the formation. Our standardization instructor pilot (SIP) went by Attack 10, the master gunner was Attack 11, and I used Attack 13. Most of these designations are standard across the Army. Unfortunately, there are people in Army aviation who don't get or don't care about the difference between Hollywood and ATO call signs, even when you try to explain it to them. For them, doing anything that is different or isn't directly related to our brothers on the ground isn't considered worthy of their time. The taint of anything that remotely involved our sister service (read, Air Force) is not "hooah" and therefore is a waste of their time. It's not pervasive but it's enough to cause problems when the real world intrudes.

Up until Operation Iraqi Freedom, even though Army aviation was supposed to operate under the ATO, most organizations gave the ATO lip service at best. After some confusion resulting from the use of Hollywood call signs during a downed-pilot event, most of Army aviation saw the light and began to get with the program. But there were some, such as the commander, who thought the ATO call sign was just like our Hollywood call signs (Attack) and intended to use them in the same way and even signed his email messages using that moniker.

The funny thing about it is that Crazyhorse wasn't even the call sign most of us thought we had submitted for. About a month or two prior to deployment, we were asked to submit our request for a call sign for use in theater. We downloaded a document that gave us the available call signs, and attempted to choose a primary and two alternates. The list has hundreds of possible call signs; some are neutral (Ford, Chevy, Apple, Cherry, etc.), some have an air of badass about them (Infidel, Gunmetal, etc.), and others were kind of humorous (Yoda, G-string, etc.). What I do know is we didn't submit a request for Crazyhorse. But when the commander returned from an advance visit to Iraq, he announced that our ATO call sign was going to be Crazyhorse. Most of us assumed he made the change, and the thing that caused most of us not to care for it too much (at least at first) was that it was the call sign of a well-known Kiowa Warrior (OH-58D) squadron, and it was too long to say quickly on the radio. I guess some of the hatred also stemmed from the fact that Attack 6 liked it. But whether we liked it or not, we were stuck with it for the duration, and now everyone knew about it. I suppose someone should have submitted this as a security violation, but I think most of us were too busy thinking about packing up and leaving to really care about that anymore. In a few short days the battalion would leave for Kuwait and then, after a month or so of training, go north to Baghdad for the duration.

The night of departure finally arrived. I drove my car to the rental space I had leased for the duration. Being single and wanting a vehicle available immediately upon my return home, I've been forced to do this. The Army provides storage, but it is outside in a vacant lot with no overhead cover. Having no desire to return to a car with ruined paint from being left in the blistering Texas sun for at least twelve months with no care and the ever-present possibility of hail damage, I choose to pay out of my pocket for a little piece of mind. After driving the car in, shutting it down, and then disconnecting its battery, I gather my stuff up and lock the door. It's not a good feeling. There is an air of finality to it that I do not like. I hitch a ride to the bag drop point from the S3; it's around 2100, and the flight doesn't leave until 0500 (the next morning). After dropping our bags off and standing around for the first of what will seem like a thousand roll calls, to make sure we are all there, we're told to go over to the Blackhorse Gym, about a block away, where we'll wait until the buses come to take us to the APOD (aerial port of debarkation). Going into the gym, I show my ID card, which they check against a roster. I'm allowed to enter (Have they ever turned anyone away?) and I find a seat in the bleachers to wait. I am reminded of the last time I deployed, where I was waiting in the bleachers in another gym. Only that time, we had ear bleedingly loud music being played by a DJ named "Smokey," who, in between playing such tunes as the Sugar Hill Gang's 1981 hit, "Apache (Jump on It!)," would tell us things like "I'm not turning this music down because it's all for you!" Yeah, you SOB, I've got something for YOU. But tonight, there is no DJ Smokey (thank GOD!). Families are gathered around their loved ones as they spend the final moments together for quite some time. Many soldiers tell their loved ones goodbye at home because they don't care for this extended agony of waiting for the bus and the semipublic display of separation anxiety that goes on here. You know the bus is coming when the band shows up and some general I've never seen before arrives to shake everyone's hand as they walk out the door, telling us something meant to be inspiring, but most of us aren't listening anyway. The band plays "Garryowen" as we mechanically walk out and get on the bus. After being in the brightly lit gym, it's pitch black outside. All I can see are the flashing lights of the bus that will take us to the airfield. I'm thinking, "Let's get this show on the road."

CHAPTER 2

CAMP BUEHRING, KUWAIT: SEPTEMBER 2006

When we get off the plane at Kuwait International Airport, it is either dusk or dawn. I don't know and I don't care what time it is. After nearly an entire day on that airplane, I want to crawl into what passes for a bed around here and sleep for a few days. As we disembark the aircraft, we move toward a cluster of buses that will take us to Camp Buehring, our home for the next couple of weeks. Once on board the bus, we are told that a single soldier needs to volunteer to be the "bus guard" or something like that. This soldier is given one thirty-round magazine for his M-16, just in case. I don't know what possible calamity we could face that a random single soldier with thirty rounds would be appropriate for, and I didn't want to find out. With the guard situation sorted out, we were asked to perform a head count again. So, starting at the back of the bus, we sounded off: 1, 2, 3, and so on. Since every seat on the bus was full, it should have been easy to figure out how many people were on it, but we were asked to count off four or five times. Nobody said so, but someone was obviously nervous and wanted to make absolutely sure that we had everyone before the buses rolled out of the airport. Eventually, after thirty minutes or so of counting heads, we moved out for our temporary home in the Kuwaiti desert.

As long as one didn't pull back the blackout curtain on the bus windows and watch the traffic weaving in and out and around our little convoy, the trip to Buehring was quick and painless. Sometimes ignorance IS bliss. We eventually arrived at a gravel parking lot beside a huge, white, domed tent. We were told to form up in the parking lot and then go inside the tent and sit down. We were immediately greeted by some NCO reading mechanically off a script, welcoming us to Kuwait. What followed were several briefings about combat pay and entitlements that I am quite sure nobody got the details of. We were then handed some preprinted rules of engagement (ROE) cards and other stuff about the theater of operations and the rules that applied there. Finally, we were being released to go get our stuff and, more importantly, go to sleep, but first we had to go forward and swipe our ID or, as they were now called, common access cards (or CAC cards, to be redundant) to make sure our tax-free status and combat pay would start (finally, something useful!). Leaving the tent, it was obvious, now, that it was morning in Kuwait, since the bright sun was already beginning to roast anything silly enough to remain in the direct light. Fortunately, I had a pair of sunglasses in the cargo pocket of my ACUs, so I was able to see where I was going. We were told that our temporary homes were about 200 meters in the direction of that bright ball of gas in the morning sky. If one squinted hard enough, you could see about twenty to thirty tents, just like the one we just walked out of, standing in the distance. I numbly walked toward the tents, knowing, the way my luck ran, that I would be assigned the tent as far away as humanly possible from where we were, right then. Good fortune smiled, however, since it turned out that we had the tents that were closest to where we had just been briefed.

Now off to find my bags. It sounds like a simple enough task, but imagine, if you will, eight hundred bags all of the same color, the only difference being that one end is marked with a 2-inch dot featuring the company color and your name along with the last four of your social security number. If hell has a baggage claim, it probably looks a lot like this. The bags had all been thoughtfully stacked just outside the tents we were going to be staying in. Of course, only about half of them were where you could see whom they belonged to. Some guys had thought ahead and placed individual tags on their bags that made them stand out just a little from the others. Eventually, with enough people working together, the bags were finally distributed to their rightful owners, who then dragged/carried them into the tent and tried to find a cot to call their own for the duration of our stay here.

It may be turning fall back home, but it is still blistering hot here, and I can't get to Iraq fast enough. I don't know if it was by design or by accident, but living at Camp

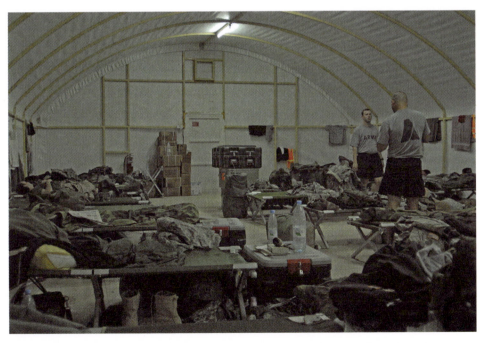

Sleeping arrangements inside the big dome tent in Kuwait, September 2006. *Photo by author*

Buehring is so infuriating and nasty that I can't wait to go north and face the possibility of a fiery death in Iraq rather than stay here another stinking day. Unfortunately, even though we've spent a year training prior to arriving here, we have to complete more training and get briefed, rebriefed, and briefed some more before we are deemed ready to face our enemies in armed conflict. I've got the crud, an upper respiratory malady I always seem to get when first arriving in this awful country (my apologies to the Kuwait Chamber of Commerce), so I'm hacking up phlegm and suffering from congestion and feeling lousy. It's made worse by the fact that it's hotter than hell, and the entire battalion is jammed into two giant tents.

We go about the business of getting our aircraft off the ship that brought them to Kuwait from Texas and get them flyable and ready for war. The pilots attend theater-specific classes and get ready, when aircraft are available, to participate in what is called "environmental training." Soldiers who will never leave the FOB go to Humvee rollover training, IED identification training, and close-combat weapons drills, which, it is hoped, they will never have to put to actual use.

Finally, I have reliable access to the SECRET INTERNET, known as SIPRNET, which is sometimes shortened by soldiers to just SIPR (pronounced SIP-er). Back at Fort Hood, mostly due to an entity known as DOIM (pronounced as DO-em), it was next to impossible to get reliable access to information regarding day-to-day activities in theater, due to the security classification and lack of a SECRET network connection. This situation, in my opinion, made training that much more difficult, because it was next to impossible to get the accurate, up-to-date information I needed to train pilots on enemy tactics, techniques, and procedures (TTP); the actual threat weapons systems we would face; and their real-world capabilities against our protective systems and the aircraft itself. From the time the BN had returned from OIF2, I had tried to get SIPRNET connectivity in the BN headquarters building. Even though there is a regulation requiring SIPRNET connectivity at the battalion level, we covered up for our lack thereof by showing the inspectors, during a US Army Forces Command inspection, a work order to get the appropriate work done and by telling them we had access to the SIPRNET through a drop at BDE. While it was true you could get on SIPRNET at BDE, it was also true that you had to wait in line, and BDE headquarters was located 5 miles away from the battalion on main post. Unfortunately, gaining SIPRNET access wasn't seen as a priority by DOIM or too many people higher than BN level, and nobody was holding their feet to the fire to get this stuff done. We didn't acquire a dedicated network connection until a couple of weeks prior to deployment. This meant I had to scramble to make up for lost time and dig through the various sites to see if I had missed anything during the train-up and to get current info on what was going on up north, so I could brief the pilots prior to moving forward. The US Army, aside from Army aviation, isn't aviation oriented, and, as a result, information regarding surface-to-air fire (SAFIRE) and enemy actions against Army aircraft was scattered around various sites on SIPR, or not even posted on the network but held internally by units currently in theater. While most, if not all, the information we needed to brief the pilots on was available on SIPR, the trick was finding it. Fortunately, I was able to locate the bare-minimum information required in the time we had available. There is no telling what we could have accomplished if we had more time available to browse and cross-reference the available information, but we made do with what we had. The regulation that allowed us to have remote access to SIPRNET has subsequently been changed, and now units BN and higher are required to have access at their work location, but, at that time, the lack of ready access was a real pain in my and other planners' asses.

With all the required work that was occurring to get us ready for the trip north, there were still things that reinforced my opinion that the commonsense gene was being surgically removed from the attendees at places such as the Command Sergeants Major Academy and the Command and General Staff College.

Upon every unit's arrival in Kuwait, they were given a list of training that all soldiers had to accomplish, regardless of their job or assignment prior to that unit being approved to go north into Iraq. In theory this was a good idea, especially considering what had happened earlier in the war to what are normally considered "second echelon" units that were thrust into situations they were unprepared for. But, as usual, problems occur when nobody can possibly deviate from the plan. We faced a compressed timeline that required us to do all this training and get downrange at our assigned time. Since I have only ever been an aviator during my time in the Army, I can't comment on what nonflying units have to do to make ready to roll north, but I can quite assertively tell you that we had more things to do than we had time for.

One of the first things I was taught in the Army was how to manage tasks and time. It was a simple lesson taught when I attended the US Army Warrant Officer Candidate School. Our TAC officers intentionally gave us more tasks to do than we had hours in the day; what we had to figure out was what could be put off or possibly disregarded altogether. If one chose wrong, you would pay a price that usually involved wearing your Class A uniform and marching up and down the street with a rubber M-16 in the hot Alabama sun during what was supposed to be your free time. It's a lesson that has served me well over the years. I'm sure others had the same experience, but for one reason or another they weren't allowed to separate the training wheat from the chaff. So, while our maintainers are working their butts off trying to get the aircraft put back together, install new aircraft survivability equipment, and ensure it works correctly, as well as support environmental training, they are also required to stop everything they are doing, pile onto a bus at 0400, drive into the desert, get off the bus, fire a few rounds through their assigned weapon into a group of targets, get back on the bus, and drive back to the base. Before you know it, four or five hours are gone just like that, and the folks on the night shift are ruined for almost an entire day. Something as simple as that had a ripple effect on the entire training schedule.

Despite some folks' best efforts, things are actually getting done, and we slowly progress toward the time of our departure to the "great adventure" known as combat.

Getting on the bus to go shoot our guns. Kuwait, September 2006. *Photo by author*

The sun rising on another day in the Kuwaiti desert, September 2006. *Photo by author*

Of course, we weren't the only unit at the camp, and we had some interesting interactions with other folks at the great social-gathering place known as the DFAC. One of the more "interesting" conversations I had was with a soldier who didn't like the business end of my M-9 pistol pointing at him in the chow line. I was wearing a leather holster that was a direct copy of the Army-issued aviation shoulder holster. When the pistol was holstered, it faced to my rear, with the barrel perpendicular to the ground. In Kuwait we had no ammunition and carried no magazines on our person or in the weapon itself. Given all of that, we were still required to clear our weapons each time we went to the chow hall to eat. So here I am, standing in line, waiting for chili mac or some other like delicacy after clearing my pistol, which I have no bullets for, and having placed it back in the holster on safe, when I feel a tap on my shoulder.

"Sir, please don't point your weapon at me." At least he was polite.

"What?"

"Your weapon it's pointed at me, and it makes me uncomfortable."

"Well, that's the way the holster is made; sorry."

"Well, I don't like it."

"Then don't stand behind me."

Yeah, I get it. "Eddie the NRA Eagle" says never point a weapon at something unless you intend to shoot at it. But here's the deal with the M-9 pistol that apparently SPC Schmedlap (not his real name) doesn't know; when an M-9 is placed on "SAFE," the firing pin is physically rotated out of the way, so there is no possible way the weapon can fire. Not to mention that there is a leather strap across the hammer that prevents the weapon from cocking or the fact that there is no magazine in the pistol, and I had just cleared it. Finally, when the weapon is in the holster the trigger is covered, so it cannot catch on anything. So, I have no idea how this "devil gun" was supposed to go off, but the good specialist was clearly concerned about his safety. I guess I just have that look about me.

The DFAC in Kuwait was always a scene of mixed emotions; you were hungry and wanted to get a meal, but you were jammed into this area that was probably too small for the number of people in it. The air conditioner was struggling to keep up, and if you were unlucky enough to get the last seat on the row, you were more than likely getting hit with the gun barrel of every soldier with an M-16 draped over his shoulder as they walked by. If you were extra lucky, when you finished eating, on your way out of the chow hall, if the wind were right, you could catch the wafting smell of the SST (shit-sucking truck) cleaning the latrine 50 or so meters away. It was truly a five-star dining experience. But if you didn't like that, you could always walk down to the Burger King and have a Whopper with a side of blowing sand with flies.

All good things must eventually come to an end. The day prior to our scheduled departure for Iraq, we were told to be at the maintenance hangar at 1500, so Attack 6 could give us his version of a pep talk.

So here we are. Even out of the direct sun, it is still incredibly hot. Bets are placed on how long the speech will last. There's a workstand that measures about 6 feet tall sitting in the middle of the hangar; this will obviously be the platform from which the great speech will take place. I'm standing next to Capt. Morton and some folks from the S2 shop. The CSM calls the formation to attention. OK, here it comes. But first we hear a prayer from our Muslim chaplain. Now here it comes. Capt. Morton is providing a running English-to-German translation of the speech at first, but he abruptly stops when Attack 6 cuts loose with this gem: "You guys are like the pit crew in the Indy 500 preparing to play for the Stanley Cup. It's the bottom of the ninth in the Super Bowl, and we all have to keep working for that big win . . . lean forward in your foxhole . . . it's going to get sporty . . . when I say mighty, you say awesome, thank you, and hooah." Or words to that effect.

"Bless his heart" is what some folks might say back in Texas about Attack 6. He wants so badly to be THAT guy. The person everyone wants to follow into battle. The man they make movies about. Unfortunately for him, it isn't working. Most of us don't care one way or another. We really don't want that. We just want someone who will back us up when we need it, and take care of the problems heaped on us from "higher" and stay out of our personal lives as much as possible. We didn't need or want a speech, but we got one, and after it was over, those of us who would be flying north to Camp Taji went about preparing for the trip.

When I consider putting my bags into an Apache to move anywhere, there is an expression about trying to stuff 20 pounds of shit into a 5-pound bag that comes to mind. Obviously, the AH-64 is not a cargo helicopter, but when we move it is

Packing the Apache for the trip north to Iraq. *Photo by author*

especially nice to have some of your gear when you get there. So, you now have the spectacle of two pilots trying to shove all their flight gear and at least two duffel bags into an Apache, repeated twelve times across the airfield. Somehow or another we made it all fit.

So, the day of departure has arrived. We are armed with the appropriate codes, procedures, routing, etc. to get us over the border between Kuwait and Iraq and on up to Camp Taji, with a fuel stop along the way at Tallil Airbase. The aircraft have been moved to a corner of the airfield, since they now have live rounds on board. Not a full weapons load, but enough to protect us and allow us to suppress and bypass in case we are engaged on the trip north.

The briefing for the movement is short and sweet. The route packets are handed out and the flight air mission commanders brief the tasks each aircraft is responsible for. Most of us have been to Camp Taji before, so this has a feeling of familiarity to it. The briefing wraps up quickly, and we saddle up with all our flight gear and associated equipment and head to the aircraft, a mere half mile or so across a blazing-hot asphalt ramp.

Finally, we crawl into the cockpit and begin the process of starting the beast. There's a bit of awkwardness to it since we are doing tasks we don't normally do back in the States. Several weeks from now, we will fly through these checks as they become second nature to us. Finally, we are all running and ready to go. Lead calls the tower and we're off.

There is always a certain bit of anxiousness when one crosses the border into a war zone. Even though all we can see are miles and miles of desert and it is no different, visually, than Kuwait, we are now in Iraq. I know because the moving map in my aircraft tells me so, and we can see the tank ditches that were dug back in the 1990s, after Desert Storm, along the border. The ARM/SAFE switch in every aircraft now goes to ARM as we cross "the fence." Our weapons are now "hot." With the flick of a thumb and the squeeze of a trigger, I can now send 30 mm shells ten at a time crashing into my enemies.

We have also enabled our self-protection equipment. New to all of us was the system just installed called CMWS (pronounced "Sea Moss"). It consisted of a set of sensors and flare dispensers designed to protect the aircraft and crew against attacks from shoulder-launched heat-seeking missiles, commonly referred to as MANPADS. While we had been briefed extensively on its operation and capabilities, this was the first time we had actually flown the aircraft with flares on board and the system fully operational.

In all the briefings we had on the CMWS, nobody had bothered to inform us about possible false alarms. Like just about any other system made by man, there were some shortcomings or peculiarities with the CMWS. One of the things about CMWS, at that time (it has since been modified), was the number of false alarms it generated. When this occurred, flares were launched but there was no actual missile in the air for the flares to spoof. When a flare cocktail is launched, a female voice comes over your intercom, telling you that a missile had been launched at you and the direction it was coming from. A warning about a missile launch from the left rear of the aircraft would sound like this: "MISSILE, MISSILE LEFT REAR." This warning generally occurred about the time the flares that had been automatically deployed came even with the cockpit. Just after we crossed the border heading north, I had the pleasure of experiencing this for the first time. So here I was, fat, dumb, and happy, flying over the desert sands of Iraq about 10 miles north of the Kuwait border, and BAM—flares go flying past my right side, and "Bitching Betty" says, "MISSILE, MISSILE RIGHT FRONT." After pulling the seat cushion out of my ass, it was apparent to me that we hadn't been engaged. When my heart rate slowed down enough to make a radio call, I asked the rest of the flight if they had seen anything, just to make sure, and of course nobody had (HA, HA, stupid American). But shortly, they would all get their own special initiation to the CMWS. For a while, false declarations became so common that we developed a call within the flight to let everyone know we weren't actually being engaged. At first, some guys said, "NO MISSILE," but some genius figured out that if your microphone picked up only part of what you said or someone was distracted and heard only the MISSILE part, bad things could follow, so the call was changed to "NO LAUNCH." If you did the actual math, considering the missile speed and the distances involved, if you were still alive and flying to hear the warning, the system had done its job, but that didn't stop me from jumping like I had been hit with a cattle prod every time it went off, for a week or so, till I got used to it. Some training on this thing using actual flares in the States would certainly have been nice; I guess they spent that money on more black berets for everyone or on camouflage flight suits that nobody liked or wanted.

Fortunately, other than the cardio workout I was provided by the inadvertent flare launches, the rest of the trip north was uneventful. The closer we got to our destination, those who had been there before began to recognize the familiar sights surrounding Camp Taji. Places not so fondly remembered; places we would soon be asked to visit again.

AH-64 punching off countermeasure flares over Baghdad. *Photo by author*

CHAPTER 3

ARRIVAL, CAMP TAJI, IRAQ: OCTOBER 2006

It was obvious to even the most casual observer that our hosts were happy to see us as we arrived. In fifteen months, we too would be the most-gracious hosts anyone had ever seen, because the sooner the new guys were up and running, the sooner we could go home, and, by the way, did you know I have a TV and refrigerator for sale . . . cheap?

As soon as we shut down, there was a guy from the unit we were replacing who was standing next to the aircraft, asking us if we needed anything, even offering us an ice-cold bottle of water.

They call the process RIP or relief in place, and for those leaving, it can't go fast enough. For those just arriving, it always seems as if you are being rushed and pushed into a position you aren't quite ready for. During this RIP we were in a little better position, having just left the same place and area of responsibility about nineteen

A pair of Apaches from A Company, 1-227th AVN, arrive at Camp Taji, October 17, 2006. *Photo by author*

months prior. After I got out of the aircraft, I began pulling my bags out of the survival kit bay and repacking my flight gear so I could hump it all like a pack mule to my new home.

Thinking I was smarter than everyone else because I had been there before, I decided to take the "shortcut." I headed for the barbed-wire fence I knew separated the flight line from the trailers, where we made our home. It was a matter of simply stepping over the single strand of wire or at worst stepping on it and then moving over to the other side and then off to the hooch. Well, at least that's the way it used to be. Now there sat a 10-foot-wide and who-knew-how-many-feet-deep drainage ditch, filled with water, that separated me from what was now a 6-foot fence.

Well, so much for the shortcut.

Unwilling to accept defeat, I headed farther down the line, looking for a crossing, knowing there had to be a gate down there that would be closer to the trailer than going the way I was told originally. Of course, I was wrong, and I eventually ended up going twice as far as if I had gone the "long" way. I arrived at my trailer, a steaming pile of fail, dragging my bags through the dirt.

At least my trailer had a shower. Being a senior warrant officer in the BN, at Camp Taji, had at least some privileges. I was going to be living in what is called a "double wet." A "double wet" is basically a single-wide trailer home cut into thirds, with a bathroom separating two living areas. The last time I was here I lived in a triple dry, which was a trailer divided into three living areas but having no bathroom. I lived in the middle room and told one of the guys who lived beside me, Geoff Horvath, that he and the guy on the other side, Wayne Turner, were my buffer in case of mortar attack. He didn't seem to think that was too funny. I had no such buffer this time, but there was a wall of sandbags piled against the side of the trailer, which were better than a WO1 or a CW2, and his belongings, as far as protecting me from shrapnel. I was going to share the bathroom with CW4 Tom Frierson, the battalion safety officer who lived on the other end of the trailer. All in all, it was not too bad a setup, and things could certainly be worse.

We spent the next several days getting our things together, making sure we had internet, buying things for our room to make life easier and going to classes and meetings. We also had meetings about meetings. By the way, did I say there were meetings?

One meeting that stood out was a gathering for all the BN pilots, hosted by the outgoing unit. Aside from the ubiquitous PowerPoint briefing about their flight schedule, procedures, and organization, what stood out in my mind was the presentation by the outgoing brigade commander. He had his own presentation, where he bragged about his crews having "tactical patience," and then he showed some gun camera tape that pretty much outraged me and, I know from comments that were made after the meeting, quite a few others as well. The tape began in the middle of a TROOPS IN CONTACT (TIC) situation. The presentation showed several US vehicles and troops on a street just outside a mosque in Baghdad being fired on by some people on the high brick wall surrounding the mosque and from a minaret on the grounds. It appeared to me that it was entirely possible to engage these people within the rules of

Home sweet home. The pilot's trailers at Camp Taji for OIF 06-08. *Photo by author*

engagement that were in effect at the time. Additionally, it also appeared to me that they could have done so without causing any significant collateral damage. But they didn't engage. They watched as American troops were being shot at, and did nothing, and their commander held them up as an example of what was right.

As I was watching the tape, I was thinking, "SHOOT!" At the same time, I heard several people in the room mutter the same thing under their breath. The longer we stayed in the room with that COL, the more obvious it became why they didn't shoot. He was an ass. It was obvious that he wouldn't stand behind his troops about anything that was questionable unless it was to push them under the bus. SO, if you were out there flying around over dangerous ground, why take the risk? Why ruin your life over something that, at best, would net the deaths of a couple of AIF assholes in a city full of them? It appeared the ground forces made it out of there safely, but then again so did the bad guys. That was their thought process at that time. I had a difficult time understanding it, but things within that BDE had progressed to the point where people watched their own six but were reluctant to do anything that might raise the ire of the BDE commander. We, on the other hand, were full of piss and vinegar and would soon butt heads with the good COL before he left the country and turned over the mission to the 1st ACB.

I met with my counterpart, who (fortunately for me) was really squared away and had developed an efficient system for the distribution of airspace deconfliction information generated through the airspace control order (ACO) and escape-and-evasion data contained in the daily SPINS (SPecial INStructions). Airspace deconfliction was aided by a product that was derived from a graphical representation of the ACO. By using a route-planning program called Falcon View, we could change the words and data contained on the ACO into an overlay placed on a map. After doing some work on the product, we produced an 8.5-by-11-inch map that aircrews could take with them that gave information on restricted operating zones (ROZ) and other special-use airspace within our AO, to include valid times and owning agencies. This product was produced every single day of our deployment. It was very necessary because we were operating in the airspace owned by up to eight different ground maneuver brigades who wanted to launch their UAVs (Ravens) or fire their own artillery. You could trust in the big-sky, little-bullet theory or you could try to be informed; we chose the latter.

We adopted an Excel spreadsheet application, created by the previous BN. Prior to each mission, an aircrew would enter their names and mission call signs, and a sheet containing the secret code words and numbers for the day and other pertinent information would be generated, saved to a database (in case of shoot-down), and printed out for use by the pilots if needed. A key bit of information that came in handy as the deployment went on was the RAMROD. Like its cousin the SARNEG (Search and Rescue Numerical Encryption Grid), the RAMROD married up a number with a letter in the alphabet so you could encrypt a number quickly. For example:

B	L	A	C	K	T	H	O	N	G
1	2	3	4	5	6	7	8	9	0

It was highly effective if everyone was on the same page. The word that was used had to be ten letters, and it was supposed to be something you could commit to memory, so it was usually something to do with sex. Obviously, this was a code that could easily be broken over time, so it was considered single use. This information changed weekly unless it was compromised or used, and then it changed sooner. Keeping up with the changes was a task in and of itself, which often proved frustrating since there was no real system in place to alert users when there was new info out. We ended up bookmarking the various web pages on SIPRNET and checking them several times a day to ensure nothing had changed.

The two things that took the most time and effort during the deployment, however, would be what were called an airport sector diagram and the aircraft mission load. On first impression, one might think that the airport sector diagram wouldn't be that big of a deal. The diagram, which was made for every airfield in Iraq (and there were a lot of them), consisted of a 5-kilometer-radius circle divided up like a pie, with each section having a letter or number assigned to it. Bigger airfields had more segments. It allowed us to communicate our direction of approach over an unencrypted radio frequency without giving too much away to anyone who might be listening and who also didn't have a need to know what we were doing. Normally during that period, the sectors were updated and changed about once a month. But just after we arrived, the airfield diagrams were changing frequently, sometimes daily. This is because pilots were flying with the diagrams in open cockpits and losing them out the door, thus compromising the information. I don't know about any other units in country back then, but we were going through reams of paper just trying to keep up, not to mention the reprogramming that was involved with the mission loads for our aircraft.

A digital mission load, at that time, was unique to the SOF and AH-64 communities. An Apache Longbow helicopter has so many functions and pages to electronically display that there is a computer program installed on the AMPS to allow pilots the ability to preprogram a lot of functions and data into a PCMICA card (the size of a credit card), which is then carried to the aircraft and uploaded to cut down on the workload during run-up. I was fortunate in that my counterpart had a rather good load that they had been using over the year they had been here. So, by taking the load they had and taking out their aircraft and codes and entering ours, we now had a workable load, at least until the good-idea fairy showed up and started asking for changes.

My ideal mission load tried to strike a balance between giving everything I would need and keeping the display uncluttered and usable. I wanted to include as much information as I could without filling up the moving map display or taking up all the usable space in the mission load for targets (at that time, we were limited to fifty targets). There were some who had a different idea and wanted everything possible to be included on the card, reducing the button pushing required during the run-up process. The downside to this approach was that it tended to use up all the available space for data in the aircraft, and unfortunately, when everything was already entered into the aircraft, a lot of people eventually forgot how to manually enter targets, waypoints, etc. from lack of practice. I tried to strike a balance, including many things but letting the pilots enter things such as named areas of interest (NAI) that changed on every mission. Needless to say, the mission load was a moving target that changed constantly throughout the deployment, according to the mission requirements and the whims of fickle commanders who would go to bed and wake up with a grand idea to "improve" the AMPS load. One of my primary tasks was to modify and make sure that the load was serviceable, so I was the one who ended up dealing with this and the complaints from the pilots that resulted from such changes.

I was able to continue a tradition that I'd seen since I started flying Longbows, though—the "Cheer-Up" file. One reason for this was because I'm pretty sure the CO didn't know how to find that page on the TSD and therefore didn't know such a thing even existed. One of the features of the AH-64D was the ability to add BMP image files to use during flight. These files were located on the image page, which was buried down in the menu of available items on the TSD. You had to know where to find them. Our load usually included a Battle Handover (BHO) checklist, an Inadvertent Instrument Meteorological Condition (IMC) recovery plan, and what some folks called a "Cheer-Up file," which usually consisted of a young lady in various

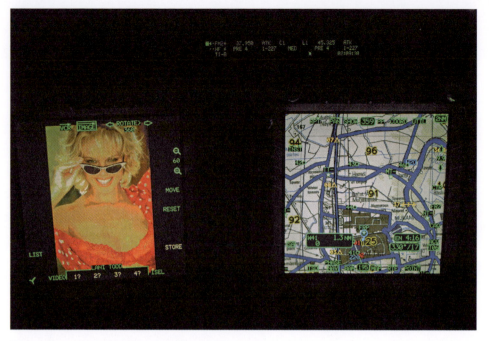

Typical picture from the "Cheer up" file. *Photo by author*

stages of undress, usually of the PG-13 variety (at least in my unit). In retrospect, I'm quite sure it violated all sorts of equal-opportunity/sexual-harassment regulations, but the funny thing about it was the person who showed me how to add the pictures was a female aviator. While we weren't allowed to have nose art on our aircraft, at least the spirit of that World War II tradition lived on with the "Cheer-Up" file.

The RIP progressed quickly since most of the folks in the unit had been here before and had an idea of the responsibilities we were going to assume. What was going to present a challenge for us down the line was the flight schedule we were going to have to maintain. Multinational Division–Baghdad (MND-B) wanted at least one AWT up in the air 24/7/365, weather permitting, so to meet that requirement we came up with a schedule. First, the day was broken down into four-hour blocks of time, which resulted in six separate mission windows. Next, there are three flight companies in an attack helicopter battalion; with eight aircraft each and with six mission windows of required support, each company would end up with two missions flying at least sixteen blade hours every day. Each mission required two aircraft to launch for at least four actual flight hours and be available for two hours on the back end for standby in case they were needed for other missions. The primary aircraft also needed at least one maintenance spare in case the primary went hard down and couldn't launch. Add to that the fact that normally each company had an aircraft not available because of scheduled maintenance, and you can see where things begin to get a little tight. This is all to cover just the base mission. Later in the deployment, when "the Surge" went into effect, the BN would at times have three teams in the air at once. As you might imagine, this operation tempo (OPTEMPO) would cause a severe strain on everyone in the battalion, but especially on the aircraft and the people who maintained them.

Eventually all the left-seat/right-seat rides and local-area orientations were done, and we had the controls. Our helpful hosts had packed up and left, and we had the mission . . . at least this was the case at BN. Our BDE, the 1st Air Cavalry Brigade, was still moving in, and a transfer of authority wouldn't take place from the outgoing and incoming BDE commander until late November. So, anything we happened to do that he didn't like we would answer for. That didn't take too long.

One of the first missions we flew came under fire while conducting a recon mission, resulting in damage to the aircraft. A sworn statement that the AMC, 1Lt. Michael Hutson, filled out after the mission, transcribed unedited, describes the action:

On 07 November 2006, I was the Air Mission Commander for a Combat Air Patrol mission involving two AH-64s, callsigns CRAZYHORSE 07 and CRAZYHORSE 08. My Pilot-in-Command was CW3 Brian Haas. The wing aircraft was crewed by CW2 Terry Eldridge (PIC) and CW2 Daryl Hosler (CP/G). During our mission window we received a dynamic re-tasking to zone 26 in support of (a) 1-66AR Cordon and Search extraction. Enroute to zone 26, CW2 Eldridge reported to me that he had received small arms fire. Immediately, CW2 Eldridge reported hearing and [*sic*] explosion which sounded like an RPG detonation below the aircraft. At the same time, he lost communications with his front seat crewman, CW2 Hosler. The decision was made to divert to Baghdad Airport to assess damage to the aircraft and determine Mr. Hosler's condition since we were unable to communicate with him. On arrival at Baghdad, we determined CW2 Hosler was not injured; however, his ICS system wiring was damaged by small arms fire. Post-flight inspection of the aircraft revealed small arms damage to the number 1 blade spar, ECS pressure line, area weapons system and ICS system. Further inspection revealed a small piece of sheet metal absorbed the round, preventing injury to Mr. Hosler.

When they arrived back at Camp Taji, they were told to report to the outgoing BDE commander, where they had their ass chewed about their radio telephone procedures, their flight discipline, their use of suppressive fire—in fact, just about anything you could think of. I was beginning to understand how a UAV managed to kamikaze itself into the window of his office shortly before our arrival here.

There existed a fundamental difference between the outgoing unit and us in the command philosophy regarding the methods used to hunt down and kill the enemy. When we arrived, we were told all about flying friendly and trying not to upset the locals, who, we were told, didn't like us flying low over their homes and such. This was followed by the tape where the crews failed to engage obvious hostiles. It was obvious that their chain of command subscribed to the theory that if we just showed the AIF what nice guys we really were, they would eventually see things our way and quit blowing up stuff.

My personal experience with and reading about the mindset of the people we were fighting told me just the opposite. They, in my experience, view the "good guy" type of philosophy as weakness. The technique we had used here previously that seemed to work well (to borrow a line from the film *The Untouchables*) was "If you send one of ours to the hospital, we'll send one of yours to the morgue." The enemy understood and respected that. The proof was in the fact that 90% of the people would flee from the battlefield when they heard our aircraft approaching. We would take care of the 10% who wanted to stand and fight.

It is important to understand that we aren't talking about wanton mass destruction, but targeted violent action against a positively identified hostile force. If you do bad things to us or the people we care about, we will hunt you down and take you out. From our interactions with the ground guys we supported during OIF 2, the enemy in Baghdad knew the big horse patch that we wore on our shoulder, they knew our aircraft, and they also knew what to expect from us on the battlefield. And they were about to get another taste.

GOBBLE, GOBBLE!
NOVEMBER, 23, 2006

When I think of Thanksgiving in Iraq, I am reminded of a line from the movie *Apocalypse Now*: "The more they tried to make it seem like home, the more you would miss it." You really couldn't fault the contractors or the cooks at the DFAC for going all out to try to put on a good Thanksgiving dinner for those of us who were deployed there. They honestly tried their best. Unfortunately, their best would never match the dinner my family would serve on Thanksgiving. Also, it was a bit of a chore to feel entirely enthusiastic about it when I had been away from home three of the last four Thanksgivings. Little did I know at the time, but I would be at this DFAC for Thanksgiving again in 2007, and 2009 as well. But it was a big deal, and EVERYONE was going, so we went and enjoyed the pleasure of each other's company. Which is, after all, the real reason for Thanksgiving.

We were warned earlier in the week not to wear our cavalry Stetsons to the DFAC on Turkey Day, but we were invited to carry them to the DFAC, and we would be welcome to put them on once inside. I devoted several moments thinking about what the logic behind this might be, because on the face of it this just sounded like the ravings of a mad man. Of course, this was a legitimate order that violated no ethical standards (other than the implication that someone somewhere was ashamed of our history), so we were obliged to follow it. It wasn't that the hat afforded us less protection than the headgear we were wearing (a patrol cap), so *that* couldn't be it. In fact, if it was protection from the sun that they sought, we should all be wearing

Stetsons every day. So what could it be? The possible answers I came up with were not all that appetizing. Either someone was entirely ignorant of the history of the cavalry and the 1st Cavalry Division and the significance of the Stetson headgear with respect to that history and tradition, or they knew about it and were scared that someone in a position of greater responsibility than themselves would frown upon this custom and that they would have to "explain" why we were wearing "unauthorized" headgear if that person saw any of us. I don't know this for a fact, but knowing some of the stalwart individuals in charge, I choose to believe the latter. It WAS interesting to note that the folks from 2-8 and 1-7 CAV were wearing their traditional headgear when I approached the DFAC and got into the long line waiting for chow.

I was standing in line with the BDE master gunner, CW4 Steve Kilgore. Steve used to be the master gunner in our BN; we had attended the FAC-A ground school and shared an office together back at Fort Hood. He had moved up to BDE to take the master gunner position earlier in the year. Waiting outside among the throngs of people waiting for their serving of mass-produced heartburn, I continued bitching to Steve and those within earshot about not being allowed to wear my Stetson. In retrospect I don't know why wearing that damn hat meant so much to me at the time, but it did. Then we reminisced about the Thanksgiving we spent here in 2004 and wondered if the contractors who ran the DFAC were going to dress up the Pakistani workers in Pilgrim outfits like they had back then. I remember at the time asking one of our RLOs who had a camera in his hand if he was going to take a picture of the "war crime." When he looked at me funny, I told him that I'm sure there was no harm meant in this, but I'm also pretty sure that these men, mostly Muslim, probably wouldn't find it amusing to find out that they are wearing costumes of Christian pilgrims. Not to worry, though; when we finally made it inside, the Pakistani workers were in their normal white uniforms, but there were a couple of female soldiers wearing faux buckskin mini dresses (where the hell did they get those things over here?) as if they were Native Americans. So instead of the anti-political-correctness home run of the pilgrim outfits, I would call the fake Pocahontas, her miniskirt, and the resulting potential sexual-harassment complaint waiting to happen a solid double. I wondered what the brigade equal opportunity (EO) representative might say about all of this. At least I had something other than my Stetson to talk about now.

We finally made it to the head of the food line, and there, in accordance with Army tradition, the unit leadership was standing ready to serve us our holiday dinner. Back home on Thanksgiving, commanders in the Army will don their dress blue uniforms and go to the DFAC that is designated for their soldiers, and serve the Thanksgiving Day meal. Here, they weren't wearing their dress blues, but there they were standing on the serving line, dishing out turkey, dressing, and all the fixings and wearing their Stetsons.

It was obvious that the folks in charge of this shindig had spared no expense in bringing in all the goodies that make up the typical American Thanksgiving Day meal. As I said before, there was no way on earth that they could duplicate the meal

I had grown up with, but for what it was, it was excellent.

There was also dinner music!

Someone had thought it a good idea to invite the 1st CAV Division Band or at least a part of it, and they were sitting at the opposite end of the DFAC from the food line. Every now and then they would break out with a song or two, which would reverberate through the metal building. I think at this time, I should point out, that it obviously wasn't dinner music they were playing; it was what might be described as a sprightly marching tune. It was, in fact, so loud when they were playing that you had to shout to the person sitting next to you in order to be heard. I openly wondered if they put the band in there not for entertainment but to get people to leave as soon as they had finished eating and get back to work. The effect was sort of like trying to eat your Thanksgiving meal in the middle of a high school football pep rally. Thinking back on it now, if there hadn't been a brass band playing during my Thanksgiving meal in Iraq, it just wouldn't have been Army enough.

According to the unit history, on December 19 Camp Taji hosted the sergeant major of the Army's Hope and Freedom Tour. Sergeant Major Kenneth Preston of the US Army visited the soldiers of Camp Taji. Celebrities such as Al Franken, Chris Matthews, Keni Thomas, Leann Tweeden, the Washington Projects, Mark Wills, Darryl Worley, and Laura Beke and Shenythia Willie of the Dallas Cowboys Cheerleaders appeared to boost troop morale and show their gratitude to the soldiers serving in Operation Iraqi Freedom. I'll take their word for it, because neither I nor anybody I know saw any of those fine folks. In fact, I would constantly see references to things like "Salsa Night" at the Taji Community Center and wonder who had time for that stuff. Well, I knew who. They were called FOBBITS. The term "FOBBIT" referred to someone who, once they arrived at the FOB, stayed on the FOB and left the FOB only to go home on leave or when it became time to redeploy. Most of us knew and understood that everyone had a job to do, and some people had a job that allowed them to remain on the FOB; it was when those people became insufferable that there was an issue.

You generally didn't refer to people you liked as a FOBBIT.

Most of us, on the other hand, had work to do. For a typical noon departure, a mission day for a flight crew member went something like this:

WAKE UP: 0730
PERSONAL HYGIENE: 0730–0745
BREAKFAST: 0745–0845 (make sure to allow for the time needed to walk ¼ to ½ mile to/from the DFAC)
BRIEFING: 0900–1015 (Once we finished briefing, it was about a mile walk to the aircraft.)
PREFLIGHT: 1030–1130
APU START/RUN-UP: 1140 (Cooling down the electronics usually took

twenty minutes or so. In the summer it took much longer to get the FLIR down to the proper operating temperature.)

TAKEOFF: 1200 (The goal was to depart on the scheduled time, which meant taxi out and then conduct the daily engine health indication test (HIT), weapons boresight, and before-takeoff checks in order to be ready to lift off at the scheduled time.)

SCHEDULED LANDING: 1600 (We would normally have a three-to-four-hour mission if the BHO took place on time. If you were extended on station, either because the mission went long or your replacement had maintenance issues, all the following tasks would shift backward or right on the schedule.)

POSTFLIGHT/DEBRIEF: 1600–1830 (If you had nothing significant to report, the debrief could go quickly. If you had an engagement, however, depending on what happened you could be doing paperwork for quite some time.)

DINNER: 1830–1930 (This all depended on which DFAC you chose to eat at or if someone brought you a sandwich down to the flight line.)

QUARTERS: 2000

If you wanted to work out or do anything else, you either had to get up earlier or do it before you went to bed at the end of the day. The PX was located about a mile from our trailers, so if you wanted to go there you had to allow for the walk to and from. Most guys waited till they had a day off to go to the PX. The goal was to fly pilots five days and have one day off, but during the Surge period, beginning around April and lasting till our redeployment, that didn't occur often. The maintainers (crew chiefs and their supervisors) worked even longer hours.

The plus side of this was it kept you busy, and time passed quickly as a result. You could, however, if one looked closely, see the physical toll it took on people after several months of doing this.

On days I wasn't on the flight schedule, I came in around 1400 or so. This enabled me to check email and the SIPR for anything I needed to work on prior to the daily battle update brief (BUB). The BUB had not improved very much since we were at JRTC. On most days, sitting there in that meeting, listening to some of the things being said made me want to gouge my eyes out with a pencil. After the BUB, many of us would go to chow and replay the lunacy that we had just heard in the BUB, just to make sure we weren't hallucinating or mishearing things. After finishing up with chow, I'd go back to my desk in the back of the big building we used for all the BN and BDE TOCs. I shared a portion of a large room (15 by 30 feet) in the back of the building with my counterpart from the 4-277th, CW4 Matt Silverman. The front half of the room contained a table and chairs for briefing, maps of Iraq on the walls, and all the regulatory publications required for planning and flying in Iraq. Back in our area, I had a desk with a computer hooked up to the SIPRNET and a printer (which was a constant source of aggravation). My AMPS sat on a table to the right side of my desk, where I also had a small refrigerator that I attempted to keep stocked with a supply of Dr. Pepper. On the wall I had hung a plush toy, which represented the perpetually stoned character, "Towelie," from the TV show *South Park*. He was there mainly because when you would press the toy's hand, a computer chip would play the words "I have no idea what's going on," which was a suitable response to many of the questions I received while sitting at that desk. I would work in there until the SPINS and airspace info came down for the next day. When that info arrived, I would create the products for the next day and then go back to "the house." Usually, I'd make it back to my trailer between 0100 and 0200.

As the days passed, we developed what in the Army is referred to as a battle rhythm. Other people might call it a "daily routine," but we really couldn't use that term in the Army because "routine" sounds like something a lady in Dallas would have and is not representative of a formation of dealers of death and destruction. Besides, what we do is not considered "routine" . . . therefore we had a "battle rhythm."

"ARE YOU STAYING SMALL IN YOUR FOXHOLE?"

Part of the battle rhythm for OIF 06-08 is the launch of the "Attack Team." The Attack Team was an AWT consisting of the BN commander and the three "lucky" aviators who got to fly around Iraq with him. It was launched in addition to the regularly scheduled missions, and not in place of them, about three to four days a week. The good thing about the Attack Team is that the commander rarely flew a four-hour block of time like the regular missions did. We would be scheduled for a four-hour block of time, but the commander usually became bored and returned to Taji after a bag of gas (2–2.5 hours). The bad thing about the Attack Team is you had to fly with Attack 6. The challenge was to find something to do that you couldn't get out of so you didn't have to go trolling the area around Camp Taji with the commander, looking for things to shoot.

There were no set crews for the Attack Team, at least initially. People were rotated through and everyone got their turn in the barrel, so to speak. One of those folks was an experimental test pilot, CW4 Don Hunter, who was temporarily assigned to the unit to evaluate the aircraft in combat and then write a report to suggest upgrades or changes to hardware or software on the basis of actual needs that he saw. One day, early in the deployment, he was flying with Attack 6 on the Attack Team. As they flew west into the afternoon sky, the CO was searching around using the TADS in the FLIR mode.

The commander spoke over the intercom to Don, saying, "Looks like there's a hole in this TADS or something, at least part of it." On the cockpit video tape, he could be seen reversing his FLIR polarity from black hot to white hot over and over, trying to figure out what the "hole" was.

Don replied (no doubt looking at the CO's video on his TSD) without missing a beat, "I think that's probably the sun."

"Yep, that's what the sun tends to do," Attack 6 replied.

It was in fact the sun he was looking at. FLIR uses heat levels to produce a visible image on the viewing screen. The hottest thing in the sky is of course the sun, so it would appear as a large white (hot) spot in a cold sky on the screen if viewed in "white hot," and a black spot if viewed in "black hot." I don't know why the commander couldn't figure this out; even though he was relatively new to the Apache, he had operated the FLIR as an OH-58D pilot . . . or should have.

Naturally, when something like that happens, you aren't going to keep it to yourself—especially if it's on tape. As a rule, aviators would make fun of anyone who screwed up, regardless of rank, and the CO was no exception. So, when the tape was presented to the S2 video production crew, they set about making a little presentation to show at the pilot's briefs, for everyone's entertainment. They ran a loop of ATK 6 saying, "I think there's a hole in this TADS" over and over, with the song "Black Hole Sun" by the band Soundgarden playing in the background. The pilots thought the presentation was hilarious, but it would be a lie to say the same for some others in the battalion.

After the Black Hole TADS incident, the Attack Team became an unofficially assigned crew position. CW4 Kevin Smith (our aviation maintenance officer) eventually became the commander's designated PIC, and the wingman position was filled by a rotating cast of characters from across the battalion's assigned aviators. I generally flew as a PIC on this mission at least once a week.

The commander really wanted to go out and kill the bad guys. He also wanted to support his old brigade, 1 BCT, to which he was assigned when he was in 1-7 CAV as an OH-58D pilot. So, as a result, most of the Attack Team activity was centered on the 1st BCT area of operations, which was located within a 10–15 km area surrounding Camp Taji. That was fine on the face of it. I'm sure 1 BCT didn't mind the support. But it caused other crews who were flying to stay down in the Baghdad sectors, exclusively. An attack helicopter generally isn't going to sneak up on anyone, so we would attempt to vary times and locations to randomize our coverage, attempting to keep the enemy off balance on when and where we would be. It was good for our survivability, and it was good for the units we supported, because the enemy could never count on where we might be at any given moment. As part of this tactic, if I was working a sector in central Baghdad, I would break up that coverage by planning to move 20 kilometers north to the 1 BCT area sometime during my mission window, in an attempt to randomize my presence. If the Attack Team was working north in 1 BCT, it precluded using that strategy and resulted in a flooding of the zone, so to speak. My concern was that over time, the enemy would recognize this pattern and take advantage by setting up some type of antiaircraft ambush. We knew from reading captured documents and transcripts from interrogations that they feared our aircraft and desperately wanted to shoot one of us down. The commander's insistence on operating in 1 BCT area of operations essentially trapped the other aircraft, forcing them to fly over the city itself while he was up. A more effective technique might have been for the Attack Team to shift south into the city when one of the other teams left, going north. There would be no change in coverage, but it had the possibility of catching those observing us unaware, at least for a time, and maybe catch some bad guys in the open, but we rarely used that technique much, if at all.

Attack 6 attended the AH-64D AQC just prior to taking command of 1-227 AVN, and that was part of his problem, as far as I was concerned. He made mistakes that everyone who was new to aircraft would make. He had absolutely zero sense of humor about himself, so pilots, being the kind of people they are, would bring up his mistakes repeatedly just to watch his reaction. He would never admit that he needed help and, in fact, tried to cover up his ineptitude, even insisting that he was ready to take a pilot in command (PIC) check ride when he probably could have been busted back to training status (readiness level 2) if someone had really wanted to. He would have been much better off if he had learned to laugh at himself, just a bit, but I guess that just wasn't in his personality.

He was in command for over two years, but he still didn't know the names of a lot of his pilots. During the tour he asked one pilot several times when he had gotten back from leave, when he had been back for months. He attempted to say hello to another pilot, but when he saw his name tag was partially covered by his holster, he stuttered and then called him "Mister B," noting that the only part of the name tag that was uncovered was the first letter of his last name. He was these officers' senior rater, responsible for writing their annual fitness reports, and he didn't even know who they were.

He had a habit, when shaking hands, of pulling the person he was shaking hands with closer to him. One day he shook hands with one of the pilots and, as usual, tried to pull the pilot closer to him, but the pilot pulled back, which resulted in a short wrestling match. It ended with the CO telling him, "You don't do that; I do that."

He regularly quoted from the Mel Gibson film *We Were Soldiers*; it was fun to watch him address soldiers who weren't familiar with this routine. He would randomly ask soldiers if they "were staying small in their foxhole?" This was a line from the film that meant something to a soldier who actually had a foxhole, but when that question was asked of someone whose "foxhole" was a sandbagged bunker, which was maybe 100 feet away from a single-wide trailer that they slept in from time to time, it tended to get you a look like you were maybe a little crazy.

He got that look a lot.

While flying missions, he operated with the philosophy that almost everything he saw was part of a cunning enemy plan. If we saw a piece of plywood lying in the middle of the road, it was a pressure plate switch for an IED. If we saw something white drying on a plastic sheet, it was homemade explosives that had been cooked up by AQI. He was dogged and determined to find the "evildoers." The problem was that a lot of the time, he applied evil intent to common, everyday activity. Fortunately, the rest of us were normally able to tamp down his enthusiasm for engaging inanimate objects in the name of total victory.

There were times that I literally expected him to order a search for some missing frozen strawberries, just like in the film *The Caine Mutiny*. Fortunately, that never occurred, and there wasn't a cabal of officers plotting against him, although maybe there should have been.

He was a bizarre fellow who believed that catch phrases and quotes from war movies could take the place for an actual personality and relating with his soldiers as human beings. He wasn't a bad person; he just wasn't a very good combat leader, in my opinion.

It was going to be a long deployment. In the end, we succeeded because we had great soldiers who were professionals, who ignored the noise and did their jobs.

CHAPTER 4

HAPPY NEW YEAR! DECEMBER 31, 2006– JANUARY 1, 2007

I can quite honestly say that I've never spent a New Year's Eve quite like this one. I'm sitting in the back seat of an AH-64 flying south of Baghdad, pulling security over-watch for a cordon-and-search operation. It's pretty orderly and not too exciting as the ground guys do their thing. They are methodically going from one building to the next, kicking in a few doors, searching for a person of interest. Time creeps by as we keep a watchful eye on our charges. I check the clock and the fuel burn and see that unless the ground guys wrap it up, we'll still be out here after the new year arrives. Not that I had anyplace else to go anyway.

We continue in our left-hand orbit of the target area, and as the clock strikes midnight, I punched off a couple of flares to celebrate the arrival of the new year. I transferred the controls to my front-seater for a couple of minutes so I could move around in my seat as much as possible and try to get the blood moving in my aching butt. It's been a slow night. Business was about to pick up, which isn't always a good thing.

EASY 40: JANUARY 20, 2007

Easy Four Zero was the call sign of a UH-60 helicopter that was flying as the second ship in a flight of two on the afternoon of January 20, 2007, when they were shot down by enemy fire east of Baghdad. A story from UPI reporter Pamala Hess detailed the event:[1]

Sgt. Terry L. Evans (one of the lead aircraft's) gunners.

"We saw the aircraft get hit initially. I saw they were in trouble. I told [the pilot in command, Chief Warrant Officer Max Timmons]—I told him they were hit. I immediately started returning fire and Mr. Timmons banked left toward Easy 40.

"Easy 40 was on fire and we knew they were in trouble. We had moved into a position where we could possibly help them if they went down. The aircraft impacted the ground. That's when I told Mr. Timmons and Lt. Neely to put our aircraft on the ground so we could go secure the aircraft," Evans said.

They landed 75 yards from the burning helicopter, but Evans and gunner Specialist David L. Carnahan, 33, jumped out before the bird was even on the ground. Armed with just pistols, the two raced to Easy 40 to rescue the wounded and protect their aircraft from ground attack.

Unfortunately, there was nothing their brothers could do. The crew was dead, and the aircraft, which contained fuel and ammunition, was on fire, and the enemy was beginning to engage the other aircraft and personnel.

At 1457 the 1st Cavalry Division Headquarters (DIV MAIN) received a report via telephone of a UH-60 crash east of Baghdad from the 36th Combat Aviation Brigade (CAB) of the Texas National Guard. DIV MAIN immediately relayed the information to the 1st ACB TOC. The TOC then directed Crazyhorse (CZ) 10/11 to the site at 1500. Because CZ 10/11 was already up in the air on patrol in the eastern part of Baghdad and had heard the mayday call on Baghdad Radio, they were well on their way to the crash site by the time they were contacted by Attack Mike. Due to the site's location in the far eastern part of our operational area, radio contact was sometimes difficult with the TOC, so aircrews often did what they needed to and then got in contact with Attack Mike when they could. By 1502, CZ 10/11 arrived on scene to provide area security for the downed UH-60. Upon arriving on station, the AWT found two UH-60 aircraft on the ground (Easy 71, 56), two UH-60 aircraft in the air, and one UH-60 on fire at the crash site. CZ 10/11 coordinated with a second AH-64 team from 36th CAB, as well as Air Force CAS, to secure the crash site. At 1511, CZ 10/11 identified a small pickup truck with a mounted DSHKA (a Russian-made heavy machine gun) in the bed. The vehicle was facing south with the headlights on, in the vicinity of the crash site. At 1520, CZ 10/11 engaged the truck and the surrounding structures with 30 mm cannon fire and 2.75-inch rockets, destroying the vehicle. At 1605, CZ 10/11 conducted a battle handover with CZ 06/12.

At 1605, after conducting BHO with CZ 10/11, CZ 06/12 coordinated with a USAF A-10 to drop a bomb on the target area. After a long discussion, the aircraft ended up not dropping the munitions because an Air Force controller called a JTAC, not on site but sitting at a TOC somewhere in downtown Baghdad, jumped onto the frequency and called an abort because he deemed CZ12 a "rogue FAC." At 1610 a ground element call sign HOOLIGAN 12 (2nd Brigade / 2nd Infantry Division [Strike]) secured the crash site. At 1633, CZ 06/12 received clearance of fires from the ground element to fire Hellfire missiles on the vehicles and structures in and around the crash site. CZ 12 then engaged one of the vehicles with a Hellfire missile, and CZ 06 engaged a nearby building with a Hellfire as well. On subsequent gun runs, the AWT fired two additional Hellfire missiles. CZ 06/12 reported targets destroyed at 1636. At 1645, CZ 06/12 engaged a house in the target area with seventy rounds of 30 mm. CZ 06/12 reported three structures and one technical vehicle with mounted DSHKA destroyed at 1648. At 1702, CZ 06 reported observing a possible 14.5 mm machine gun, which also appeared to be fully operational. At 1718, HOOLIGAN 12 found an SA-7 box, a functional SA-7 surface-to-air missile (a.k.a.

AH-64D on patrol over the northern part of Baghdad

a MANPADS), and a fully serviceable .50-caliber machine gun with ammunition in the first structure CZ 06 had engaged.

I went out to the area later that evening, and then again the next day, since our BN was tasked to provide security to the site until the remains and aircraft could be recovered. It was immediately obvious to me when we arrived that first night why the enemy has chosen this spot to set up an ambush on a helicopter. Flipping down my NVGs and looking north toward Balad Airbase (where Easy 40 had taken off from that morning), one could see a line of helicopters flowing as if on a highway in the sky. We could preach about being unpredictable until we were blue in the face, but unless crews took it to heart, we were making the enemy's job that much easier when we set patterns like that. It was obvious this was a well-established route that aircraft used to skirt Baghdad proper to the east while flying north and south. We were still doing the same sort of things that got that RAF C-130 shot down the last time I was here. To me it was infuriating. Unfortunately, this was only the beginning of the things to come.

BLACKWATER DOWN:
JANUARY 23, 2007

The morning of January 23 dawned nice and clear and a bit chilly as we prepared to go out. It was great weather for flying.

In the city, around 1030 Baghdad time, a private contractor personal security detail (PSD) provided by a company called Blackwater was escorting a US State Department official to a ministry meeting in Baghdad. During the journey, the convoy began to take small-arms fire. They called for help, and a Blackwater quick reaction force (QRF) team responded from the Green Zone. The Green Zone was the area where the US embassy, Iraqi leadership, and various military facilities were in downtown Baghdad. The QRF was also ambushed by machine gun fire as they approached, from multiple locations along the road. They limped back to the Green Zone with two blown-out tires and an unknown number of casualties. Subsequently, two more Blackwater QRF teams were dispatched, and they too were violently attacked. During these attacks, the attacking insurgents also took several casualties.

Blackwater then dispatched two of their MD-530 Little Bird helicopters to provide aerial cover and suppressing fire. Blackwater had several MD Helicopters Little Birds (like the OH-6 Loach of Vietnam fame) based out of the Green Zone. They carried armed personnel in the rear of the aircraft but had no externally mounted weapons such as rockets or mini guns.

When the Little Birds engaged the insurgents, one door gunner was killed and the rotor blades on one of the aircraft were damaged, but it managed to return to base in the Green Zone. The second Little Bird was shot down, and that is where we came into the picture.

Blackwater MD-530 helicopter like the one shot down on January 23, 2007. *Photo by author*

Downtown Baghdad as seen looking west from RT PLUTO near Sadr City. *Photo by author*

I was flying that morning as lead in an AWT with 1Lt. Smith Griggs, a West Pointer from Dothan, Alabama, as my CPG. We were operating in the northeastern part of Baghdad checking NAIs when we heard a mayday call on Baghdad Radio. We rushed toward the area, just north of the Green Zone, where the Blackwater aircraft was calling from. I called Washington Tower, the entity that controlled the airspace in the immediate vicinity of the Green Zone, and told them we needed to shut down the airspace to the northeast due to a Fallen Angel. Trail called Battalion and Baghdad Radio as we established ourselves in zone. I was talking with one of the Blackwater aircraft pilots, who was desperately searching for the lost aircraft. He thought they had possibly gone down in the Tigris River, so we worked back and forth in the vicinity of the river, looking for signs of a downed aircraft. We could see no signs of anything resembling a helicopter or a crash site. There was no smoke, fire, or even massing of people that might indicate the location of a downed aircraft.

In the meantime, another AWT from 4th Batt showed up, as well as a couple of UH-60s. We formed a stack above the Blackwater aircraft, with everyone desperately looking for our fallen brothers, knowing that time was running out.

Minutes went by as we continued to search, with no results. After about fifteen to twenty minutes of fruitless searching, we were retasked by Attack Mike to respond to a ground unit a couple of kilometers away on the east side of the river that was in contact and receiving fire from enemy forces. I felt bad about leaving the Blackwater guys to continue their search, but they did have the other aircraft above us to lend them assistance as needed. We pushed over to the ground unit's frequency and quickly flew to their location.

We found the unit easily; they were moving through the congested city streets of eastern Baghdad in Stryker Infantry vehicles. A Stryker was as big as a small bus and green in color, so they were typically easy to spot among all the tans and browns of Baghdad.

I made one turn around the friendlies, and as I came around I saw the muzzle flash from an automatic weapon that was firing out of the open door of a side building that was attached to a mosque. A person inside the mosque was obviously shooting toward one of the Strykers moving down the adjacent street. The friendlies didn't have any dismounts out at the time, so while what I saw made me concerned, it was something that we could take a bit more time to get set up on. As you might imagine, a mosque is a sensitive area, and we needed to be careful about shooting up a church. I called out the muzzle flash to Lt. Griggs. "I've got a muzzle flash off the nose in the mosque."

"I don't see it."

"It's right off the nose."

I didn't know how he could miss it. So, to make my point, I entered a dive, pointing the aircraft directly at the offending doorway. Aggressively pushing forward on the cyclic, I said, "It's right there in front of us."

"OK, got it."

It wasn't the textbook way of handing over targets from the back seat to the front-seater, and if I had it to do over again I would have done it differently, but it got the job done.

I don't know if it was the dive or the noise the blades on the aircraft make when they get loaded in a turn, but the firing stopped. We continued to circle but could never break out anyone with a weapon near or in the mosque. It happened this way most of the time when we responded to a TIC call. As soon as the enemy heard the approaching aircraft or saw us, they would break contact. It was rare that they would stand and fight if they knew we were about. We jokingly called such situations TWICs (troops were in contact). Seriously, though, if we were able to get the enemy off the backs of our ground forces, we had done our jobs. We relayed the info about the shooter to the ground unit and provided security for about fifteen to twenty minutes.

In the meantime, the downed Blackwater aircraft had finally been located. Once again, we received a change of mission from Attack Mike and headed back to the area of the downed Blackwater aircraft. This time we linked up with the US Army ground force QRF that was moving to the crash site, to secure it, giving them overhead cover.

Even after getting the actual coordinates for the downed aircraft, it was hard to find. It wasn't near the river, as everyone had first thought. The aircraft came down several blocks east of the Tigris in a congested neighborhood. The MD 530 had wedged itself between two buildings in what was essentially a slum. No wonder we couldn't find it. If I took my eyes off it for too long even after we found it, finding it again took a few seconds even though I now knew where it was.

As the QRF was making its way to the site, we were running out of gas. Doing some coordination with Attack Mike, we arranged a BHO with CZ 20/21 so we could hit the FARP. About thirty minutes after the handover, they engaged AIF that were attempting to interdict the recovery effort. This resulted in capture of one wounded AIF fighter and no friendly casualities. The operation concluded with the recovery of the crew and the transport of their remains back to the Green Zone. We wrapped up our day by doing some CM2RI around Camp Taji, with nothing more significant to report. We landed back at Taji with just a shade over four hours of flight time for the day, aggravated that CZ 20/21 ended up with our engagement, and beginning to wonder if there was something a little bit different about what was going on in our AO.

FALLEN ANGEL . . . AGAIN: JANUARY 28, 2007

The way it started, January 28 was a typical mission day. The AWT that I was flying with had the noon takeoff for a scheduled four hours of flying, followed by a two-hour standby on the back end in case we were needed for anything else. Our call signs that day would be Crazyhorse 10 and 11. It was nice weather, with the sun shining in a mostly blue sky when I showed up to the TOC, three hours prior to takeoff, to get the mission briefing. I was going to be flying with CW2 Jay Hunte, who had arrived at the unit out of flight school just prior to our deployment. We

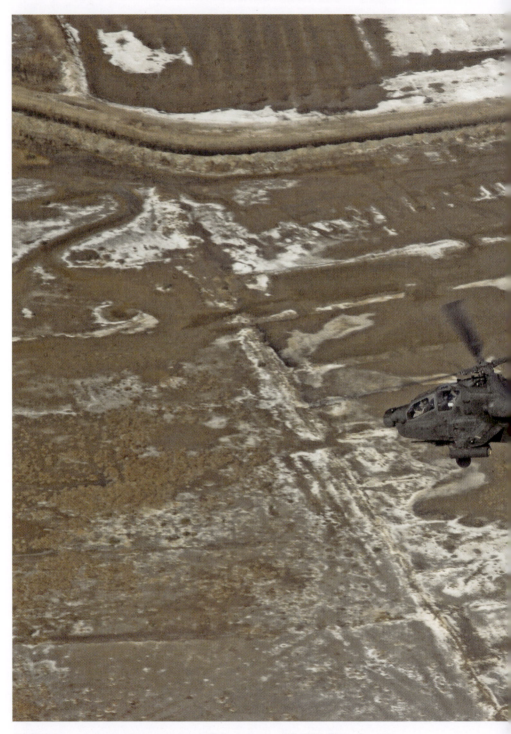

AH-64 flying over the test-fire area west of Taji on January 28, 2007. *Photo by author*

were going to act as a wingman to CW4 Troy (Dawg) Trentholm, who was flying with 1Lt. Griggs as his CPG in flight lead. After the normal routine of briefing and preflight, we taxied out to the active and began our mission. The AWT we were supposed to relieve was in another part of the AO, doing something that they preferred to finish themselves, so we were free, for the moment, to do some administrative tasks before getting on with the tasks at hand.

The guns on the aircraft we were flying hadn't been fired in a while, so, immediately after takeoff, we went to a test-fire area northwest of the airfield to check our weapons and make sure they were functioning correctly. Since I hadn't fired any flechette rockets this rotation, I opted to fire a pair during the test fire just to see how they functioned and to rotate the stock (I would soon wish I hadn't). A flechette rocket is a 2.75-inch rocket that contains over a thousand steel antipersonnel darts. If they are allowed to sit too long in the aircraft, the darts tended to clump together when fired instead of deploying like they should. After finishing up with the test fire, we were directed to fly about fifteen minutes south of Baghdad to the vicinity of the city Salman Pak and link up with a ground patrol in Zone 202 that was searching for some individuals who had taken a shot or two at them earlier. We were working this contact, looking in the reeds around the Tigris River for these shooters, when I got a call from Capt. Daigle in the TOC.

The words send a chill through me: "Fallen Angel." Another aircraft had gone down.

Unbeknown to us, earlier that day a US Army Special Forces team along with their Iraqi counterparts had been ambushed near the city of An Najaf by what ended up being a force of over eight hundred enemy combatants. Our sister battalion 4-227th AVN (call sign: Big Gun) sent an AWT (BG 52/53) in response to the call for help. While engaging enemy forces just north of the city, Big Gun 53, an AH-64D flown by the crew of CW3 Cornell Chao and Capt. Mark Resh, was brought down by multiple hits from various weapon systems. Unfortunately, there were no survivors. Their flight lead, Big Gun 52, being flown by CW4 Johnny Judd and CW2 Jake Gaston, had taken battle damage that disabled their 30 mm gun, but they remained on station guarding their fellow troopers until help arrived in the form of another Big Gun team. We were dispatched to relieve that team and pick up the fight.

As soon as we explained the situation to the ground unit we were working for, we checked off with them and proceeded south as fast as the aircraft would go. Having already been on station for an hour or so, I recommended to Dawg that we go to the FARP at Kalsu (which was on the way) to get some gas, since we had no idea how long we would be on station. At the time, with the limited information we had been given, I was under the impression that we would be pulling security on the crash site like we did with Easy 40 until the remains could be recovered. This impression would soon change. As our flight raced toward Kalsu, we kept receiving intelligence updates from the TOC about the situation in An Najaf. The first call we received was soon after we were tasked with the mission, which told us there was an ongoing fight with what was believed to be twenty to thirty insurgents. The next call corrected that number upward to one hundred plus. The next went up even more. After the battle, I found out that the actual total was somewhere near eight hundred armed fighters.

I found the situation rather concerning, and unfortunately the amount of time that it took to fly there gave me a lot of opportunity to contemplate all the bad things that could occur to my aircraft and me while doing things such as this. I would be lying if I didn't say that I was a bit scared.

We got a quick splash of gas at Kalsu, and then our flight was off, heading south to do a BHO with Big Gun 64/71 north of An Najaf.

We approached the fight from the north, swinging out wide to the west to stay clear of the fight until we were invited in. After getting a situation update from Big Gun, we took over the fight around 1500. Flight lead was talking with the JTAC on the ground, TITAN 01, while I maintained contact with the Big Gun CP at Kalsu. After we made a couple of turns in an orbit out to the west, I heard Jay exclaim, "Man . . . oh, man." I snuck a look at my left-side TSD, where I had Jay's video displayed, and saw two groups of armed men, each numbering between ten and fifteen, arrayed along an east–west-running earthen berm, firing at friendly forces to their north. I called Dawg on internal and asked him, "Do you guys have eyes on the two groups of individuals on the east–west berm?" Dawg replied immediately that they did. We divided up the targets. On the next pass, lead would take the far group and we would take the near targets.

I was trying to stay out of Jay's cockpit and let him set the aircraft up so he could be ready to engage as necessary. But this was going to be the first time he would fire at anything in anger, so I wanted to talk to him about how I saw the engagement going. I reminded Jay that on the basis of my previous experience, once we started firing I expected them to scatter, so he should take his time and engage whatever targets he could get after the first burst.

I had lagged back a bit, so when Dawg broke off his attack run, I'd be in a position to cover his egress and engage. I saw him break off to the left and I called visual and inbound. As soon as lead was clear of us, I informed Jay he was cleared to engage. His first burst of 30 mm was a little left, and he got no immediate effects on target, so he adjusted and fired again. We got three bursts off on the first pass. The weird thing is that I was wrong; the AIF stayed in place even though 30 mm rounds were bursting around them. We found out later in the after-action review that the ground unit found atropine injectors and other types of drugs among the bodies. They were apparently higher than a kite at the time, which might explain why they didn't move. In retrospect, I wished we had fired rockets on our initial pass, since a group of individuals in the open is a classic rocket target.

On the second pass we got a little better weapon effect on target. We broke off our gun run and were in the turn to pick up lead, who was outbound. I looked back over my shoulder to ensure that nobody was trying to shoot us in the ass. Just then, I saw a huge explosion just to the north side of the berm. I immediately called Dawg, since he was the primary guy talking with the JTAC, and asked, "Did the Air Force just drop a bomb?"

"Say again?"

"Did the Air Force just drop a bomb? We just had a huge explosion on the side of the berm."

"Not that I know of."

Whatever it was had caused the people who were able to start moving off the berm and down toward a trench line at the base of the hill.

It was, in fact, a bomb dropped by an F-16 from somewhere up in the ether. I was amused to read in an article in *Stars & Stripes* newspaper a few months later that this bomb strike turned the tide of the battle, and the pilot of the F-16 received a Distinguished Flying Cross for his actions that day. Unfortunately, nobody bothered to tell those brown dudes on the ground that the battle was over, so we turned inbound and fired all our remaining flechette rockets into the trench line. We couldn't tell till we reviewed our tapes, back at Camp Taji, but we did get good effects with the rockets, which we followed up with gun, also getting good hits.

This was a good lesson in trusting the aircraft to help you out. Flying inbound, I told Jay we were going to do what is called a cooperative or co-op rocket engagement with our four remaining flechette rockets. In a co-op engagement, the frontseater lazes the target, giving the aircraft targeting computer information, which changes the symbology for the pilot. The pilot lines up the rocket cues, and when everything is where it is supposed to be, he pulls the trigger and like magic the rockets hit the target . . . in theory. In actual practice it didn't always work as advertised. So, when we got everything set up, I noticed that the rocket-steering cursor was way off to one side.

I asked Jay, "What the hell are you looking at?"

"The target." He said.

"Okay."

"Match and shoot."

"Firing." I guess he knows what he's doing; everything looks right on the symbology, other than being way off to one side of what I thought was the gun/target line. I thought to myself trust the instruments, and I pulled the trigger. Sure enough, the flechettes deployed and were all over the trench line. Unfortunately, at the time we didn't realize that all we could see was the spent rocket motor impacting beyond the intended target in a puff of dust, so we were really unsure of what the weapon effect was. The "problem" with the steering cursor was that the wind had picked up and was now blowing with a crosswind of about 25–30 knots, and the aircraft recognized and corrected for that but I didn't at that moment in time. Looking at the symbology after the fact, there were a lot of clues that the wind was howling, but under stress I failed to pick up on those things. Fortunately, I trusted the aircraft, and the flechettes went where they were supposed to. Sometimes the aircraft is smarter than the pilot; well, in this case a lot of the time.

While that was occurring, I got a call from a Big Gun AWT saying that they were coming to do a BHO with us for our maintenance problem. I told them we didn't have a maintenance problem, and if they would stand by for a minute, we were in the middle of something and I would get back with them in a moment.

After we finished with the trench line, TITAN 01 informed us that they were taking fire from a building north of the trench line, near the crash site of Big Gun 53. They wanted us to engage the building with 30 mm. We quickly repositioned, found the target, and engaged with several bursts of 30 mm. TITAN 01 reported that they saw secondaries, as we pulled off target. We were starting to run low on 30 mm and were out of flechettes, so I suggested to Dawg that we BHO with Big Gun.

We did a quick BHO with Big Gun and gave them the location of the trench and the house that we shot. After deconflicting airspace, we headed north back toward Kalsu. When we arrived at the FARP, they stripped off all but one of our Hellfire missiles, since the FARP had run out. We fully expected to return to Taji since there were at least two teams sitting in parking, waiting their turn to go. We had been flying for over four hours by now, and with the sun going down, according to our crew rest policies, we would need an extension on our duty day in a couple of hours. But when we checked in with the Big Gun command post (CP), they told us to head back to the battle and BHO with the Big Gun team that had taken our place just thirty minutes ago. I told the battle captain that we were going to need an extension on our flight time (we were going to exceed the maximum allowable flight time for the day), and he said OK.

So, we headed south once again, BHO'd with Big Gun, and checked in again with TITAN. There was kind of a lull in the fighting, and for the next twenty to thirty minutes we pulled security for the ground units as they maneuvered to secure the crash site and take out the remaining enemy fighters. Eventually, as the sun finally set, we were relieved by an AWT from our A Company (Avengers), which was led by CW4 Frank Almeraz and Capt. Jesse Fleming. Instead of going directly back to Taji, we were told to go back to the FARP at Kalsu. We had landed in there twice now, but that was in daylight. Attempting to get into a place you are unfamiliar with at night is always an adventure, especially when they are using minimal lighting such as Kalsu. When we finally crept into the pads, we filled up with gas and they took our last missile.

Finally, we were released to return to Taji. After takeoff, Dawg punched in a direct route back home and we flew as fast as the aircraft would go. We arrived back at Taji and taxied into parking, shutting down with over eight hours of flight time for the day. I hadn't left the cockpit or moved out of the seat once in that time. As the APU wound down, I sat in the back seat, enveloped in the dark and a sudden silence. The flight line seemed so quiet. I let out a long sigh and massaged my aching right hand. I realized I had been squeezing the cyclic grip the entire time; it was something I did as a nervous habit. There was no feeling of triumph or victory . . . I was just tired, and we still had a long way to go. I hope we don't have many more days like this.

I climbed out of the aircraft, gathered up my gear, and walked back to the TOC. Someone had gotten food for us, and it was sitting in the debrief area. I ate it so fast I don't think I even tasted it. I did my part of the debriefing paperwork and then knocked out my TACOPS duties for the day. I ran into the 4th Batt commander in

This aircraft (REAPER 331) belonged to B CO 1-227 and was flown by my wingman on February 28, 2007. *Photo by author*

the hallway, and he thanked me for going down there; he was emotional about losing two of his soldiers, and I mumbled something about it being something they would have done for me if the situation were reversed. I went back to my trailer that night feeling washed out and sick and tired of it all.

The battle went on all night as the USAF and our attack helicopters continued to pound the enemy positions. After the battle was over, ground forces found at least six hundred enemy dead. During the night, two AC-130 gunships expended all their ammunition. It was the most extensive air battle of the entire Iraq war. Our BDE maintained aircraft on station over the fallen aircraft until everything was recovered. The A Company AWT remained on station in excess of eight hours as well and ultimately escorted one of the friendly units south through the city of An Najaf before returning at the end of mission to Taji.

During the unit's next deployment to Iraq in 2009, word was received that 4th BN, 227th AVN, 1CD, had received the Valorous Unit Award for their actions near An Najaf, Iraq, on January 28, 2007. To date, the elements from 1st BN, 227th AVN, that participated have yet to be recognized by the Army for the part we played that day.

CHAPTER 5

CAMP TAJI, IRAQ, FEBRUARY 2007: WORST. MONTH. EVER!

What started with the shoot-down of a UH-60 with the call sign of Easy 40 on January 20 escalated over the month of February. Eventually a total of eight helicopters would be brought down by enemy fire, resulting in the loss of twenty-four lives between January 20 and February 22. Most of these incidents were in or near the Crazyhorse area of operations. To some of us it appeared that something we had feared for a long time was coming to pass. The AIF and AQI were beginning to specifically target helicopters, with teams trained specifically to shoot them down.

FEBRUARY 2, 2007

I knew something was wrong almost as soon as I got out of bed that morning. When I tried to check my email, the internet was down. I stuck my head outside the trailer, and it was unusually quiet. Something just didn't feel right. Since I wasn't on the schedule to fly that day, I took my time putting on my uniform and set out for the TOC.

It was immediately apparent when I opened to door to our CP that something terrible had occurred.

We had an aircraft down and the crew was lost.

When they came to work that morning, CW4 Keith Yoakum and CW2 Jason Defrenn attended a mission briefing with their wingman and flight lead Crazyhorse 07. They walked out the door as Crazyhorse 08, did their preflight, ran up, and took off just like every other mission they had flown in Iraq during this deployment. Because the BN had experienced some gun failures during attempted engagements in the last several weeks, the commander had instituted a policy to have crews test-fire their guns in the beginning of the AWT's mission window. Unfortunately, at that time there were only two approved test-fire areas. One was in Zone 101, east of Taji, which was regularly patrolled by coalition forces. The other was northwest of Taji, just past a road called Route Redlegs, which was in an area that had not been regularly visited by ground patrols since we had last been here in OIF 2. This was the test-fire area that the team of CZ07 and 08 chose that morning.

As they approached the test-fire area, the flight ran into an antihelicopter ambush. Much like the crew of Easy 40 almost two weeks before, Keith and Jason were surprised by a coordinated attack by multiple weapon systems, designed to bring maximum firepower to bear against an airborne target. Using a model first developed by Communist guerrillas in Vietnam, the enemy arrayed themselves either in a triangle or square, with heavy weapons (usually .50-caliber machine guns or higher) at each corner. They would typically wait until a flight had entered the ambush zone, engaging the last aircraft. To counter this tactic, some units preferred to use a technique known as combat spread. In the combat spread, a flight of two basically flew line abreast with at least 1,000 feet between aircraft. It required a good deal more communication and practice to operate more effectively than traditional formations, but it had some advantages. Most of us in 1-227th chose to use a modified free-cruise formation, where we would remain between 30 and 45 degrees off lead to either side. This allowed lead to see his wingman and allowed them freedom of maneuver without having to announce a turn ahead of time. All these formations had strengths and weaknesses. There was and still is considerable discussion about what formation(s) should be used in combat for attack helicopters in this type of scenario.

On that day, Keith and Jason were flying slightly behind flight lead as they entered the ambush area. As is their want, the enemy chose to engage the trail aircraft, since he was in the middle of the ambush zone. Keith and Jason's aircraft was struck with multiple rounds in its aft part, near the rear avionics bay and the hydraulic-fluid reservoir. In the cockpit of CZ 08, they knew the aircraft had been hit. They pushed through the ambush and attempted to evaluate the damage to their aircraft. Keith announced to lead that he had received enemy fire and had a utility hydraulics failure. The emergency procedure for that failure would have been for them to make the five-minute flight back to Camp Taji or, in the worst case, pick a spot and find a place to land.

But Keith and Jason elected to stay and fight.

During the rapid, turning, turbulent fight that followed, CZ 07 never noticed the fire that had begun burning through their wingman's tail section. Keith and Jason had no way of knowing that they were on fire, since there are no sensors to detect one in that area of the aircraft. So, minutes after initially coming under fire, as they were attempting the engage the enemy with 2.75-inch rockets, the aircraft finally gave up, coming apart and falling to earth. Crazyhorse 08 was lost.

CZ 07 first noticed that there was a more serious issue when they attempted to call their wingman and received no answer. Then they spotted the smoke. They flew over to what used to be an AH-64D Longbow Apache and saw a burning, twisted wreck in a field, in the middle of Iraq. After seeing this, they managed to tamp down their feelings of rage and despair and did their job. They called in the Fallen Angel to Attack Mike, established security, and guarded their fallen comrades until the cavalry arrived.

A QRF was air-assaulted in to secure the site initially. It took a ground convoy from 1 BCT over seven hours to fight their way through multiple IEDs, taking causalities in the process of getting to the site, but they persevered and eventually made it. It was a particularly bitter pill for those of us who had been here during OIF 2, to see that this area that had been cleared of AIF was again riddled with IEDs and other enemy activity. The pilots' remains were secured and returned to Camp Taji, where they were prepared for their journey home. The rest of us were left to think about how this event occurred and how we could work to make sure something like that didn't happen again.

In the aftermath, we applied lessons learned from this event, and we put our heads down and drove on.

Anytime a unit loses someone, there is a ceremony that according to tradition must be carried out. This occasion was no different.

A military memorial can be quite affecting. I sometimes think that the Army sat down and tried to make something so emotional that it would get it all out of your system at once so you could go on and get past this painful experience.

For those who are unfamiliar with a military memorial service, at the front of the room is a wooden stand, on which is a rifle with its bayonet thrust into the ground for each soldier who has left us. On top of the rifles today rest the flight helmets of Keith and Jason. Draped around the rifles are their dog tags, and at the foot of the rifles are their boots. Because there are no caskets present, those are the physical representations of our lost comrades.

After everyone available to attend (missions continue nonstop) is present, the ceremony begins. The chaplain gives his remarks, which are for the most part standard for a funeral service. Then ATTACK 6 makes his remarks:

Battalion Commander's Remarks, CW4 Keith Yoakum and CW2 Jason Defrenn Memorial, 6 Feb 2007.

Troopers and friends of the First Team, the Warrior Brigade, and the troopers of the 1-227th ARB. A special recognition to SGT Brandon Brown (CW4 Yoakum's nephew from the 618th Eng Co. up north). Thank you all for attending this memorial in honor of our two American heroes. Thank you all for your outpouring of support; thank you Garry Owen for taking care of my guys and helping to bring them home. Thank you, Sustainment Brigade, Mortuary Affairs, for the sensitive job you perform every day taking care of fallen American soldiers.

On Friday, February 2nd, 2007, the Battalion suffered an immense loss of two American heroes who both chose to embody a cause bigger than their individual aspirations or their families. While we do not risk lives unnecessarily, we have all chosen a profession with the very clear understanding of the dangerous nature of this profession during our period of setting history for others to follow. With this danger brings the possibility of loss, and despite our best efforts we don't always succeed in bringing all of our soldiers home.

Such is the case tonight as we mourn the deaths and celebrate the heroic life of two of our own, Chief Warrant Officer Four Keith Yoakum and Chief

Warrant Officer Two Jason Defrenn. I will not be able to appropriately express the great loss of these two heroes to the 1-227th Regiment nor the great loss to their families and friends back home. Words alone cannot describe their split-second decision to place the lives of their lead aircraft pilots ahead of their own.

With extraordinary valor, Keith and Jason led the Battalion by attempting to destroy an enemy anti-aircraft machine gun position north of Camp Taji. They pursued this valiant effort while never giving up, protecting their lead aircraft from enemy fire. Their heroic achievements on that day were extraordinary as they provided the aerial security to their lead aircraft while maneuvering to a position to engage a heavy anti-aircraft machine gun position that threatened other aircraft teams operating in the same area. This single action, in the face of the enemy fire, saved his lead aircraft from further harm and other aircrews operating in the area. Keith and Jason knew this anti-aircraft system posed a grave danger to other aircraft operating in the area. They understood the grave dangers of enemy anti-aircraft systems very well as only approximately 13 days ago, they were one of the first responders to the UH-60 aircraft shoot-down known as Easy 40 east of Baghdad on the 20th of Jan. In this extremely high-threat environment and enemy-infested area, Keith and Jason identified and destroyed an anti-aircraft system in Zone 207, ensuring this enemy threat was eliminated before other aircraft arrived on the scene. As Keith and Jason's determination and valor was evident during the Easy 40 shoot-down on the 20th of Jan, so too was their determination and valor on the 2nd of February during the period leading up to their perilous crash.

During their valiant efforts, their aircraft, after receiving extensive enemy anti-aircraft machine gun fire, losing power and hydraulic pressure in a severely crippled condition, crashed and this led to their tragic loss. Listening to the voice of Crazy Horse 08 on the radio, it was very clear to me that the lives of their lead aircraft and other aircraft teams operating in the area were of higher importance than their own. Protecting their brothers in arms was very important to Keith and Jason.

This is a significant and life-changing loss to all of us; however, I believe we must have confidence that somehow their death serves the greater good for Freedom and mankind. For now, we can find comfort in the fact that they fought valiantly while demonstrating the best of our American tradition and that is Selfless Service. They are our heroes. They are First Team heroes. And, they are America's heroes.

This is our story, and I ask you to tell it to all. You tell them this story is one of great courage and sacrifice that Americans and America should know. You tell them we are hurt but we are not broken. While our grief is great, this grief must be channeled into a greater faith and resolve for mission accomplishment and defeating those that chose to do further harm to any American soldier. This is our commitment.

These brave men put their lives, their families, and their dreams on hold because they wanted to make a difference for America. And that they did! Both of these officers touched every one of you in the First Attack in very close and personal ways. Personal courage, extreme loyalty, selfless service, honor, and laser-sharp duty first are core attributes that these two showed every day and on the 2nd of February 2007. Keith and Jason are a part of each and every one of us here as soldiers and leaders.

Their bright stars will always shine high above us, and their gallant light will guide us in darkness till dawn's early light. And this will be our motto, "In God is our trust." And, the Star-Spangled Banner in triumph shall wave. Both Keith Yoakum and Jason Defrenn, you now reenter the land of the free and the home and hall of fame of the brave you will always be, in our hearts.

Keith Yoakum and Jason Defrenn, Crazy Horse 08, you are mission complete. Rules of Engagement complete and precise; call sign retired from the Crazy Horse rolls; aircraft logbook of Aircraft 02-05337 complete and closed out; cockpit clean and ready, SPARKLING as always; fuel sample checked and found okay; this is Crazy Horse 6, we bid you farewell, Heroes and Brothers at War, until we meet again in some place afar.

After the commander finished, CW2 Brian Carbone, a member of A Company and friend of both pilots, performed a guitar melody that combined "Amazing Grace" and the "Star-Spangled Banner," which was most touching.

The final gut-wrenching thing is the roll call, followed by the firing of the volleys and "Taps."

For the roll call, the company first sergeant stands up at the back of the auditorium and calls out a name or two of soldiers who answer "present" or "here"; he then calls out, "Mister Yoakum." Again, he calls, "CW4 YOAKUM" louder.

Finally, he shouted, "CHIEF WARRANT OFFICER FOUR KEITH YOAKUM" even louder.

Then the same procedure was done for Jason.

"Mister Defrenn."

"CW2 DEFRENN."

"CHIEF WARRANT OFFICER TWO JASON DEFRENN."

Then you could hear the muffled commands to the firing party just outside the open door. Then the snap and pop of the rifles being readied, followed by . . .

READY. AIM. FIRE.

FIRE.

FIRE. The sound of the rifles echoes through the building.

Then comes the sound of "Taps" played by a single bugle. It just rips right through me. I stand there at attention with tears streaming down my face, looking straight ahead.

As the final notes drifted away into the smoke-laden sky at Camp Taji, one by one we all filed up to the helmets sitting on the rifles at the front of the room, said a prayer or a goodbye, and then went out of the building and went back to work.

AH-64D 02-05337. This is the aircraft that was flown by CW4 Yoakum and CW2 Defrenn on February 2, 2007. *Photo by author*

Several weeks later, 1 BCT caught the bastard responsible for planning the helicopter ambush; last we heard of him he was in jail, which was too good for him as far as we were concerned.

"HOW ABOUT THROWING A 'SIR' IN THERE SOMEWHERE, SERGEANT MAJOR?"

I was brought up to be respectful of authority. I always called people older than me or in a position of authority "Sir" and "Ma'am," long before I ever thought about entering the military. I generally don't have an issue with following rules, and I don't break the law. But the one thing I can't stand is people who use a position of authority, assumed or legitimate, to harass and badger in the name of rule enforcement without attempting to apply even a modicum of common sense.

To illustrate exactly what I am talking about, I give you the BDE command sergeant major. As "King of the FOBBITS," he has not left this FOB once since we arrived here on a combat mission. He fills his days roaming about the FOB, concentrating on minutia. Lord help the poor soldier who is checking IDs at the DFAC if he/she fails to yell, "At Ease" when the CSM enters (even though there is a colonel already seated, enjoying his meal), and pity the specialist who chose to drive a Gator across the flight line without wearing a Kevlar helmet. He is the man who must stop the outbreak of people wearing civilian clothes to go 50 feet to the shower trailer at 0200. He will make sure that everyone riding a bicycle around the FOB is wearing a reflective belt. He is, in short, a man without much to do and is hellbent on pissing off everyone he can.

Heaven forbid the CSM might do something constructive, such as give a door gunner the day off and fly a mission or two in his place or go down to the flight line and see if there is anything the soldiers working there needed . . . such as water.

Even though he isn't technically in the chain of command, he speaks with the authority of the BDE commander, which he believes gives him license to address lieutenants and captains as if they were his subordinates. But his favorite target for derision and harassment seems to be warrant officers. At least in our eyes.

For those who have never been in the military, and for some who have but never really figured us out, the idea of a warrant officer is a strange or unknown concept.

A warrant officer is an officer who does a specific job his entire career. He is considered a tactical and technical expert in his field. In the rank structure, a warrant officer was above all NCOs and just below a second lieutenant. There are five grades of warrant officers: WO-1 through CW5, with 5 being the highest.

During the Vietnam War there was an explosion in the number of warrant officers in the US Army because the Army needed helicopter pilots. Unlike the other branches of the armed forces, most aviators in the Army are warrant officers. It was during the Vietnam War that the aviation warrant officer first cultivated the image of a mustachioed renegade, something the Army and sergeant majors have been trying to smother ever since, with varying degrees of success.

So here we are at Camp Taji, Iraq, warrant officer dogs and CSM cats living together. It could be a disaster of biblical proportions.

On the evening in question, I wasn't scheduled to fly, so I went to work around 1430. It was especially bright out that day, so I wore my approved sunglasses to shield my eyes from the glare and to function as the eye protection we were required to wear when we were outside. I finished up my work that night about 0200, and as I was leaving the TOC on my way back to the trailer, I realized the only eye protection I had was a very dark pair of sunglasses. I decided that the risk of falling over something I couldn't see in the dark because I would be wearing sunglasses was greater than catching a rock or splinter in the eye due to enemy activity, so I made the decision to forgo wearing my glasses in the interest of SAFETY.

According to the CSM, I chose WRONG.

I was about halfway to the trailer when I heard crunching gravel under boots, which was followed by a shout.

"HEY!"

I stopped, turned around, and saw the BDE CSM approaching out of the darkness. He must have been lurking in the shadows, waiting to catch an out-of-control, rule-flaunting soldier without a reflective belt or eye protection (a.k.a. "eyepro").

I could easily guess who was yelling at me, because word had gotten around about his habit of lurking in the dark, trying to catch evildoers. I don't really appreciate being yelled at in the dark in a rather dismissive tone by someone I legally outranked, and I took the opportunity to let my displeasure be known with an abrupt return shout of "WHAT?!?"

"We've talked about this before; where are your glasses?" He had failed to address an officer properly (repeatedly), but I failed in my duty to him by not giving him an on-the-spot correction.

"No, we haven't talked about this before. I forgot my clear-lens eyepro, so I chose not to wear my sunglasses in the middle of the night. I thought I would be safer that way."

"You've got to wear eyepro."

"Like I said, all I have are sunglasses. Wearing sunglasses at night isn't very safe. You can't see anything."

"You've got to wear eyepro."

"Look, I went to work, the sun was out, I wore my sunglasses, and I forgot my clear glasses. I thought it would be MORE dangerous to wear sunglasses in the middle of the night than to go without my eyepro."

"You've got to wear eyepro." It was like his computer was stuck in a do loop.

"Is that all you're going to say?"

"You've got to wear eyepro."

"This is stupid; I'm going to bed."

"You've got to wear eyepro."

"OK."

"We'll talk about this later, and you've got to wear eyepro."

"Yeah, no we won't, and how about a salute there, buddy?" As I walked away, I thought maybe I should have locked him up at the position of attention. If I had, I would have been in front of the BDE commander the next day . . . it just wasn't worth the hassle. Fuck that guy.

This wasn't the first run-in the guys in my battalion had with this pompous buffoon. Previously, several aviators had been accosted after finishing flying a mission late at night, in December, for having "concealed weapons."

When we flew, a lot of us chose to carry our assigned pistol in a shoulder holster. We didn't have a jacket that was approved for wearing during flight at that time, so we wore our body armor over our fight suit, with our sidearm and survival vest over the top of that. When it was cold, most of us kept a jacket to wear later under the seat or in a compartment called the "saddlebag." When we finished flying, we would slip on the fleece jacket and walk to the TOC. The pistol remained safely in its holster under the jacket.

One night while walking back to the TOC area after flying a combat mission for four-plus hours, two aviators walking down the flight line were accosted by a figure that literally appeared out of the shadows.

"Where's your weapon, sir?"

"Under here . . ." Lifts his jacket to show he's got his pistol.

"You can't have a concealed weapon; it's against the Geneva Convention."

"As soon as I go outside the wire, I'll remember that."

"You can't have a concealed weapon!"

"What about my knife?" the pilot asks as he reaches into one of his pockets and pulls out a large folding Gerber knife and shows it to the sergeant major.

"You can't have concealed weapons!" This guy was big on repeating himself, like he was in some sort of trance. Maybe the COL was hypnotizing him to do these things every night during their meetings.

"OK." The pilot then unzipped the armpit vent and pulled his pistol out of the vent hole. "Is that good enough for you?" He then walked off, leaving the sergeant major standing there in a sputtering rage.

On another occasion, the CSM stopped several pilots walking in a light rain who were wearing fleece jackets, haranguing them for several minutes and telling them that the Army bought them rain gear and they should wear it . . . causing them to get soaked.

It is people like the CSM who make an already unpleasant, difficult experience almost unbearable at times. I could deal with flying in combat. I could deal with a less-than-desirable commander or boss. But a person who uses his position to harass and badger soldiers, who tries to enforce rules that he doesn't even seem to understand and is unable to apply even a modicum of common sense—that, my friends, is almost enough to make you want to drink . . . that is, if we could drink.

As bad as all of that is, the most galling situation was this person's involvement in the vetting of awards submissions at the BDE level. While I acknowledge that the BDE commander could involve whomever he pleased in the awards process, the inclusion of a person who has never been at the controls of an aircraft in combat for even a second in the process of approval or disapproval of awards for aviators was at the very least puzzling; in action, it was frequently enraging. It became infuriating when award packets were returned to company commanders with a sticky note from the CSM that read, "Standard troops in contact, no valor involved."

I have a great deal of respect for our BN CSM and the first sergeants whom I served with during this deployment, but this gentleman literally took the cake. If NCOs really are the "backbone of the Army," that backbone had a slipped disk or, more appropriately, suffered from scoliosis. There is a phrase for a person like that: "oxygen thief." He would be a thorn in our side throughout the deployment.

TIGRIS RIVER, FEBRUARY 17, 2007: "YOU GUYS REALLY ARE ANGELS ON OUR SHOULDER!"

This weather sucks. I am walking to the TOC from the trailer, trying to avoid mud puddles and occasionally looking over toward the tall antenna on the west side of the camp, next to Route Tampa, to see if it is visible. It's usually a reliable indicator if we have the visibility required to launch on a mission. This morning a scud layer floats by, and sometimes you can see it, sometimes you can't. I resolve not to look over in that direction anymore because a lot can change in four hours anyway, and it wasn't worth worrying about yet.

I arrived at the TOC a bit before the scheduled brief time, so I could check my work email and grab a package of peanut butter cheese crackers and a Dr. Pepper out of my stash to tide me over till dinner. I never liked flying on a full stomach over there, so that snack would last me until we ate dinner later that evening. A quick conversation with the battle captain revealed that there was nobody flying, currently, due to the weather being below minimums.

I met the rest of the team in the S2 briefing area a few minutes before our scheduled brief time, three hours prior to takeoff. If the weather allowed us to fly today, I'd be flight lead with 1Lt. Griggs. Our wingman would be CW3 Sebastian Cousins (a.k.a. Seabass), who would have CW2 Aaron Fish as his GPG. After the S2 entertained us with the latest depressing news about IED strikes and indirect-fire attack on FOBs, we got our stack of scheduled AMRs from the battle captain. When the battle captain finished up, we briefed the plan on how we were going to cover all the assigned tasks we had just been given, when we would go to the FARP, and the commo plan. After we finished with that, I decided to go down the hall and talk with the Air Force weather people and see what they had to say about the clouds that were currently keeping everyone grounded. It took about ten minutes of talking to get out of them that they weren't sure what the weather was going to do, but they were pretty sure it would clear up sometime.

At the time, our policy was that no matter what the weather was doing, we would preflight, run up, and taxi out just in case the weather lifted. So even though we couldn't see the control tower, located about halfway down the runway, when we walked out to the aircraft we continued the premission ritual. By the time we got on the APU, it appeared that the clouds were starting to burn off a bit. By the time we cranked engines, the ceiling had lifted considerably, and by the time we rolled out for takeoff, the weather was within our limits. So, we lifted off the Taji runway on time to start our mission window, headed for Baghdad. As it turned out, we would never leave the traffic pattern that day.

While we were going through our preflight routine and procedures, a patrol from 1-7 CAV (call sign Comanche White One), led by 1Lt. John Dolan, was conducting the first reconnaissance operations on the Tigris River with their Iraqi counterparts in what essentially amounted to modified bass boats. While moving down the river, they came under fire near an island in Zone 100, not even 5 miles away from our runway at Camp Taji. During the intense firefight that followed, one of the boats ran ashore on the island, and another became separated and ran aground on the eastern bank of the Tigris near a village named Falahat.

A story by correspondent Loriann Moss fills in some of the details:[1]

Only a few minutes into the four-boat patrol, [Sgt. Ken] Thomas, 23, of Utopia, Texas, heard a machine gun unload on the boats from the river's shore.

Then, numerous insurgents popped out of buildings on both sides of the river and peppered the unconcealed blue boats with bullet holes.

"Bullets were everywhere. It was pretty wild," said [Sgt. Thomas]. The soldiers had a gut instinct that the mission wouldn't be a quiet cruise down the river, so they brought extra ammunition. Thomas estimated that he shot off at least 570 rounds from his M-4 rifle in the firefight.

First Lt. John Dolan, Thomas' in the lead boat, had no choice but to give the order to turn back. But it was too late for the first two boats.

While steering around, an Iraqi policeman, driving Dolan's boat, was fatally shot in the stomach and fell against the wheel, making the boat veer toward an island where it ran aground.

Thomas' crew in the second boat went to help but his two-engine boat lost power when bullets destroyed one of its engines. The boat also got stuck in shallow waters, forcing the six soldiers to bail out into the polluted river.

Weighed down by roughly 80 pounds of combat equipment, the soldiers struggled to swim in the murky water to another island about 50 meters away, Thomas said.

Staff Sgt. Allen Johns ordered Thomas to climb the steep, muddy riverbank and look for a way out while the rest hunkered down. As he climbed, Iraqis armed with AK-47 rifles as close as 50 feet away were taking aim and machine-gun fire continued from across the river.

Soaking wet, Thomas went about cutting through an electrical fence to gain access to a building where his group took shelter. A second group with a wounded 1Lt. Dolan was isolated, pinned down by enemy fire on the island in the middle of the river.

We had just taken off and were turning downwind in the traffic pattern when I got the call from the TOC about a TIC in Zone 100. I knew a lot of the zones by heart, but I didn't recognize this one, so I told Lt. Griggs to punch in the grid when he got it and give me a steer. Unfortunately, the different zones of MND-B were named in a random fashion, so even though I knew where Zone 101 was, there was

A pair of AH-64s take off Camp Taji in support of another mission. *Photo by author*

no guarantee that 100 would be next to it. Even though I needed navigation info, I resisted the urge to get into Lt. Griggs's cockpit, since he was getting frequencies, call signs, and grids as well as trying to get the standard after-takeoff checks done, and I waited, not so patiently, for a direction to the contact.

Absent a steer, exiting the downwind I turned in the likely direction of the TIC, southeast toward the city. Clearing the Taji fence, I turned the smacks (anticollision lights) off and the CMWS on. Then I armed our weapons with the master arm switch. I got the "saddle" call from trail, so I sped up and gained just a bit of altitude. The clouds had continued to burn off, and the weather was solid VFR now. We passed over a set of high-tension power lines just where they crossed the Tigris River on our way east. I didn't know or see it at the time, but out our left door, less than 500 meters away, was the island Lt. Dolan's unit was pinned down on.

Finally, after doing a fighter check-in with Ironhorse Main, we were pushed down the Garryowen Mike (1-7 CAV) and then eventually Comanche White 1. Along with that, we finally got a good grid for their location. As Lt. Griggs talked with them, I could hear gunfire in the background. They had KIA and wounded; they were under attack and running out of ammo. They needed help now. Lt. Griggs entered the grid and made it the active "fly-to" in our navigation system. I didn't see the carrot on my symbology telling where the "target" was, so I said, "I don't see it."

Lt. Griggs said, "It's behind us."

I called Seabass on internal and said, "I'm coming hard left," while cranking the aircraft around and descending, heading back toward the TIC. Lt. Griggs got on the radio and told them, "ETA one minute."

I pulled the guts out of the aircraft as we sped toward the river. Comanche White called and said he was popping smoke.

When we came into view of the soldiers trapped on the island, Lt. Dolan made a radio call and said, "You are really angels on our shoulder." For a split second, what he said made me wonder if he'd watched *Saving Private Ryan* one too many times, but having heard his situation report, I knew it was real and not some attempt at being funny.

Unfortunately, when we cleared the village that sat on the banks of the Tigris, all that was left of the smoke that Comanche White 1 had popped was wisps of an orange haze that hung over the island. So, as we circled the island, we couldn't immediately pick up the location of the friendlies since they were hidden in the scrub brush and tall grass, trying to avoid enemy fire. I could, however, see where their boat had run aground on the island. They must have been traveling fast, since it had slid up and onto the island, about 100 feet or so from the bank.

I called, "NO JOY" on the ground forces back to Comanche White. Immediately after my radio call, some crazy dude in ACUs stood up waving an orange VS-17 marker panel. That "crazy dude" was SSG Mathew Shilling, who would later receive a Bronze Star with V device for his actions that day. I was quite shocked to see him and took my left hand off the collective and waved at him to get down. I could still hear gunfire in the background when Comanche White acknowledged my call of

"VISUAL." I would find out later that they had been told by their interpreter that the loudspeakers on the mosque in the village had been giving the call for everyone to gather to kill the Americans. This, no doubt, added to their anxiety about being stuck on an island in the middle of a river, surrounded, waiting for help.

Comanche White requested immediate suppression to the south of their position on the island. From above I could see an area south and east of the island that was full of reeds, and it had me concerned that someone might be hiding in there, waiting for a chance to attack. We were down to about 100 feet AGL as I turned inbound and slowed; I had control of the gun, and it was slaved to my helmet sight. I called Comanche White once more to make sure: "Confirm there are no friendlies south of your position?"

He called back immediately, "Negative friendlies." And I fired.

I put three ten-round bursts of 30 mm into the reeds and tall grass on the south-eastern and southern end of the island, near the disabled boat. I was about to fire again when Lt. Griggs said, "That's enough."

I had bled off quite a bit of airspeed, and the high-tension wires that crossed the river were about 100 meters in front of me, so I turned, climbed, and accelerated to the left, calling the break to Seabass in gun 2.

Our break took us directly over the village on the east side of the river. When we arrived seconds prior, there were people everywhere in the streets. Now the streets were empty as we continued the turn to the north, so I could get sight of Seabass. Seabass asked for permission to engage, since we didn't see anything on the first pass; I told him to go through dry (not firing). Talking with Comanche White, we determined that the enemy firing had stopped for the moment. This lull allowed us to get a better idea of the situation on the island and the rest of the battlefield.

We climbed back up to a higher altitude and established a wide orbit over the village and the island. I could see Lt. Dolan's section hunkered down in a low spot near the middle of the island. His boat was abandoned on the southern end of the island, about 100 feet from the shoreline. There was a second boat that was run aground on the eastern shore of the Tigris, near the village off the northern tip of the island. That was where the group with Sgt. Thomas had crossed the electrified fence. We had no idea of their current location or condition at that time.

While we were assessing the situation, it became apparent that Lt. Dolan and others needed medical attention. I asked Seabass if they could contact Attack Mike and have them get with 2nd Battalion to get medevac headed out to the island. In my mind, it shouldn't take that long because we were almost in the traffic pattern for the airfield.

Additionally, we were talking with Garryowen Main, who helpfully reminded us that it was very important that we try not to damage the boats any more than they already were, since they were brand new and Ironhorse 6 didn't want them destroyed. Unknown to me and Garryowen Main at the time was the fact that SSG Shilling had already thrown a grenade into the boat on the island to render anything in it useless to the enemy. It would have made me feel better if I had known about the grenade, since I was now worrying about the holes I had more than likely put into the boat with my 30 mm fire earlier. I was seriously wondering if there was a statement of charges in my future for destroying government property or something.

Our conversation with Garryowen was interrupted by a radio call from some other boats belonging to 1-7 CAV, who were now a couple of miles up the river, near the bridge to an area we called Airfield Island. They were apparently under fire again.

We widened up our orbit to see if we could see what was going on up there, but I was extremely reluctant to leave these guys on the island, who were exposed and almost out of ammo. It smelled to me like a ruse to lure us up there, leaving the guys on the island exposed. We monitored the situation, and the guys in the other boats were eventually able to break contact.

In the meantime, I hadn't heard a peep out of medevac on the tower frequency, so I asked Seabass what was going on. He told me they had sent the request and they would ask again about their status. It seemed like it was taking forever.

After hearing that info from Seabass, I called Comanche White and asked him how they were doing. The voice on the radio said he was OK but that he was feeling kind of woozy. After hearing that bit of news, I told Lt. Griggs that if the medevac wasn't there in the next few minutes, he was going to get out and strap himself to the outside of the aircraft, and we were going to transfer these people ourselves, using a technique known as a spur ride. It wasn't the way I wanted to do it, but I'd be damned if I flew around listening to these guys on the radio while someone bled out when the damn medevac bird sat on the ground less than 5 miles away.

I was just about to give up hope on them ever taking off when I heard Bandage (medevac's call sign) call for taxi over the Taji tower frequency. We made contact with the crew pretty quickly and relayed info about the LZ. At the same time, I told Comanche White that the bird was inbound, and we were about to get them out of there.

About the same time as the medevac UH-60 and his wingman touched down on the island, a patrol of Stryker vehicles rolled into the village on the east side of the river, where Sgt. Thomas's group had taken shelter. I didn't have comms with them and didn't know whom they belonged to, but they were a welcome sight.

The '60s on the island loaded up quickly and departed without any issues. Garryowen had informed us of their intent to recover the boats and asked if we could remain on station to cover that. We replied in the affirmative. Having been on station for over an hour and with the guys on the island, now safely out of harm's way, I thought this would be a good opportunity to top off our tanks, because really, who knew how long this recovery effort would take. We told Garryowen Main that we were going to the FARP to top off, and that we would monitor their freq while there. If they needed us, it would be a simple matter to unhook the hoses and relaunch.

After getting gas, we returned to our spot, on station over the stranded boats. While we were waiting for 1-7 CAV to get a recovery team together and move the mile or so down the river to get the boats, we began doing a route recon to ensure nothing was awaiting these guys when they got going. Additionally, we were told that we were to support a cordon-and-search operation on the west side of the river that was to kick off as soon as assets got into place. If the people responsible for the ambush were still in the area, 1 BCT was determined to root them out.

Moving up and down the river, we found no prepared fighting positions, but the banks of the river had plenty of cover and concealment, especially on the east side, since date palms grew right up to the edge of the river. It would be simple for anyone wishing to set up an ambush to do so, unless the area was under constant surveillance.

About a half hour later, a new group of boats launched from about a mile upstream from Airfield Island, headed toward the abandoned boats that Lt. Dolan's men had left behind. Almost at the same time, M-1 Abrams and Bradley infantry fighting vehicles began to seal the roads surrounding the area where the ambush occurred on the west side of the river, in anticipation of the upcoming cordon and search. I also spotted a T-72 Russian-built main battle tank that belonged to the Iraqi army, which was manning one of the roadblocks. It was still odd for me to see a vehicle that for my entire military career had represented "the enemy" now rolling down the road and being driven by our allies . . . something I was having a bit of trouble wrapping my mind around.

For the next couple of hours, we alternated between the cordon and search taking place on the west side of the river and the boat recovery operation taking place on the island.

The boat recovery operation was particularly painful to watch. As the new boats arrived on scene, they put some soldiers ashore on the island. They proceeded to rig the grounded boat, which would allow it to be pulled back into the water.

I offered the suggestion to Garryowen that if they rigged the boat for a slingload that it would be no problem for a UH-60 to take it out of there as soon as the sun went down (a few hours from then), and they could fly it to wherever they wanted. I was thanked for my initiative, and they proceeded to continue to try to drag the boat off the island.

Have you ever been watching something, and you just knew something bad was going to happen? Well, this was one of those times, and I had an awesome seat for the show. Thankfully, nobody got hurt . . . that I know of. After some false starts and a lot of southern engineering, the guys on the island got a tow strap hooked up from the grounded boat to the towboat in the water. I wasn't read into what was going on, but obviously the plan was for the boat in the water to gun its engine and pull the stranded boat off the island, and then with it back in the water for the trip back to the dock. I am sorry that I didn't have the presence of mind to have Lt. Griggs tape this, because if we did it would have probably won us some money on *America's Funniest Home Videos*, if it was still on TV. On second thought, maybe not, especially since nobody got hit in the crotch with something hard.

When everything was ready to go, the towing boat gunned its engines. The water was boiling white and frothy at the stern of the little vessel, but nothing was moving. After a few seconds of no movement, the throttles were pulled back. Then it was balls to the wall again, with more boiling white water but no movement . . . until the strap broke.

Physics immediately took over, and Sir Isaac Newton was heard laughing as a couple of soldiers in the back of the towboat fell overboard into the nasty waters of the Tigris, along with their weapons and other sundry equipment. Fortunately, the water was shallow where they tumbled in, and they would be able to scramble to safety, but now their weapons and other gear were in the murky water somewhere. The mission immediately shifted to the recovery of those "sensitive items," and radio traffic started discussing the possibility of blowing the boat in place or having us put a Hellfire missile into it.

Personally, I was all for blowing the boat up, not only to cover up the evidence of my 30 mm attack earlier (and save me some $$$) but to allow us to concentrate on the cordon and search that was going on not 100 meters away. As it was, even though we were attempting to cover both operations, we were probably doing a piss-poor job. Between the two aircraft in the flight, we had four FM radios. We were using one for internal comms between the two aircraft, one for Attack Mike and one for Garryowen, which left none to push down to the freqs being used by the different operations we were tasked to support . . . so the only information we had on these operations was what Garryowen was giving us. It is difficult if not impossible to be proactive and anticipate the needs of the ground unit if we can't monitor what they are doing, but we were doing the best we could.

Ironhorse 6 had overheard the conversation about destroying the boat, and he quickly put a stop to that nonsense by breaking in on the net and telling everyone that no, we wouldn't be blowing up the boat today, and get your ass in gear and get that stupid thing off the island.

DAMN . . . foiled again.

So, while the guys on the boat played in the water and flirted with hypothermia, we shifted our focus over to the cordon-and-search op. They had collapsed the perimeter since the search had progressed well through the buildings on the west side of the river. We didn't have any info on whether anyone had been detained or not, but we were fairly sure they hadn't come into contact because we hadn't heard anything on the net.

Shortly after that, Seabass called me with the news that we were being relieved by the next AWT. He was conducting the BHO with them now on BN internal. I informed Garryowen Main that we were being replaced, and gave him the call sign of the next AWT. As soon as I heard them call for takeoff, we headed for the FARP to get out of their way and to gas up before we went to parking.

During the AAR process we were told that there were twenty-plus confirmed AIF killed, along with fifty wounded that day by 1-7 CAV. One Iraqi police officer who was shot in the stomach and would later die of his wounds was the only death for coalition forces.

After we returned from Iraq, we were able to meet the newly promoted Capt. Dolan and some of the soldiers who were on the island that day. I was humbled and embarrassed when he thanked us for saving his life that day. I told him we were just doing our jobs, that anyone in our battalion would have done the same thing. He also told me then that he didn't know how it was we didn't get shot down that day when I made the gun run on the island, because the AIF were all firing at me. Thank GOD they were bad shots, because my aircraft returned with zero damage. Thankfully, I never heard anything about paying for damages to the boat either.

FEBRUARY 19, 2007:
ALAMO IN TARMIYAH

The town of Tarmiyah lies about 15 miles north of Camp Taji. About halfway to the sprawling airbase at Balad on the banks of the Tigris River, Tarmiyah had long been the home of insurgent activity. During OIF 2 it was a known hotspot to us and was the place where a UH-60 carrying soon-to-be-senator Tammy Duckworth was shot down. Just west of the town in January 2006, we had lost a good friend from 4ID, CW3 Rex Kenyon, when he and his copilot, CW2 Ruel Garcia, had their '64 hit by a MANPADS. So, to say the events that occurred on February 19 were unexpected wouldn't exactly be true, at least to those of us who had been here before.

Early that morning an AWT belonging to B Company (Reapers) 1-227 had taken off from Camp Taji and was working in the 1st BCT sector, just west of Camp Taji. Flying that day as CZ 03/04 was 1Lt. Brian Haas and CW3 Brian Haas (yeah, not a typo); their wingman was Capt. Mike Hutson and his CPG was CW2 Erik Hoskinson.

At 0708, AIF forces launched an attack on Joint Security Station North in the city of Tarmiyah, using a truck bomb. Inside the station were elements of 2-8 CAV's Demon Company.

The situation was described in an AP report that was posted by NBC News in 2010:[2]

Popcorn popping, thought Army Staff Sgt. Jason Fisher. That's the sound the bullets made as they hit the wall of the American outpost.

It was early morning and Fisher's comrades were still asleep. But he had stayed up overnight, processing suspects wanted in the killing of an American soldier two days earlier. His outpost often took gunfire, usually sporadic, but this time it didn't let up. Then he looked out the window and saw it: a white truck barreling toward the converted police station.

Fisher turned to run. Suddenly, he was flying through the air.

The blast sheared off the front of the building, burying some of the soldiers. Others rushed to dig them out and find their weapons and flak vests in the rubble.

Coated in cement dust, the soldiers looked ghostlike as they made what would become a more than four-hour stand, outnumbered nearly 3-to-1 by militants.

The truck bomb destroyed most of Demon Company's communications equipment and Humvees. But the soldiers managed to start a Humvee engine for just a couple of minutes—long enough to turn on the radio and report being under fire.

Twelve miles away, at the large American base at Taji, battalion commanders watched the battle on video from an aerial drone. Word spread quickly. So many soldiers gathered at the operations center, pleading to go to Demon Company's aid, that commanders ordered them out of the room. Most continued to linger by the door.

Help soon came in the form of the two Apaches, flown by Haas squared and Hutson/Hoskinson.

In the meantime, SFC Freddie Housey had retrieved a Harris Radio from one of the damaged Humvees and climbed to the roof of the building to direct the incoming AWT.

After the truck blast shook Demon Company's JSS location, the AIF fighters initiated a ferocious ground assault, firing on the position with automatic weapons and RPGs. SFC Housey, on the roof of what was left of the JSS, pleaded with CZ 03 to get there as soon as they could.

For their part, CZ 03 and 04 were flying toward the beleaguered unit as fast as they could go. CW3 Haas was on the radio trying to make sense out of a very confused situation on the ground, so they could place fires upon the enemy as soon as possible. Unfortunately, SFC Housey couldn't give grid coordinates to the approaching helicopters, but he did describe the direction and type of fire he was receiving. By 0720, CZ 03/04 had reached the town and began to develop the situation.

"The Apaches were the first ones on the scene," said Housey, "It was the best view in the world. Everyone felt better."

Capt. Hutson describes what happened next in an article written for the August 2011 edition of *Knowledge, the US Army's Safety Magazine:*[3]

CW3 Haas was in radio contact with Demon while I was flight following as Hoskinson updated our TOC of the developing situation. After transmitting our situation report to the TOC, we off-tuned to Demon's frequency and then realized the seriousness of their situation. The JSS had taken a direct hit from a vehicle-borne improvised explosive device (VBIED) through their front gate.

They were taking sustained small-arms and rocket-propelled grenade (RPG) fire from all directions and had suffered casualties. Due to the intensity of the firefight, the soldiers were unable to get to their casualties and believed the enemy was inside the compound. The fear in the kid's voice on the other end of the radio drove home the urgency of the situation.

As we arrived on station in the vicinity of the JSS, the damage we saw was chilling. The VBIED had ignited the JP8 fuel storage tank [at] the facility and left it burning out of control. Also, most of the wall around the area had collapsed.

Our first goal was to locate the source of the enemy fire so we could set up close combat attack runs. The ground unit reported they were taking RPG fire from adjacent buildings to the north and east. We looked but could not find anything. Then the ground unit reported the enemy had adjusted fire from the JSS to us.

Lead was hit multiple times on the first run, but was able to stay in the fight. Unbeknownst to them, they had taken an anti-aircraft round in the tail rotor gearbox. As we attempted to vary our orbits around the station, lead spotted a motorcycle fleeing the area where the JSS was reported to have taken fire. We tracked the motorcycle into a palm grove to the east of the JSS, approaching from the south to get a better look.

As I maneuvered back into formation with lead 175 feet above ground level, I felt a firm jolt underneath the aircraft and saw Hoskinson's overhead canopy pane crack, obstructing my forward field of view. Hoskinson shouted over the intercom that we were descending rapidly into a palm grove and quickly made a Mayday call. Crazy Horse 3 [lead] turned 180 degrees to cover us when they received our call we were taking fire. It turns out they just turned around into the same maelstrom of bullets we had just flown through.

I recovered the aircraft and got it as straight and level as I could with my limited field of view. I took over lead, and lead became our wing to keep an eye on our aircraft. We wrapped around the north side of the city and, once we cleared the western edge, [we] proceeded directly to Taji. During this time, the cockpit voice was going crazy announcing the various emergencies caused by the battle damage we had just taken. Cockpit indicators told me I had taken damage to the utility hydraulic system, rendering our 30 mm gun inoperative. We had also suffered flight control damage, illustrated by the "BUCS FAIL" message on the [heads-]up display.

Our wingman, now flying trail, was able to see and relay to us that our wing stores were on fire. I looked out the left side of the aircraft and saw the rockets beginning to cook off. I punched off the stores and began looking for a place to set down the aircraft.

However, after conferring with our wingman, we decided the tactical situation did not permit this. After assisting me in getting the initial emergencies under control, Hoskinson, by peering through the small windowpane in front of him, began to guide me back toward Taji. Trail took care of the radio calls so I could concentrate on flying. He also relayed the events to our TOC and requested a follow-on air weapons team (AWT) and ended up conducting a battle handover with them.

After establishing a heading back to Taji, I suspected Hoskinson had been hurt and asked him about his condition. His reply was "I'm fine. Just fly the aircraft." I knew when we got hit that he'd been hurt, but I didn't know to what extent. Hoskinson ignored his injuries and kept me concentrated on getting the aircraft home to Taji. Hoskinson performed incredibly well during this emergency. As we surveyed our damage, he reported that a round had penetrated his floor and damaged the cyclic, which had fallen over to the stop. I later discovered that same round had hit the bottom of his seat and sent fragments into his calves. Since we couldn't transfer the controls, I had to depend on him for obstacle avoidance, as I was practically flying blind. I knew there was a set of high-tension wires between Tarmiyah and Taji, but I could not see them. Thankfully, Hoskinson spotted the wires, which gave me ample time to negotiate them.

CW3 Haas and 1st Lt. Haas did everything they could to assist us getting home. They took over all radio calls for us and helped us assess our aircraft damage, allowing us to control the aircraft and monitor our own systems. On our way back to Taji, we passed the replacement AWT. Crazy Horse 3 relayed our situation and the tactical situation on the ground in Tarmiyah to them, including a warning that we had taken fire by some heavy-caliber weapons in the eastern palm groves.

After landing, Capt. Hutson counted at least twenty-two bullet holes in his aircraft. His wingman had a bullet in their intermediate tail rotor gear box, but it continued to operate and returned them safely to Camp Taji. CW2 Hoskinson's wound had been caused by a 12.7 mm machine gun round that had struck the aircraft immediately underneath his seat. Erik returned to action, flying missions a week after his wounding.

There are not too many aircraft that can take that kind of punishment and keep flying. There is no doubt in my mind that if I ever go to combat again, the Apache is the aircraft I want to fly.

The second team of Apaches CZ 18/19 assumed the fight from 03/04 and rushed toward the besieged JSS. They were flown by CW3 Matt Skiver and 1Lt. Clint Burleson in CZ 18 and CW2, and Micah Johnson and CW2 Troy Moseley in CZ 19 were conducting their regular combat air patrol when they heard Capt. Hutson's mayday call. They immediately broke station, flying en route toward Zone 99 and Tarmiyah.

Around 0810, CZ 18/19 arrived from the east, passing Hutson and Haas on the way in. Once they determined that CPT Hutson was going to be able to recover his aircraft successfully, they assumed CZ 03/04's mission at the JSS. Not getting a complete battle handover from the previous flight for obvious reasons, the flight checked in with Demon 06, who gave them a quick situation update. One aircraft then pushed down to Blue 4 (SFC Housey), who informed the flight that the JSS was still in danger of being overrun. They also received grid coordinates of an enemy position and clearance to engage by Stallion 06 (2-8 CAV's commander), who was developing the situation through a UAV feed, back at Camp Taji.

While all that was going on, the flight began to take heavy fire from enemy fighters in and around the JSS. After about ten minutes on station, Micah Johnson in CZ 19 reported to lead that they had been hit and had problems with one of their Hellfire launchers, as well as having indications in the cockpit of a utility hydraulics failure.

The flight disengaged and flew northwest into a clear area to assess the damage to the aircraft. Flying alongside CZ 19 in his aircraft, CW3 Skiver reported that he saw visible fluid all over the tail of the aircraft, but there was no fire or smoke visible. After checking his cockpit pressure indications and assessing that he could continue the fight, CW2 Johnson told lead that he was good to go. So, the flight returned to the JSS to provide security and close-combat attacks until a BHO could be made with another AWT.

At about 0840 a medevac UH-60 proceeded inbound to evacuate wounded from the JSS. It was going to land in a field adjacent to what was left of the building.

As soon as the UH-60 touched down, Blue 4 reported that the JSS was now taking fire from a building 100 meters south of the JSS. CZ 19 dove down out of his overwatch position in a north-to-south gun run directly over the top of the UH-60, sitting on the ground in the LZ, engaging the enemy position with twenty to forty rounds of 30 mm cannon fire.

After breaking off the attack run, 1Lt. Burleson reported spotting enemy fighters north of the JSS that were also engaging the JSS from a rooftop position. The flight then maneuvered to place fires upon that position, with both aircraft firing their 30 mm cannon at the enemy. On the break 1Lt. Burleson reported seeing secondaries from their attack.

On a second attack run, CZ 18 felt a solid impact on the aircraft, which violently jolted the aircraft upward. Matt told Lt. Burleson that he thought they were under fire from RPGs.

Almost as soon as that occurred, the flight received a call from Blue 4 stating that the flight was being engaged with both small arms and heavy-caliber machine gun fire. The flight maneuvered to attempt to throw off the enemy's aim. Due to the nature of the threat to the ground forces, the AWT remained on station, exposed to enemy fire, protecting the soldiers in the JSS for another thirty minutes until they got a BHO around 0930 from AH-64s Attack 22 and 26, belonging to the 36th CAB, based out of Balad, about ten minutes' flight time north.

CZ 18/19 returned to Taji. After landing they inspected CZ 19 and found damage to both wings, with the tail and main rotor blades receiving small-arms damage. There was also damage from heavy machine gun fire to the tail section, and the hydraulic return line from the tail rotor controls was severed.

After Johnson and Moseley jumped into a spare aircraft, at 1055 CZ 18/19 re-assumed the fight in Tarmiyah. The situation at the JSS had stabilized somewhat, so they began a search for the weapons pylons that had been jettisoned by Capt. Hutson earlier that morning. They were on station for about fifteen minutes when Blue 4 once again reported that the JSS was under attack.

Friendly forces marked the area the fire was coming from with tracer fire from a .50-caliber machine gun. After observing the marking rounds, the flight engaged the area and adjacent street with 30 mm cannon fire, silencing the enemy fire. After about thirty minutes on station, 18/19 was relieved by another Crazyhorse team and they returned to Taji, their flying day over.

The battalion maintained a presence in the area for the rest of the day, sending one AWT after another to provide security for the JSS and those participating in the operations around it.

An AH-64 on patrol over the morning fog near Camp Taji. *Photo by author*

An AH-64 in the forward arming and refueling point (FARP) at Camp Taji. The soldiers in the FARP worked long hours to keep all the aircraft going. *Photo by author*

That night around 1900, while on station near Tarmiyah, CZ 12/13 received a tasking from 2-8 CAV's JTAC, HAVOC 12. They were asked to investigate a Bongo truck near a house where persons had been observed trying to recover the weapons jettisoned previously by CPT Hutson. After being talked onto the target by using a video feed from a UAS, HAVOC 12 cleared CZ 12 and 13 to engage the truck, using 30 mm cannon. The resulting attack yielded a large secondary explosion and fire, which ultimately caught the nearby house on fire.

Although we wouldn't lose any aircrews in or near Tarmiyah for the rest of the deployment, it would be a place we would visit over and over again in response to enemy activity. It wouldn't be until we returned to Iraq, in 2010, that the town would eventually be considered secure.

By the end of February, the 1st Air Cavalry Brigade had participated in thirty-two separate enemy engagements that month. We had lost two aircraft, with many others damaged as well. Worst of all, we had lost four fine officers, men who were sons, brothers, and fathers. Men whose loss we mourn to this day.

We came away from that month changed. There were lessons we learned, things that we probably should have seen before, but either pride or stubbornness didn't allow us to. But we mourned, learned, and moved on. It was all we could do. It may sound cliché or corny, but we owed it to them to keep going; it is what they would have done.

CHAPTER 6

LEAVE:
MARCH 2007

Every soldier who served more than ten months in a combat zone, at that time, was entitled to what the Army quaintly called "environmental leave." Back in Kuwait when everyone put in their dates for leave, I selected a time in March, since it was at about the midway point of a twelve-month tour, and I figured when I got back from the States that everything would be downhill from there. At the time there were rumblings about a fifteen-month rotation, but nothing definitive had been put out by anyone in a position of authority. I would soon find out that I had guessed wrong about the twelve months and the downhill part.

Environmental leave, or what used to be called R&R (for rest and recuperation) leave, is something everyone enjoys, but I don't think anyone really enjoys the process of getting there.

The process started several days prior to leaving Taji, when you were required to go to BDE to get a briefing about going on leave. Those of us scheduled for leave gathered at the appointed time and place in a room over at BDE. A rather pleasant young specialist gave us a briefing about what we needed, and the time and location for our departure. We signed a piece of paper so someone could prove we had received the briefing, in case we screwed up later, and that was it till the day we left.

On the morning of my departure, I got up early and made sure everything in my room was in order. Then I put on my body armor (damn, this stuff is heavy) and Kevlar helmet, grabbed my rucksack, and went out the door, locking it behind me. I first went to HHC (the company I was assigned to), where I signed out and turned in my personal weapon. Then I walked to BDE, where I signed out, signed in for the flight, and sat down to wait for the time to go to the Taji terminal/helipad for my trip to Balad Airbase, from where I'd start the journey back to Texas.

The one thing that hasn't changed about the Army, since George Washington ran it, is the waiting. No matter what you do, no matter where you go, the one constant will be the waiting. If you removed all the waiting from my time in service, I may have actually served only five years, tops. I exaggerate of course; the actual figure is probably closer to eight years.

After waiting for thirty minutes or so at BDE, those of us going on leave that day were told to go over to Taji Pad (the name given to the passenger terminal/

helipad). I hoisted my rucksack and headed out the door for the short walk to the terminal. After arriving there, we waited on the UH-60 or CH-47 to arrive to fly us the fifteen minutes north to Balad.

As I sat at the terminal, waiting for the flight, I noticed others around me had enough bags to stay somewhere for a month. I wondered if I had missed something in one of the briefings. I KNOW I was ALLOWED to have two duffel bags, but it didn't mean I was REQUIRED to bring two duffel bags. I thought to myself, What in the hell are they taking back to the States that they need all those bags for? We weren't supposed to deploy with more than a single change of civilian clothes, so it shouldn't be that, and I certainly wasn't taking back any more uniforms than what I had on my back. Oh well, at least I'm not carrying that stuff or trying to get it all through customs.

The sun had now come up on a new morning in Iraq. I now knew I was getting a ride in a Hawk, since the 47s didn't fly in daylight. The reason that was a concern was the fact that a UH-60 carried a lot fewer people than a Chinook. I guess it really wasn't a concern; it just meant you may have to wait longer, depending on where you were in line for a ride. I was going on leave regardless, and the only thing now was how much time it was going to take to get there. The thing in our favor was the fact that your leave didn't officially start until you arrived at Dallas–Ft. Worth (DFW) airport, so all this time en route was just another form of waiting, and time when you weren't at work.

Eventually a Hawk with my name on it showed up, and off we flew to Balad. We arrived at the "Catfish Air" terminal, where all the Army helicopter passenger operations occurred at Balad. Getting off the aircraft, we eventually made our way via a bus to a holding area. There, we were told to go to a certain number of shack, which contained a bunch of cots (not a good sign) and wait for the formation at an assigned time and place to be told when our flight to Kuwait would occur. In the meantime, between formations, we could come and go as we pleased.

I took the opportunity to visit the PX to buy a pillow and marvel at the sight of all the stuff that our PX at Taji didn't have. I felt like a person from a Third World country visiting the Mall of America . . . Air Force bastards.

Come dinnertime, I went over to the nearest dining facility, which was run by the USAF. There were signs everywhere admonishing people to wear their reflective belts. A reflective belt was made from nylon or some other man-made material, 2 inches wide, which reflected available light extremely well. When hit by the beam of a car's headlight, the belt would almost glow. At the time, the Army hadn't bought into the reflective belt craze, and I laughed at how stupid this whole thing was in a combat zone . . . little did I know that soon, we too would be wearing the infernal belt of obedience, which would even be color-coded as to rank.

After every meal we had a formation to tell us that there weren't any flights going out to Kuwait, and to wait for the next formation. Initially, everyone went with the flow and nobody complained too much about it. After a day or so of waiting, the holding area started getting kind of crowded, and the troops began to get a little restless. Personally, I had to remind myself that it didn't matter; none of this was counting against my leave, and I would get there eventually . . . but it required constant effort not to get frustrated.

Eventually, after several more formations and a briefing or two, I found myself waiting in line to get aboard a C-130 cargo plane headed south to Kuwait. The crew members were ever so serious as they went about their duties getting ready to start the four-engine beast. I found myself almost laughing at the loadmaster, since he was quite dramatic about strapping on his body armor. Aside from the takeoff, we were going to be cruising at an altitude way above the range of the kind of weapons that the animals we were fighting were using. I suppose they could have tried to engage our aircraft with a MANPADS, but they had plenty of opportunity for other targets that offered a higher possibility of success than a C-130 en route to Kuwait. Now don't get me wrong, I have a great deal of respect for anyone who did their job in a professional manner, and these guys certainly fit the bill, but there was a bit of the dramatic to the way they went about their job.

I put in my earplugs and tried to get as comfortable as you can when jammed into the canvas web seating elbow to elbow with your newest best friend (in this case, Capt. Fleming, the HHC commander), who hasn't showered in a couple of days. Somehow, I managed to doze off, waking up a couple of hours later as we began our decent into Ali Al Salem Airfield in Kuwait. I always called it "Olly Olly Oxen Free," but nobody ever thought it funny, even though I kept trying the joke.

Fortunately, since we were landing in Kuwait, we were spared the combat assault approach into the airfield. Riding a 130 into Iraq usually included the combat assault landing. Designed to limit the exposure of the aircraft to enemy fire, the combat assault involved spiraling and diving the C-130 from its cruising altitude down to an abrupt landing at the chosen destination. Inside the aircraft, the experience would be what I would imagine it would be like if one were sealed inside a large metal trash can with some holes punched in it to let in light, and then rolled down several flights of stairs.

Getting off the plane, I saw one of the pilots standing off to the side. As we waited for our bus to arrive, I walked over and thanked him for the ride. He asked me what I did, and I told him I flew '64s out of Taji. He said, "Yeah, we see you guys down there all the time as we fly over; that must be exciting."

"Yeah, I try not to make it exciting. Exciting usually isn't a good thing. Small world, huh?"

When the blue Air Force bus arrived, it took us to another admin area. There, we got a few more briefings about our flight and customs, and then the yelling started.

I noticed over the course of several deployments that the pompous nature and self-importance of bureaucrats is inversely proportional to their location in reference to actual combat. In Kuwait they were at the level of a Barney Fife, the bumbling deputy played by Don Knotts on the *Andy Griffith Show*. When we arrived in Texas at the DFW airport, some of the soldiers in charge of things were full-on DMV-level a-holes. But that fun was at least another twenty-plus hours away.

Once again, after arriving and going through the process of storing our body armor and helmet, we received tent assignments and were told to be in the terminal at a certain time to get our takeoff times. In the meantime, there was a PX, a DFAC, and a string of fast-food places to pass the time. A large loudspeaker system regularly announced changes in the schedule, so you tried to pay attention to make sure you didn't miss something.

If you were traveling home to the USA, there were two places you could go to: Atlanta, Georgia, and Dallas–Fort Worth, Texas. Since I was initially going to my brother's house in Fort Worth, I knew which airport I would be flying to, but I didn't know when the plane would be leaving. It is interesting to note that when I went through this process in 2004, it took less time than it did in 2007. When I did it again in 2010, it took even more time. So instead of getting better at this as time went by, we as an institution got progressively worse. I think only a government-run program could accomplish something like that.

Eventually, our names were called to get on the bus to carry us to Kuwait International Airport to meet our chartered plane, which would then get us back to the USA . . . eventually.

After a stop in Shannon, Ireland (and don't forget, kids, GO #1 is still in effect . . . no drinking!), to refuel, our plane touched down at Dallas–Fort Worth International Airport as the sun was rising in the North Texas sky, completing our twenty-plus-hour journey from Kuwait. As we taxied to parking, two fire trucks sprayed the aircraft with a "shower of affection" from the people of the Metroplex, but that was only the beginning.

I had been through DFW back in 2004, when I came home on leave, so I had an idea of what to expect, but the welcome was still emotional and appreciated more than the people who took the time to come out and say hello will ever know. As the flight attendant opened the door and soldiers began to file out, those still inside the airliner could hear the sound of people cheering, coming from the terminal.

We arrived at DFW airport at Terminal D, which is the international terminal. When passengers disembark from their plane, they emerge onto a glassed-in walkway that overlooks the portion of the terminal where people wait to board their flights. Those people were there as part of their normal lives, traveling on business or on a vacation, and probably had no idea we were going to be there. When they saw the first soldiers emerge on the walkway, a spontaneous cheer erupted that grew louder and louder as more of us emerged. By the time I made my way out of the plane, the folks down below us were in a full-throated roar. It was almost embarrassing to me to be the object of such a welcome. I thank and treasure each one of those people who were down there, but it was almost too much to handle for me. Less than for-ty-eight hours ago, I was going about my duties at Camp Taji, and now here I was in Texas with a crowd of people cheering for us. I saw several people wearing Texas Longhorn gear who were cheering, and I shot them a "Hook 'Em Horns" sign and hurried on to the stairs that led to US Customs.

The customs inspection went quickly, given that we had all our stuff inspected before we ever left Kuwait by US Customs inspectors, so, finishing that, all we had left was to do some admin stuff regarding our leave forms and then run "the gauntlet."

Once we finished the customs, our leave forms were stamped with the date and time we arrived at DFW. We were then given some papers that told us where and when to be back at DFW for our trip back to the sandbox. What awaited us around the next corner, which I jokingly called "the gauntlet," was in fact hundreds of average Americans from all over North Texas who came on their own time to make sure their soldiers, sailors, airmen, and marines were given a welcome a lot of folks never got.

Once we finished with the admin clowns, we gathered up our stuff and went through a double set of doors. What stood on the other side was simply overwhelming. Waiting were hundreds of people cheering and clapping, all welcoming, offering assistance, a cell phone, a bottle of water, whatever you might need. We walked down a narrow corridor that split the throng of well-wishers. There were hands being thrust out, wanting to be shaken, while someone else pounded you on the back. I thought to myself, so this is how it feels to be a movie star. It was nice, but I'm glad I don't deal with THAT every day.

Some of us were looking to find our connecting flights, while others, like me, were looking for our relatives or friends to get out of there and start their leave. Some of the welcoming crowd must have thought me quite rude there toward the end of the line; as I spotted my brother at the end of the crowd line, I ignored everyone else and walked rather briskly to him, shook his hand, and said, "Hey, how's it going? Let's go."

Less than thirty minutes later, I had taken a shower and was wearing street clothes, watching sports on TV. It was at the same time normal and very bizarre.

It's been said by others that "the US Army is at war; the American public is at the mall." Driving down I-20 outside Arlington, Texas, in the spring of 2007, you would never know this nation was at war. Aside from a few faded yellow-ribbon bumper stickers, there were no outward signs that thousands of miles away, at that very moment, soldiers were fighting and dying. There was no doubt that this area is populated with those who love this nation, since the outward signs of patriotism were all there, and I loved being home in Texas, but I couldn't help feeling disconnected from the reality I had been living since last September. I enjoyed being home, but I didn't feel like answering the questions I was always asked and correcting the ignorance about what was actually going on in Iraq. Watching the news was totally out of the question, since I could literally feel my blood pressure rise when politicians would be shown pronouncing the war "lost" or "hopeless" . . . and that was probably the least infuriating thing that they did.

I went down to Fort Hood to visit friends, check on my personal effects that were in storage, and make sure the different payments I had arranged were being taken care of. This is one of the joys of being a single soldier; there is nobody to help with bill paying while you are downrange, and frankly, if you are an officer, the Army really doesn't care . . . that is, until you get in trouble for not paying your bills.

Doing recon and security north of Camp Taji. *Photo by author*

It is especially fun coming back from a deployment. Welcome home, you are released . . . good luck finding a place to live, sucker . . . see ya in four days. But all of that was waiting for me sometime in the future.

For the next nine days I enjoyed some of the things I had been missing over the last six months. I visited most of my favorite restaurants and enjoyed meals I had missed while downrange. It was a needed break that was over almost as soon as it started. Before I knew it, I was back at DFW, standing in a line with about two hundred other soldiers getting yelled at by an NCO with no combat patch (we have been at war for six years now; how do you manage that?) about the weight of our rucksacks and being told to take off our boots and belts so we could go through the TSA line. I remember a civilian yelling at the TSA person (who, let's face it, was doing what he was told) about making us remove our boots and belts. He ripped the guy running the scanner up one side and down the other about making soldiers take their boots and belts off so they could fly back to combat . . . only in Texas.

Forty-eight hours later I was back at Camp Taji. Seventy-two hours after that, I was flying with Capt. Fleming, conducting a mission on the wing of Maj. Welch and Lt. Haas over Baghdad. That night, our team had two separate engagements. The first engagement was against an individual who was attempting to emplace an IED on a road that paralleled the Tigris River, called Route Cobras, north of Camp Taji. He was spotted by the owning ground unit and passed to us by Attack Mike. Lt. Haas found him hiding in some bushes near the road and dispatched him with several bursts from the gun.

The second incident involved supporting a ground unit that was in enemy contact in the west part of Baghdad, near BIAP.

Almost as soon as we arrived on station, Lt. Haas spotted a group of insurgents. We had caught them red-handed as they fired at a group of friendly dismounts and their Stryker vehicle with AK-47s. He engaged them with the aircraft's 30 mm cannon, obliterating them. In fact, he did it so quickly that my front-seater, Capt. Fleming, was unable to acquire until the engagement was completed. Jesse was on the radio talking with Attack Mike, giving them a SITREP, when I saw lead begin to engage. I called them to assure Maj. Welch that I was out of their way, telling them, "You're clear." Then I told Jesse, "They're firing." Before he could get his TADS on the action, they fired again, and the engagement was done. That was the way things went down sometimes; over and done within a matter of seconds.

That was the first time I'd ever had two engagements in a single night, and it was a hell of a way to get back into the swing of things.

Things certainly weren't slowing down at all.

OK, break's over; get back on your head!

A 64 departs on another mission. *Photo by author*

A medevac and escort return from another mission. *Photo by author*

Looking down on my wingman. *Photo by author*

On patrol in northern Baghdad. *Photo by author*

An Apache sits in parking, ready to go with eight Hellfires. *Photo by author*

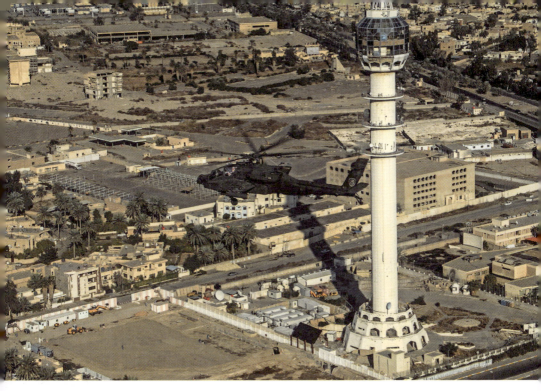

Flying the flag over the middle of Baghdad. *Photo by author*

A team lines up to do their premission checks prior to departure. *Photo by author*

An AWT departs Camp Taji. *Photo by author*

My wingman as seen over Baghdad. *Photo by author*

Punching off flares at sunset just west of Camp Taji. *Photo by author*

Sunset. *Photo by author*

For a short time, the aircraft of A 1-227 flew with pre–World War II roundels painted on their rocket pods. *Photo by author*

CHAPTER 7

SURGING:
APRIL–NOVEMBER 2007

We knew in January, when President Bush first announced it, that the Surge was coming. Most of us also knew that meant our tour would be extended, but that wasn't official until April 11, 2007. On that day, the new secretary of defense, Robert Gates, announced that effective immediately, our tour was now fifteen months long.

In a Washington, DC, press conference, he said the following:[1]

In January of this year, I announced a new set of policy initiatives to improve how the Department of Defense manages the deployment of Reserve component forces. My objective was to set clear guidelines that our commanders, troops, and their families could understand and use in determining how future rotations in support of the global war on terror would affect them.

At the time, I also understood that we faced a similar challenge in establishing clear, realistic, executable, and long-term policy goals to guide the deployment of active-duty forces, particularly the Army.

This year I learned that the then—earlier this year I learned that the then level of deployed forces in Iraq and Afghanistan would require active-duty units to flow into Iraq before they had spent a full twelve months at home. It is important to point out that this was the case prior to the president's decision to provide additional forces to support the Baghdad security plan. This reality was a significant factor influencing my decision to recommend to the president that we grow the Army and the Marine Corps over the next five years by 65,000 and 25,000, respectively.

As the next step, acting upon the recommendation of the acting secretary and chief of staff of the Army, I am announcing today a new policy intended to provide better clarity, predictability, and sustainability in how we deploy active-duty Army forces.

Effective immediately, active Army units now in the Central Command area of responsibility and those headed there will deploy for not more than fifteen months and will return home to home stations for not less than twelve months. This policy applies to all units with the exception of two brigades currently deployed that have already been extended to sixteen-month deployments.

This policy is a difficult but necessary interim step that will be kept in place only until we can shift with confidence to the twelve-month deployments and twelve months at home, and ultimately to the rotation goal for Army active-duty forces of twelve months deployed and twenty-four months at home. Without this action, we would have had to deploy five Army active-duty brigades sooner than the twelve-months-at-home goal. I believe it is fair to all soldiers that all share the burden equally.

This policy will accomplish two other goals. First, it represents a fair, predictable, and sustainable commitment to our troops that they can use with confidence to understand what the country is asking of them as they deploy. I strongly believe that we owe our troops as much advanced notice as possible, and clarity on what they and their families can expect. In other words, predictability.

Second, this policy, as a matter of prudent management, will provide us with the capacity to sustain the deployed force. This approach also upholds our commitment to decide when to begin any drawdown of US forces in Iraq solely based on conditions on the ground.

I realize this decision will ask a lot of our Army troops and their families. We are deeply grateful for the service and sacrifice of our men and women in uniform and their commitment to accomplishing our mission. In the end, I believe this new approach will allow the Army to better support the war effort while providing a more predictable and dependable deployment schedule for our soldiers and their families.

While the SECDEF was giving that speech, I was on a C-130 flying from Kuwait to Balad Airbase in Iraq, returning from my "environmental midtour leave" to Texas. I heard about the announcement while listening to AFN radio on a bus going from the passenger terminal to a DFAC on Balad. I was particularly amused by the additional announcement that due to the three-month tour extension, all environmental leaves would be extended by two days. Missed it by THAT much.

Even though we knew the extension was coming, we had all hoped that somehow it wouldn't affect us. Of course, that wasn't the case, and even though it was expected, it was still a hard pill to swallow. I could rationalize the reason for it, understood the reasons for it completely, and even agreed with the idea in principle, but it didn't mean I or anyone else LIKED it. Given we were coming off an especially bad period where eight aircraft were shot down in the span of a month, there weren't too many of us in the mood for speeches about digging deep and giving 110%. What exacerbated that mood were mission briefings where pilots were told by the briefers that the ground units were screaming for air support, and how vital it was that we were out there for every second of our mission period, only to launch and check in with a ground unit and be told that they didn't have anything specific for us to do. This situation tended to occur more often with respect to the missions being flown late at night. The teams that flew between 0200 to 0600 have always had a hard time finding useful things to do. During OIF 2, after we made the rounds of all the BCTs and checked our assigned NAIs, if there were no actual aviation mission requests (AMR) to be supported, we recovered and remained on standby until the end of our mission period. This was something during OIF 06-08 that the chain of command was loath to do.

From the pilot's perspective, if we were flying just to be flying, with no assigned tasks, we were risking ourselves and the aircraft for little gain and should be allowed to return to Taji. From the commander's perspective, the aircrews weren't trying hard enough to find something useful to do. The truth is that the commander and most of the staff had never been out there between 0200 and 0400 trying to find something to do, at least not anytime lately. We all knew that they wouldn't do it now either. While it WAS true that units WERE out there begging for more support than we were able to give, the requests generally weren't for support at 2:00 a.m. unless we were supporting some Special Operations Forces raid.

The reality was that when you check in with a unit at 0200 hrs, you aren't talking to the guy who has been bugging your S3 for support; that guy is asleep. You are talking to some bored captain who, if they don't have anything pressing going on, is either going to tell you to check the standard NAIs, give you some random thing to look at, or tell you to get lost so he can get back to his fascinating game of *Minesweeper*. It was something that couldn't be reasoned or explained to our commander, since he was convinced that his pilots were the issue. In some cases that may have been true, but for the most part, all the AWTs went out and did their business in a professional manner. So, for our sins we had to read and heed the following:

In light of an incorrect perception spread from one of the TOC staff personnel regarding our OPTEMPO and why we fly the assigned missions as we do, I want you to disseminate the following Attack 6 Tactical Command Message down to EVERY line company pilot and ensure your pilots have my command message direct from me to them:

Tactical Crazy Horse Command Message (16 Apr 07):[2] The Crazy Horse has currently and always has flown missions that have assigned and approved AMRs or assigned NAIs tied to the enemy movements. We will aggressively conduct reconnaissance to find, fix, or destroy the AIF according to the ROE and Warriors Edge MNC-I CG Letter. Every second of your mission, I expect you are using every opportunity to maximize the fundamentals of reconnaissance within your cockpit and within your team. Our OPTEMPO is based on assigned AMRs and NAIs that are analyzed multiple times a day with the maneuver battalions and adjusted based on SIGINT, HUMINT, or tactical AIF interrogations done at the maneuver battalion level. These NAIs are aggressively tracked in the Crazy Horse TOC and crews will take FRAGO directives from the TOC based on changing METTT-C. There are no surge teams, unless specifically approved by me, and pilots fly missions that are assigned a minimum of 24 hours out. NAIs are updated before the individual team briefings and the S2 briefs these NAIs at tactical team briefings. If any pilot believes they are flying without a clear task and purpose or without valid assigned NAIs tied to enemy movements or actions, it is the responsibility of every PIC or AMC to bring this to the Battalion S3 immediately or Battle Captain in the S3's absence. Company Commanders will bring this issue directly to the battalion S3 for resolution. All PICs and AMCs are responsible for NOT setting patterns with respect to executing assigned missions or aerial denial missions. The TOC will brief the previous week's aerial denial targets executed to ensure patterns are not being set by aircrews.

Misperception among some pilots regarding the hours we fly monthly and how missions are assigned:

We fly hours just to fly? [*sic*]

We are in some competition to fly a certain CAP or OPTEMPO monthly flight hour total?

We fly missions without a task and purpose?

We fly missions without an AMR or assigned NAI tied to enemy movements?

Tell all my pilots, I am proud of all their hard work and I rely on them every second of every day, as the brigade and division does, to continue to be the best they can be and improve every day as part of the Crazy Horse Team. You are making a significant difference in the Global War on Terrorism. Thanks for all you do! Crazy Horse! First Team!

"ATTACK 6"

LTC, AV

Commanding

1-227th Attack & Recon BN, "First Attack," 1st Cav

ATO C/S: "Crazy Horse 6"

Cdrs, I ask you to brief ALL your pilots on my tactical command message in the next 24 hours to ensure that there are not any of the above misperceptions among any pilot or leader. I want you to give the S3 a "thumbs" up for personally briefing this message. If you do not brief this personally, I ask you to have your "second in command" platoon leader or XO brief this. For any pilot that does not understand my command message, I ask you to personally ensure they come see me ASAP.

To my knowledge, nobody went to see him ASAP. I know I didn't, even though I really had a difficult time deciphering some of this message. I'm pretty sure we also had to sign the "Virtual Briefing Book" affirming that we read this message. The "Virtual Briefing Book" wasn't "virtual"; it was an actual three-ring binder in the briefing room that had instructions such as the commander's letter that aircrews were required to read and then initial, next to our name on a sign-in roster. In the rest of the flying world, such a thing was called a "reading file." Items that were deemed important for all pilots to read were placed in a reading file; it was one of the things that we were required to check before going to fly. That was standard

Two AH-64s return from their mission as a Black Hawk crew chief walks across the ramp with his gear at Taji. *Photo by author*

Two AH-64s exit the runway at Camp Taji. *Photo by author*

Visibility dropping at last light, an Apache dispenses a flare near Camp Taji. *Photo by author*

An Apache flies back to Taji near sunset. *Photo by author*

procedure in Army aviation since the first day of fight school. For some reason, this information was too important to be put into the reading file; hence the creation of the virtual briefing book, which was the same damn thing, only "more important" or something. This was the world I was trapped in for at least the next seven months or so.

"THERE WILL BE NO CURSING IN THE CHOW HALL"

The DFAC at Taji was a meeting place where everyone who lived or even visited the FOB came to eat. As such, the FOBBIT and the fighter were there in equal number. The grease-splattered specialist who had just spent all morning working on a helicopter in 100-degree-plus heat sat down the table from a person who worked in an air-conditioned office, who was across from a sergeant and his platoon who had just pulled into Taji after doing a route clearance mission in their Buffalo MRAP vehicle, parked outside. Sometimes it was fun to just go in there and people-watch.

I usually didn't do lunch in the DFAC, but today I accompanied Maj. Welch, the B Company commander.

After a few months deployed, it became a chore to find something I was enthusiastic about eating. It wasn't that the people running the DFAC didn't try their best, because they did. There were literally hundreds of options available. You could visit the sandwich bar and order whatever deli meat you wanted on a variety of different breads. There was a wide selection of chips as well. If you wanted a salad, that was also available, as well as the usual hamburgers and whatever selection they had, on what was called the main line. Then there was the dessert bar. There was a reason that some people on deployment to combat in Iraq gained weight, and it was called all the Baskin-Robbins ice cream you can eat, cake and pie for free, and no self-control.

So here we were, sitting at a table in the busy DFAC. I had selected a "delicious" chicken salad sandwich along with some cheese-flavored Doritos from the sandwich bar, washed down with a Dr. Pepper. Memory fails me what Maj. Welch was having, but as we sat having a discussion laced with a few choice words about the latest outrage being perpetrated upon us by others, we noticed we were being given the skunk eye by a senior NCO who was sitting with a young lieutenant a few seats down.

I knew he was a FOBBIT from his unit patch and the fact that his uniform looked brand new. The female lieutenant also appeared to be quite FOBBIT-like herself. Not that there is anything wrong with that per se; everyone has a job to do, but it seems some people lose perspective of what is going on not 200 yards away on the other side of the wire.

We continued to pontificate on the parentage of different members of the brigade and division and what they should do to themselves and others, and the NCO continued to glare ever so obviously in our direction. Eventually, either our uncouth language or the desire to protect the delicate sensibilities of the young lieutenant overcame him. He pushed his chair back, approached Maj. Welch, and cleared his throat.

"Sir, I would appreciate it if you watched your language."

"Sure, sorry about that," Maj. Welch diplomatically replied.

I sat silently, but I thought this guy was being a tool. I don't know, given that they were in the National Guard, that lieutenant could have been his daughter, wife, or girlfriend.

Now, I'd like to think that I am not really that rude of a person and that my parents taught me better than to be the kind of person who lets loose with profanities in a public place, but on that day I had failed miserably. But the thought that this guy might be offended by a few swear words in a place where people were being killed daily (some just yards away from this dining facility) kind of offended me the more I thought about it. I wanted to ask him if he didn't have some latrines to inspect or some sandbag-filling detail to monitor, but I kept it to myself.

I will be the first to admit that I was using language my mother wouldn't have been proud of, and I certainly don't enjoy eating dinner around people who use the f-word to construct an entire paragraph, but that isn't what we were doing. So, the more I thought about it, the more I wondered why, out of all the things to get pissed off about (and he was pissed, there was no doubt about that), would you pick THAT thing, here. I understand that people have their certain pet peeves, but I can assure you that if swearing is your pet peeve, serving in the United States Army in a war zone probably isn't the best choice for you. On the plus side, at least this incident got my mind off the other stupid stuff going on around Taji, so I guess the entire incident was an overall win in that regard. It did make me recall the scene in *Apocalypse Now* when the character of Kurtz talked about the fact that troops couldn't write the word "fuck" on their airplanes, but yet it was OK to kill hundreds if not thousands of people. It was kind of ironic. The Army's not real big on irony.

The incident also reminded me of one of the best Army port-a-potty graffiti statements I had ever read. In 1988, at the National Training Center, I was standing in a portable latrine, and scrawled on the wall in front of me were the words "Profanity is the linguistic crutch of the illiterate motherfucker." Indeed, it is.

LEFT SEAT / RIGHT SEAT: MAY 2007

As part of "the Surge," the area south of Baghdad that had been our responsibility was now being turned over to the 3rd CAB from the 3rd Infantry Division. As part of that transition of responsibility, we were tasked with providing a RIP for part of the incoming unit. While it wasn't the RIP we were looking for, we were more than happy to do it and wished them the best of luck.

Task Force 3-17 CAV (an OH-58D squadron with an attached company of AH-64Ds from 1-3 AVN, 3rd Infantry Division) was going to be taking over a slice of the pie we were responsible for. The process began when they sent a couple of people from their advance party to talk with us about the AO they were about to take over. As part of this process, I talked with a captain about the route their aircraft would fly coming north. I gave him some idea about areas to avoid and attempted to give him an overall picture of the enemy situation and their common modus operandi.

As it turned out, when their 58s made the journey north, either the word about the avoid areas didn't make it or they chose to ignore the advice. They flew right through the middle of a real enemy hotspot and took damage to a couple of their aircraft. Fortunately, nobody was severely injured, and no aircraft were lost. But hearing the news caused me to shake my head in wonder.

After the task force had arrived at BIAP, several of us were tasked to go over and give the pilots a briefing like the one we were given when we arrived in country, back in September. I gave a short presentation to the pilots that provided facts and analysis about the threat to helicopters in the AO, and some of the things we did to counteract the enemy's tactics. Knowing the rivalry that exists between the Apache and the Kiowa Warrior community, I took the time to ensure that the information I gave wasn't airframe specific and that I genuinely cared about their success, and it seemed to be well received. Although you never know; we were all ordered to be there, so maybe they were just humoring me. They may have been thinking the very same thing we were thinking when we got our briefing from the guys we replaced: thanks a lot, hurry up, shut up, and get out of my way. I have no way of knowing.

The first unit I served in was also the first in the US Army to receive the OH-58D, back in the mid- to late 1980s. I'd like to think I have some friends who fly those aircraft, and I have never completely understood the vitriol that some express when they compare or talk about other airframes or organizations. Some commanders seemed to almost encourage active discord, in a manner not unlike a rival in sports hating their competitor in order to get an edge on the playing field. While this may be effective in the game of football, it is not conducive to military operations, in which you may suddenly find yourself looking to your "hated rival" for help. But they did it, and I am quite sure they still do. It's petty and childish and doesn't speak well of their leadership style.

Fortunately, we didn't have a great deal of that when conducting the RIP. It seemed to me, anyway, that everyone was focused on doing their jobs and getting the task at hand completed.

After the initial in-briefs were finished, we went about conducting what are called left-seat/right-seat rides. During the left-seat portion, the new crews are following along, watching and learning the new AO and the procedures we used. During the right-seat ride, the new guys were the leaders, and we would watch them to make sure they were doing things correctly. Then the training wheels would come off and they would have all the controls by themselves. This process was kind of ridiculous because OH-58s and AH-64Ds are different aircraft with different capabilities and different ways of doing the same mission.

On one mission, I can recall us telling the 58s we were leading around to stack up in altitude above us while we assisted a ground unit that was in trouble. For a '64 that isn't that big of a deal, because we use our TADS (especially at night) to develop the situation, and another Apache would have been easily able to observe the prosecution of target from above. The KWs, however, have more of a personal touch as they get lower and closer to do their business, for the most part, and I'm sure this experience circling around above us while we shot stuff didn't do anything for their SA or aided much in their orientation to the new area of operations. But it's something THEY (the nameless, faceless pronoun people) said we had to do, so we were doing it. It was to everyone's credit that most of us endured it without a lot of gripes or complaints.

Every day, for several weeks, we would brief our mission at Camp Taji, fly over the Baghdad International, pick up a team of '58s, and do the LAO, after which we would return to BIAP, and then we would continue on with the rest of our assigned tasks for the day.

On May 31, things went a little differently for the team of CW4 Bill Ham, CW2 Cole Moughon, CW4 Steve Kilgore, and Lt. Brian Haas. Tasked with conducting an orientation flight for the '58 guys, they received their normal intelligence briefing before taking off. During this briefing they were informed about the possible location of a group of vehicles associated with an ADA ambush using gun trucks (pickups with machine guns mounted in the back), which was aimed at engaging and shooting down helicopters. The suspected location of these vehicles was near the route the team was going to take to BIAP to pick up the '58s for their LAO, so during the team brief they decided to investigate the accuracy of the intelligence.

The suspected enemy location was on the seam between the USMC area of responsibility and 1st CAV's AO. In the four years since the invasion, our enemy had learned a few things about us. One of those things was the fact that occasionally, the areas adjacent to the boundaries of units were not heavily patrolled. The sector just northwest of Baghdad, on the far eastern part of the area, which the Marines controlled, was at best lightly patrolled, and it allowed a dead space for enterprising bad guys to move about in. Coincidentally, that spot of ground also lined up with the flight path a lot of aircraft took to get from Balad to BIAP. It was a prime spot for someone who wanted to shoot down a helicopter. The previous November, farther north, almost due west of Camp Taji, along the same boundary in what was called Zone 110, the USAF had lost an F-16 flown by Maj. Troy L. Gilbert, who perished during the event, and the 160th SOAR had an AH-6 Little Bird shot down while battling insurgents manning a training camp, which ultimately resulted in one of the Little Bird pilots, CW5 David F. Cooper, receiving the Distinguished Service Cross for his actions during the same event. So obviously, the enemy utilizing the gap between units wasn't something that was new.

So today it was in this area, where several light pickup trucks (often referred to as "bongo trucks") with heavy-caliber machine guns were waiting, manned by insurgents who were intent on downing a coalition aircraft. It was a technique that we suspected had been used in the shoot-down of Easy 40 and Crazyhorse 08, and these people may very well have been involved, so naturally everyone on the mission took this situation rather personally.

After all the aircraft preflight checks were accomplished and the out-front boresight on the TADS completed, the team launched on time and departed Taji around 1830 en route to BIAP, with a small detour to check out the suspected gun trucks along the way.

As the team (using the call signs CZ 22/23) transited the area en route to BIAP, they were conducting what is called zone reconnaissance. While transiting through Zone 111, near the area of suspected enemy activity, CZ 22/23 first noted people in the area acting strangely and then noticed multiple vehicles that drove off the road once they observed the aircraft. Individuals left the vehicles and hid in nearby ditches and fields. As the AWT turned to investigate, three to four crews equipped with heavy machine guns engaged CZ 22/23 from multiple locations. CZ 22/23 immediately reported the SAFIRE to Attack Mike and Ironhorse TOC. The team immediately returned suppressive fire at one of the bongo trucks, which mounted a heavy machine gun located by a dirt road with thirty rounds of 30 mm. That truck moved west to a house nearby, where both aircraft reengaged with PD Rockets and 30 mm, resulting in one probable AIF KIA.

Then, at 1854, CZ 22/23 observed three bongo trucks with heavy machine guns moving at a high rate of speed from the engagement area. While the trucks were maneuvering west on the road, CZ 22/23 observed multiple muzzle flashes from the heavy machine guns. On flight trail's (CZ 23) tape, Brian Haas could be heard to exclaim, "GUN . . . big gun!" As the ZPU in the back of the small pickup truck fired at them, the muzzle flash of the gun pointed at the helicopter seemed to take up the entire screen of Haas's TSD.

The lead aircraft in the flight also maneuvered to engage the trucks. Bill Ham exclaimed over the aircraft intercom, encouraging his CPG, "Get 'em Cole . . ." as his front-seater attempted to engage the bouncing and weaving trucks that were now attempting to escape.

Moughon in CZ 22 attempted to engage the trail vehicle with a single Hellfire missile, but it did not impact the target, sailing over the cab as the truck hit a dip in the road.

CZ 22/23 then maneuvered to reengage the group of trucks. CZ 22 engaged with another Hellfire missile, disabling the lead vehicle, which careened off the road and into a ditch. CZ 22 further engaged with a hundred rounds of 30 mm explosive warhead (PD), and flechette rockets and CZ 23 engaged with fifty rounds of 30 mm, PD, and flechette rockets, destroying the three gun trucks and killing an estimated three AIF.

At 1900, CZ 22/23 returned to the bongo truck at the house to do a quick BDA. CZ 22/23 reengaged the truck with ten PD rockets and a Hellfire missile. CZ 23 then observed a fifth bongo truck nearby that was equipped with a ZPU, and noted that it also had a possible shoulder-launched surface-to-air missile (MANPADS) lying in the truck bed. CZ 23 then engaged the vehicle with the three bursts of his 30 mm cannon.

The AWT team engaged a total of five trucks, all with weapon systems in the back of the trucks. CZ 22/23 engaged with an approximate total of 530 rounds of 30 mm, five Hellfire missiles, eleven flechettes, and twenty-eight point-detonating rockets.

Ironhorse had requested that the AWT destroy the vehicles and weapons in their entirety, since no ground units were able to move out to the site. At 1924, CZ 22/23 reported Winchester on ammunition and stated that they were unable to destroy the possible MANPAD surface-to-air missile on the back of the fifth bongo truck. CZ 06/25 conducted a BHO with CZ 22/23 as they broke for the FARP to assess possible small-arms damage. Ironhorse directed CZ 06/25 to complete destruction of all weapons systems (since there were no ground units available to move to the location), secure it, and conduct sensitive site exploitation (SSE). At 1939, while at the FARP, CZ 22/23 reported that one 14.5 mm round had clipped the tail rotor blade of one of the aircraft. At 2010, CZ 06/25 engaged the remaining weapon systems with a total of four hundred rounds of 30 mm, three Hellfire missiles, and seven rockets, causing their complete destruction. Ultimately, the results of this engagement were five AIF technical vehicles destroyed and four enemy fighters killed in action.

There would be no LAO for the '58s that night. I don't recall anyone complaining about that too much, though. We didn't encounter any of these truck-based ADA ambushes aimed at shooting down helicopters in our AO for the rest of our tour.

Soon after this event, we finished up our left-seat/right-seat rides with 3-17 CAV. We wished them the best of luck, and with that, our AO collapsed to what was essentially the east side of Baghdad and the area around Camp Taji, patrolled by 1st BCT. But this wasn't the last we would see of our brothers and sisters in the 17th CAV.

ZONE 9, VCTY SADR CITY, JUNE 2, 2007: SAME SONG, DIFFERENT DANCE

"Crazyhorse is cleared to engage ..."

Well, here I am flying as CZ07, wingman for CW4 Kevin Smith and ATK 06. Once again, we are working in the Ironhorse AO west of Camp Taji. There is zero illumination, which means there is no moon and whatever stars are out are being dimmed by dust in the air. As a result, it is darker than a stripper's heart. We are currently flying over a rutted, blown-up, worn-out road out in the farmland west of Taji, providing security for a route clearance team that is looking for IEDs. I silently wonder how long it's going to be before the commander gets tired of flying around in the dark looking for bad guys, who, with a dust storm headed our way, are more than likely hiding inside somewhere, watching goat porn or doing whatever it is that they do when not planting IEDs or launching mortars and rockets indiscriminately in the general direction of people they had some sort of beef with. I keep looking around, trying to make sure that the weather is not getting any worse. The only way I can really tell is by keeping an eye on the lights of the surrounding villages and, from time to time, Camp Taji. The storm is starting to blow in from out west, and the visibility is slowly starting to drop. My ability to see the surrounding lights is my only clue to just how much visibility is being reduced. If we weren't careful, the visibility could drop to the point where we would be forced to go on instruments and either shoot an approach back into Taji or the more likely option of having to fly into Baghdad International or the USAF base up in Balad. Aside from that worry, all the dust in the air makes our job as an attack helicopter more difficult, since the laser energy required to get a range or designate targets gets refracted and becomes less and less reliable the more dust or other particulate matter is present in the air, and creates a condition called backscatter. Backscatter is a situation where our laser-guided missile can't tell where the desired impact point of the weapon is because so much laser energy is being reflected by the particulate matter in the air.

As the trail aircraft in the flight, we monitor the BN command network. A part of our duties is to call the TOC periodically, to update them with what we are doing and where we are. We are also monitoring the net in case BN gets word of something that we need to be retasked for, such as a troops-in-contact situation or covering a medevac mission.

Around 2130, we get a call from Capt. Paul Daigle, the battalion battle captain that evening, directing us to fly toward some suspicious activity that was going on in Zone 9, which was located near Sadr City. It is an area from which a lot of indirect fire and bad-guy activity have been occurring since forever, but especially so over the past several months.

A large observation balloon known as a JLENS on FOB Loyalty has spotted several individuals getting in and out of a van and setting up rockets in the middle of a soccer field, which were assumed to be aimed at the Green Zone on the basis of their orientation.

We were briefed by Capt. Daigle to proceed to that location in order to engage and destroy the rockets, the launchers, and any people dumb enough to be around them. Flying in my front seat tonight is CW2 Brian Carbone, who was assigned to the Avengers of Alpha Company 1-227; he rapidly enters the coordinates given us, and sends them via the aircraft's digital data modem (IDM) to flight lead.

I call ATK 06 on team internal and give them the heads-up that data we were sending them target coordinates via the IDM, by saying, "Check mail, Target 10." It was a shorthand code we had developed as a community to let someone know they were getting a message via the IDM. A chime that sounds much like a phone ringing will go off in the aircraft when a message arrives, but it never hurt to give them a warning, and the identification that info would have (in this case, the coordinates would be stored in the slot "Target 10" when the receiver accepted the message). The target handover and mission retasking end up taking longer than usual, for some reason. We don't ask them what the problem is, but eventually Brian ends up re-sending the information to lead, by voice over our team internal radio as we flew toward downtown Baghdad as fast as our aircraft would go.

When the Apache is being flown with a high power setting, it has a particular gait and vibration that reminded me of a horse at a full gallop. To fly faster in a helicopter, the pilot pushes the cyclic forward with his right hand and pulls the collective up with his left. The person who is on the controls also tends to lean forward like a rider on horseback. We were truly cavalry soldiers on the charge heading for a fight . . . we hoped it would be one sided.

About halfway there, we get another call from Capt. Daigle, telling us that Special Operations Forces (SOF) have just opened a restricted operating zone (ROZ) in the vicinity of our target. We get the center-mass grid for the ROZ, and Brian enters it into the aircraft database as a 3-kilometer threat ring, which shows up on the moving map display on my instrument panel as a red circle with a crosshatch. This gives a quick reference in the cockpit that allows us to easily see the airspace now denied us. Technology is great when it works like it is supposed to, and you know how to use it.

It is immediately obvious that we can no longer fly directly to the target, and now we will need to adjust our route to the east to avoid the operators doing their thing. I call lead on internal and let them know that we now need to fly east between the Tigris River and Route Pluto (the north–south-running road that skirted Sadr City to the west) due to the SOF activity. We really didn't want to fly into Sadr City unless we had to, because almost every time someone flew in there, they would draw ground fire from someone, so more often than not it was just best to avoid it, unless you wanted to get into a fight. We already had one of those coming, so we would just save Sadr City for another day. That left us with about a half-mile strip of land that we could use with Sadr City on the east side and the OCFI ROZ on the other as the most direct route available to the target.

The detour ended up costing us several minutes en route. At that time, we had no way of knowing if the minutes lost would mean that the enemy would be able to engage with their weapons or escape into the night. I felt antsy, and time seemed to crawl as the adrenaline began to pump through me. I realized I was squeezing the cyclic in a death grip (a nervous habit I had), so I took a deep breath and flexed my right hand to get some circulation going again and to try to relax a bit. I sneak a look off to my left; I can still see the Taji flame east of the airfield, so I know at least the weather is still holding for now. The Taji flame was the name we gave to a refinery just east of our airfield; the flame given off from the burning of waste gases was visible across Baghdad if the weather was good. Many of us used it as an indicator of reduced visibility.

As we closed in on the target, I told Capt. Daigle that we would be pushing off the BN net to the ground unit. We got to the freq in time to hear CZ 06 making his initial call to the owning ground unit, Strike Main. After the usual back and forth, Strike relayed the same basic info that Attack Mike had given us initially. We were rapidly closing to within range. Brian had slaved the TADS to the coordinates of the suspected enemy mortar team and was scanning for a target. We were still several kilometers out when Brian called that he had the target in sight. I had his video as an underlay on my left display, so I glanced down and, sure enough, there was a van and what looked like a lot of rocket launchers arrayed across the soccer field, all aimed in the direction of the Green Zone. I called lead and let them know we had a "tally" on the target.

We ended up taking a few minutes to work through some shot geometry due to the location of the SOF ROZ, to make sure we weren't shooting toward or over friendlies. Unfortunately for us, the ROZ was placed in an area that prevented us from using the most advantageous axis of attack on our target. So, we worked around to the southwest and set up an attack axis headed toward Sadr City, shooting where our rounds would cross over the stands on the south side of the field. Kevin told us that initially we should take the van and they would fire on the rocket launchers, and then we would adjust future attack runs from there.

ATK 06 then called Strike Main, described the target, and asked for permission to engage. Immediately Strike called back, "Crazyhorse 06, you are cleared to engage." Kevin had already rolled the flight inbound toward the target. I had slowed down in order to give us enough spacing behind lead to cover their break and then be able to engage our targets as quickly as possible.

Lead is pressing in on the target and then begins firing his 30 mm cannon . . . on the van.

Brian tells me they are hitting our target, so I glance down to the TSD just in time to see lead's 30 mm rounds striking the van. Not wanting Brian to try to shift targets at the last moment and possibly screw up the shot, I tell him to go ahead and hit the van again. Brian fired two ten-round 30 mm cannon bursts into the van, which caused the smoldering van to burst into flames.

Several days later, when we saw the FLIR video shot from the JLENS, we could see two individuals running away from the van toward the bleachers as our team engaged the van. I don't know about lead, but we never saw those guys with our TADS. Score another one for the legacy FLIR. A newer FLIR that had better resolution and overall performance was being used by our friends in the 82nd Airborne, up north of us, but we wouldn't receive it till after this deployment was over. Fortunately, some overhead assets saw them and tracked them to their hiding place in Sadr City, where they and their operation were rolled up in a raid a few days later.

As the flight came around for the second pass, Kevin relayed to us that he was going to take out some of the rocket launchers. First they fired two pairs of rockets, with little to no effect. Continuing the pass, they began to engage with the aircraft's 30 mm cannon. From my position it appeared that they were almost directly above the target. I could plainly see the rockets exploding as they were struck by the 30 mm rounds. Some of them were cooking off and flying around the soccer field like some pyrotechnic snake gone wild. It was spectacular. Since Kevin had slowed to almost a hover, I maneuvered around to protect him as best I could by flying a figure-eight pattern to the south and east. During this, one of the rockets lit off and launched, going just underneath Kevin and ATK 6's aircraft. I was worried that they were about to shoot themselves down, so I called a warning: "You had a rocket just go under you." Immediately after the call, lead accelerated and moved out to a little more respectable distance from the exploding ordnance.

We had fallen prey to something that was common among Apache pilots when firing from an orbit. I had done it before and would do it again in the future. It is a hard habit to break even if you are aware of it. I called it swirling around the drain. If you weren't careful while firing, the tendency was to tighten the orbit, getting closer to the target with each turn, much like water swirling around the drain in your sink. Having watched a lot of gun camera tapes, I can say this was a common occurrence. We were trying to combat it within the battalion . . . but it seemed to be something in the nature of the gun pilot to keep closing on the target.

As we widened up the orbit, the flight received a call from Strike requesting that we service the burning van with a Hellfire missile. Lead was going to take the shot, so I hung out, pulling security as we positioned ourselves for lead to fire a missile at the now-blazing van. The missile came off the rail and struck the van. Unfortunately, it didn't do much more damage to the van.

After completing that shot, someone in Strike had either spotted or gotten the word that there were individuals who had been seen fleeing the van, hiding under the north bleachers. They requested we look for these people and engage to destroy when they were located. It wasn't apparent until we started looking at them, but the stands surrounding the field were made from concrete, and from where we were looking (from over the soccer field, looking toward the stands) it was difficult if not impossible to see anything hiding under them. Just when I thought we were wasting time with this effort, one of the persons hiding underneath the stands decided he couldn't take it anymore and decided to move. We saw a figure move across one of the entranceways, and lead opened fire with his 30 mm. As they worked the west end of the bleachers, we put a few bursts into the eastern part of the stands to attempt to flush them out. I saw a lot of cement chips flying, but I doubt we did much more damage than that.

After a few minutes of that, Strike, apparently unsatisfied with the results of the first missile hit on the van, requested another Hellfire be put into what was left of the vehicle. Lead was kind enough to allow us to take the shot this time. It was then that Brian told me this was going to be his second Hellfire shot ever. His first one hadn't been too successful, since it was a "worm burner" (a missile that for one reason or another comes off the aircraft and flies into the ground at a point not intended by the shooter), and he admitted to having some concern regarding this shot. I told him not to worry, that I would give him plenty of time to set this up and it would be a piece of cake. I took tactical lead of the flight and went outbound a little more than we really needed in order to give Brian a bit more time to set up his shot. Once established inbound, I slowed down to about 60 knots. I was looking inside at Brian's setup a little more than I should have been, and we ended up climbing a bit. I corrected this, but I felt bad about making him work a little harder on the target tracking than he should have. Just as we came into range for the shot, the missile started giving a "backscatter" message from the laser return; it was either from the smoke from the burning van or all the dust in the air, since the weather was getting a bit worse. Since he had the missile set up in a mode called lock-on after launch (LOAL), Brian released the laser trigger, fired the missile, and then relased the target as per SOP. The second missile Brian had ever fired flew true to the target and blew what was left of the burning van all over the soccer field.

Soon after that shot, we were told that an F-16 with the call sign Weasel 35 was on station, and that he had eyes on an individual hiding underneath the bleachers we had engaged previously. I guess this just wasn't going to be that guy's night.

As the plan evolved, Weasel 35 would lase the target and Crazyhorse 06 would maneuver his aircraft, allowing him to engage with a single Hellfire missile. The target handover was labored, since the commander had never attended any of the air-ground integration classes or pilot's briefs where these techniques were discussed. I assume Kevin was trying his best to talk him through it from the back seat. After a couple of dry passes (quite frankly, I was worried about the F-16 running out of gas before they got it done), CZ06 finally managed to get a missile off the rail and on the target. Weasel called back with good BDA, but even after getting back to the TOC and looking at the shot on the big screen in the TOC, I couldn't tell what, if anything, was under there. I guess we would take Weasel 35's word for it.

While CZ06 was maneuvering and attempting to engage the bleachers, I received a call from the TOC on BN internal informing us that there was a brigade weather recall for the incoming dust storm, and we needed to RTB as soon as possible. I didn't want to lay more information on lead while they were trying to get a shot off, so I told ATK Mike, "Roger," and we stood by until the engagement was over. Finally, after they finished up with the BDA, I was able to relay the weather recall info.

It was a short ten-minute flight back to Taji, which went without incident. After landing we went through the postflight ritual, and the commander completed the debriefing paperwork. I dropped off my gun camera tape and aircraft data card. I finished the evening back at my desk in the rear of the TOC, knocking out some of my daily, required administrative tasks.

The next day I received an email from the S3, asking me to fill out a sworn statement on the mission from the night before. Sworn statements are usually filled out only when there is going to be an award submitted or someone is in trouble. I knew we hadn't done anything wrong, so I assumed it was an award situation. I knocked it out quickly and sent it back with a note that said if they needed anything else, to please let me know.

A few weeks later I returned from flying a mission, and I spotted a green binder on my desk. It was one of the binders the Army uses for awards. Opening it up, I saw the citation for an Air Medal for the events that took place on June 2, 2007. These types of things were usually done with a bit more ceremony; I guess it was a good thing I decided to come to work that day.

A few days later, during a rare day off at the Taji swimming pool, for his actions on the night of the second of June 2007, Chief Warrant Officer Two Brian Carbone was presented the Air Medal for Aerial Achievement (First Award) by his company commander.

SPUR RIDE-A-POLUZA, JULY 2-6 2007

Greater love hath no man than this,
that a man lay down his life for his friends. —John 15:13

On the morning of July 2, a team of OH-58D Kiowa Warriors who were assigned to our friends from 3-17 CAV were conducting a recon and security mission in Zone 308, south of Baghdad, when they came under fire, as described in a report by *Washington Post* writer Ann Scott Tyson:[3]

"We're taking fire!" Chief Warrant Officer 2 Steven Cianfrini, 27, yelled to his co-pilot as he looked out the helicopter door and saw tracer rounds flying his way.

Hearing Cianfrini's warning, Chief Warrant Officer 2 Mark Burrows, 35, banked right to evade bullets from a heavy machine gun that had opened up across a field. Then a second machine gun began firing at them. Burrows turned again, only to face a heavier barrage.

"The whole world just opened up on us, it seemed like," Cianfrini said in a telephone interview from Iraq. "We zigzagged, whatever we could do, to get out of the guns' target line. Then we started taking rounds from behind. That . . . took the aircraft down."

At 0655, while conducting recon and security in support of the strike brigade in southeast Baghdad, the AWT call sign CZ 16/17, flown by the crews of CW2—Allan (Al) Davison, CW2 Micah Johnson, CW3 Troy Mosley, and CW2 Seung Choi—monitored a call on Baghdad radio indicating a possible Fallen Angel at a location in Zone 308, which was about a ten-minute flight from their current position. The team immediately headed for the downed aircraft and, more importantly, the now-evading aircrew. They also gave Attack Mike a heads-up to inform them that they were responding to the call for help.

In the meantime, Burrows and Cianfrini were running for their lives:

"We determined our only option was to go into the canal," said Burrows.

Cianfrini . . . initially stayed behind with the survival radio at the aircraft, while Burrows rushed about 30 feet across the road and into the canal. Cianfrini followed.

Burrows waded into knee-deep water, stepped off a steep underwater embankment and started sinking into the mud. Weighed down by his armor, he thought he would drown. As the water reached his neck, he hit firm ground. Cianfrini was in up to his chin.

The pilots had planned to cross the canal to reach a field on the other side, but the mud made it hard for them to move. Moments later, they realized that being stuck probably kept them alive: Insurgents were waiting on the opposite side.

About 15 or 20 insurgents with AK-47 assault rifles and other weapons then converged on both sides of the canal and started firing.

"We couldn't move," Cianfrini said. "I was thinking, 'This is it.'" Bullets were hitting the water, chopping off the reeds and zinging over the pilots' heads.

At 0711, CZ 16/17 received a refined grid for the Fallen Angel and began to search for the downed aircraft.

They arrived at the general area where the aircraft had gone down, and assisted three Kiowa crews (already on-site) in searching for the downed helicopter. One of the Kiowa pilots said over the radio that he had spotted the aircraft on the ground.

It was burning.

In an interview for the 1st Cavalry newspaper,[4] Davison said, "He gave it to our team. We headed over there and found the 58. It was on its side; the nose was burning."

Meanwhile, one of the Kiowa crews had landed and checked the wreckage.

The pilots were gone.

"Their helmets were there, but they weren't there," Davison said. "Our immediate response was 'Well, that's good—but they're not there. Are they evading, or did they get picked up by the enemy?' That kind of sat heavy with us."

CZ 16/17 immediately started looking at the roads in the area for any traffic that might be fleeing the scene with the missing aviators on board. After several minutes, one of the Kiowas reported that they had spotted the missing crew hiding near the crash site. A few seconds after the sighting, the '58s asked CZ 16/17 if they could execute a spur ride extraction. Davison responded in the affirmative and then maneuvered CZ 16 to land near the crash site. They waited about thirty seconds without seeing anyone. Exposed and vulnerable in an area where one aircraft had already been shot down, time crawled by.

They couldn't wait forever. As the aircraft was lifting off, one of the scout pilots called that the crew was on the opposite side of the crash site, in the reeds. Davison maneuvered the aircraft, and, sure enough, there they were. He set the aircraft down about 20 meters away from their hiding place.

They came out the reeds, running toward the waiting Apache. Micah Johnson, who had gotten out of the front seat of the aircraft to assist, said that when he first saw them, he wasn't sure those guys were even pilots, since their flight gear was soaked and stained with canal water. As they boarded the aircraft, Johnson placed one of the aviators in the front seat where he had been sitting. The other went on the left side, where he assisted in hooking him up. Finally, Johnson hooked himself to the outside of the right side of the aircraft.

After Micah gave Davison the thumbs-up, signaling everyone was ready, the AWT and friends departed and began the ten-minute flight back to BIAP. Al was understandably a bit amped up and was flying around 110 knots. For anyone who has ever stuck their hand outside your car window at 70 mph, imagine doing that at 120. The guys on the outside took quite a beating, but they held on to make it back to the 3rd Infantry Division area at BIAP.

The downed aircraft was later destroyed by a USAF A-10 to prevent sensitive materials from falling into enemy hands.

Micah and Al would later be asked (ordered) to appear on CNN, ABC, and other media venues to relate their story to the folks back home. I'm sure they ran it in between stories about Britney Spears, or breaking news regarding whatever celebrity had photos of their private parts posted on the internet that day.

Four days later, on July 6, an AWT with call sign CZ 01/02 from Charlie Company (Vampires), 1-227th, conducted another unconventional CASEVAC (spur ride) in Zone 22, which was near Sadr City.

CZ 01 was flown by CW3 Felick Vallot and CW2 Brent Gruber, with CW3 Scott Sweat and CW2 Briley Beaty flying in CZ 02. At 0450 they were providing area security for a group of SOF operators following an IED strike. The operator's vehicle had struck two IEDs along Route Gold inside Sadr City as they were exfiltrating from their objective area, following a raid. The element traveling in military vehicles reached COP Ford, just outside Sadr City on Route Pluto, with three WIA and two KIA. According to the guys on the ground, they were unable to contact medevac to get an evacuation to the hospital, so they asked CZ 01 if they were medevac capable. Following the request, the team had a quick internal conversation about the feasibility of doing a spur ride, especially with a wounded person on board. The decision was made that if the patient were conscious and could be placed in the front seat of the aircraft, they would do it.

CZ 01 landed in the small LZ at COP Ford. The LZ was not much more than a dirt parking lot, and barely big enough to accommodate CZ 01. Entering a cloud of dust, the aircraft browned out just prior to touching down. As soon as the aircraft was down, an SOF operator with a serious leg injury was strapped into the front seat. The front-seater, CW2 Gruber, hooked into the left-side avionics bay outside the aircraft and braced his feet against the inboard hellfire launcher. CW3 Vallot then flew about 5 miles directly from the COP to the combat surgical hospital (CSH, pronounced "cash") without incident.

After CZ 01's departure, CZ 02 began an approach to the LZ to pick up the other wounded operator. Ultimately, he was waved off because the other causality was strapped to a backboard and wouldn't fit on the aircraft. A while later, an SOF MH-6 arrived and transported that individual to the CSH.

It was later relayed to the BN and later by the SOF chain of command that if it weren't for the quick thinking and actions of CZ01/02 that morning, there would have been at least one more KIA that day.

What is "interesting" to me is the reaction of our chain of command regarding these actions. After the mission in the early hours of July 6, the reaction by BDE and the rest of the chain of command could in no way, shape, or form be characterized as positive. The brigade standardization instructor pilot called the aviators in our battalion "cowboys," essentially saying that we were out of control. In the next breath, however, he also called us "pussies." This was essentially calling us cowards. Maybe we were cow pussies? They also said they had a "concern" that pilots were doing spur rides just to be doing them. It was a ridiculous allegation that fell apart as soon as anyone put some serious thought into it, but it didn't stop some people from saying it.

Regarding spur rides, every AWT that I was a part of briefed the possibility of extraction during every mission briefing. Nobody wanted to see anyone left down among a horde of savages, just waiting to be torn apart or to be captured and have your decapitation shown live on the internet. As such, our plan was that if the downed crew wasn't being secured by a coalition ground unit, we were going to extract ourselves if the tactical situation allowed for it. The people who were now griping about spur rides knew this because they had sat in on our briefs when they flew with us

The Avengers of Alpha Company featured a picture of "Captain America" on the tail of their aircraft, and for a short time a pre–World War II USAAC roundel on their rocket pods. *Photo by author*

A more detailed look at the "Captain America." *Photo by author*

and never said a word about it one way or another. Better safe than sorry, I always say. Or as the more cynical among us might say, "Better to be judged by twelve than carried by six," and the ever-popular "Fuck them if they can't take a joke."

This incident also highlighted a trend that I felt was not healthful and that, if not changed over the course of time, would end up affecting morale. It seemed to me that there was an inability by some at the brigade and division levels to separate the heroic on-the-spot decision to risk the safety of the aircraft and crew to save another soldier's life from the after-action review process that says, "Good job, but maybe that's not the way we'd like things to go on a regular basis." While having a conversation with someone about this problem, I tried to relate it to another action in the history of the US Army. There was an incident during World War II when a decorated soldier described an incident where he was overcome by grief and rage about his best friend being killed. Full of anger, he left cover and directly assaulted a German machine gun nest by himself, armed only with his rifle. After killing all the German soldiers there, he picked up their MG-42 machine gun and began to work his way down the line, killing even more Germans. I am quite certain that isn't

Photo of the soccer stadium where the engagement on the night of June 2, 2007, occurred. *Photo by author*

the way they teach how to assault a fortified position at the infantry school, but it didn't stop them from giving Audie Murphy a medal for it. Awards aren't supposed to be given for perfect doctrinal exercises; they are supposed to be awarded for going above and beyond the call of duty . . . a concept that seemed beyond the grasp of many in our chain of command back then, and even now, for that matter. There seemed to be an attitude in our BDE that was essentially this: if you didn't do something perfectly, then you wouldn't be recognized for it; in fact, you would be threatened with punishment. One of our platoon leaders was told by the BDE commander that his "award" for placing himself and his aircraft between friendly forces about to be overrun and the enemy was not getting a statement of charges for the battle damage that was inflicted on his aircraft by the enemy.

The consistent refusal to recognize performances that were above and beyond the call of duty and placing others before self was counter to the "Army Values" (see appendix A) and could be considered lazy at best, and petty and jealous at worst. Their actions disgusted me at the time, and my opinion of them hasn't improved since.

HAPPY FOURTH
OF JULY!, 2007

Aside from being our nation's birthday, the Fourth of July was always special to me. When I was a kid it was even more so, because it meant my birthday was just three days away. One of the local department stores in Waco always had a huge firework show, and as luck would have it, at least when I was small, the show was held just down the street from my house. The holiday also meant ice-cold watermelon, homemade ice cream, and burgers on the grill.

Here in Iraq, all the Fourth of July meant was one less day in Iraq and another mission to be flown. We had the afternoon go today. As you might imagine, Iraq in July is extremely hot. I was not looking forward to the long walk down the flight line with my gear. Not to mention the fun that comes with doing a preflight on an aircraft that is painted a dark color and made of metal in the noonday sun. These were truly the dog days of summer. On the other hand, I could have been an infantryman out walking patrol wearing full battle rattle in downtown Baghdad. It was never a bad idea to try to keep things in perspective.

Not willing to forget the great Stetson incident of Thanksgiving 2006, I let it be known to my teammates that for the mission we were scheduled to fly on Independence Day, come hell or high water I was going to be wearing my Stetson. 1 ACB and 1st CAV could go straight to hell as far as I was concerned. I still don't know why I had chosen this particular hill to make a stand and possibly die on, but I had made up my mind. I was pleased to see when we sat down for the mission brief that Capt. Daigle and Lt. Haas had brought their hats with them as well. So, with that, our merry band of insurrectionists went to work.

The brief began in the normal manner, as one of the members of the S2 section turned on the projector and brought up the PowerPoint presentation that contained the day's situation brief. They usually started the brief with a humorous video or cartoon just to lighten the mood. In my opinion, their greatest triumph in terms of morale-boosting entertainment was the day they showed a video of a French performer who goes by the name Alizee. It looked like she was on the French version of *America's Got Talent* or some such show, singing her song "J'en Ai Marre." The image of this singer on the big screen in our TOC, dancing and singing a song that for all we knew was about killing baby rabbits in a sacrifice for the devil, is forever etched into my memory. If I knew the name of the soldier who first found that video, I would have submitted him/her for an Army Achievement Medal.

The S2 Section did a great job every single day we were there. They overcame a lot of obstacles internal and external to accomplish their mission. None of them were aviators, so I'm sure it was a culture shock when they were assigned to us, not to mention the verbal abuse they suffered at the hands of several of the pilots. They also had to deal with the crazy ideas such as the bird tracker slide, which tracked the areas of Baghdad where our aircraft had struck birds. They handled these for the most part much more seriously than they deserved to be. Their brief to us that day was pretty much standard. These briefs usually included the weather outlook, the significant acts in our operational area for the last twenty-four hours, and, finally, highlights of anything that might be of particular interest regarding our mission. From time to time, we would be treated to slides featuring photos of enemy weapons rounded up during operations we had supported. Invariably these caches would include pornography, often of the homosexual male variety. I always thought that kind of ironic, since these good soldiers of Islam were supposed to be fighting to keep that stuff out of their country. If we take them at their word, I suppose they believed in knowing their enemy.

After the intel guys finished their spiel, the battle captain arrived and gave us a stack of paper about an inch tall, which represented all the mini-missions or individual tasks we were expected to accomplish that day. Simply put, our primary mission was to fly two AH-64D aircraft on a combat air patrol over Baghdad for four hours. During those four hours we would be given many separate tasks to perform. For example, a mission package could contain tasks to conduct CM2RI for Ironhorse between the hours of 1400 and 1530, provide route recon and security for a patrol from 1530 to 1600, and support a cordon-and-search operation starting at 1615 until end of mission. Usually, we would be retasked in flight, and all these little missions would go out the window for something of a greater priority such as a medevac or TIC. But we would brief as if we were going to accomplish every task we were given.

After the battle captain finished, we briefed the order and timeline for all the tasks we had been given. The biggest concern was to figure out where, in all these tasks, we could take a break to go get fuel and still cover all our assignments.

On the desktop in the briefing room was a handy AWT briefing checklist to help make sure we talked about all the necessary information. We covered things such as which aircraft on the flight was responsible for what radio calls, and what we would do in the event we became separated or went into the clouds in an unplanned fashion. Most of these things were covered in our SOP, but we touched on them before every flight just in case someone was unclear about their responsibilities.

After finishing up the brief, we walked over to the Air Force weather folks; first, to see if they had switched people out again, and then to get a weather update before we went out to do the preflight. It seemed (to us anyway) that every time we went to brief, there were new people in there. The USAF had a different policy in place on tour length than the Army, at least for the folks who staffed our weather facility. They changed out personnel several times during our deployment. The downside of that, for us, was that it seemed as soon as they learned the local weather patterns, it was time for them to leave. The result of all of this was that the weather forecasting wasn't as accurate as it could be, which, for someone who flies for a living, can be quite aggravating.

Other than the weather being ridiculously hot, the forecaster told us it was going to be okay for the duration of our mission window. So, with that information in hand, we gathered up our kneeboards and assorted paperwork and began the walk-over to the crew chief trailers on the flight line to get our tail numbers and check the logbooks to see what, if anything, we needed to be concerned with regarding maintenance on our assigned steeds that day.

When we walked out the door of the BDE TOC, I slapped my Stetson on my head, and we began the long walk over to where our crew chiefs hung out. During our sunny stroll, I remarked to my copilot that day, Capt. Daigle, how—if the Army were serious about protecting its soldiers from the ravages of sun-damaged skin— you'd think they'd wholeheartedly support the wearing of this kind of headgear. To be honest, I think if they were to adopt this kind of headgear, they would do well to pick something other than the color black, since that baby tended to get a little warm ... but it did an excellent job of deflecting the sun's rays as we walked defiantly across the base toward our waiting aircraft.

Surprisingly, nobody said a word to us about wearing our hats that day. I suppose the CSM was sleeping in his CHU, waiting for the evening to come out of the shadows and provide corrective guidance to renegade warrant officers, who, through their blatant violations of uniform standards and policies, threatened to undermine the entire chain of command and military discipline in general. But today we had some-how managed to avoid that craptastic bastard, and I would be able to enjoy the Fourth of July pretty much douchebag-free.

When we arrived down at the BN area on the flight line, I raided the freezer for a bottle of water. It was frozen solid, but if I left it out in the sun it would be nice and slushy by the time we finished the preflight. Walking into the trailer, I looked on the whiteboard to see what tail number I had today. I hoped it wasn't 331, not that there was anything wrong with it, but because it was located at the end of a line of twenty-four helicopters, about a half mile away. I lucked out and got an aircraft in the middle, somewhere near the trailer that held our flight gear. That crisis averted, I gave the computer logbook from my aircraft a careful look. There weren't any major discrepancies or showstoppers with the aircraft, and we had enough available flight time before the next scheduled service to fly our mission. Hanging out with the crew chiefs for a few minutes, we admired their collection of *Maxim* magazines, raided their box of snacks for a piece of beef jerky, and just enjoyed the air-conditioning for a few more minutes. I finally decided that I couldn't put off the inevitable too much longer and still launch on time, so I walked out into the blast-furnace-like heat of midday central Iraq to get my M-4 from the arms room and then walk out to our aircraft to start the preflight. As I opened the door, the heat slapped me in the face, and I let out a long sigh. Here we go again.

A few minutes later, I arrived at the storage shed down on the flight line and went inside to collect my flight gear. My helmet bag and survival vest were there on the shelf, where I had left them the day prior. I collected my stuff and walked to the aircraft, which was a couple of revetments down. The bird was already opened and ready for preflight. The crew chief (who had driven down in a Gator four-wheeler) was hanging out in the shade, available if Capt. Daigle or I found anything that we thought needed attention. Before I began the preflight, I went about building my nest in the cockpit. I put my rifle in its mount inside the cockpit, plugged in my helmet, took my pubs bag and put it in its place on the left side of the instrument panel, installed the PCMICA into its slot, put my kneeboard and checklist on top of the dash, and finally placed all the AMR requests between the sun shield and the dash for easy access. With all that done, I fished out an extra pair of flight gloves to wear while preflighting and then tossed my now-empty helmet bag into the survival kit bay.

Capt. Daigle had already started on the left side of the aircraft and was working back toward the tail, so I started at the nose on the right side and would meet him back at the tailwheel. I am glad he did the left side, because I hated the damn catwalk between the engines and its cowlings, which never seemed to match up. I always seemed to end up in a wrestling match with the doors and the pins, which held them in place; it was easily my least enjoyable thing to preflight. We finished up finding nothing to squawk about, so we were rapidly running out of reasons to cancel the flight. About thirty minutes prior to our scheduled launch time, we climbed on board and started the APU to begin the process of launching our team. Due to the extreme heat, we needed to start that early to give the electronics a chance to cool down. According to the book, we weren't supposed to turn on several systems until the expanded forward avionics bays (EFAB) reached a certain temperature. Believe it or not, that temperature was nowhere near the 120°F we were experiencing on the ramp. This precooling was done, of course, to avoid damaging the various electronic systems on the aircraft. On the plus side for the pilots, at least, the cockpit was cooling off . . . our crew chief, who was wearing a headset that was attached to the aircraft via a long cord, had no such luxury. He stood in the hot sun, waiting for us to start the aircraft or tell him about some issue we were having and then try to fix it before we had to launch, or get us moved to a spare aircraft.

Fortunately, today, the aircraft didn't wake up stupid, and we didn't have to do what we called the Boeing reset, which amounted to turning the aircraft computer off and then back on . . . which, as one might imagine, can be a real pain in the butt, especially when you are up against a time schedule you have to meet. So as soon as everything cooled off, we set up the IDM, completed the internal boresights, and accomplished all our required commo checks. Now we just waited for our "crank time," when we would start our engines, taxi out, do our out-front boresight of the TADS, and then depart Taji to, we hoped, accomplish all those little tasks we had been given at the briefing. I was fortunate and got an aircraft that had already been flown once today so I didn't have to do the "HIT check" (an engine health indication test), so that was one less thing we had to do before we took off.

I adjusted the vent on the dash to blow cold air in my face, and took a drink of water from the bottle I took earlier. Finished drinking, I threw the bottle on the top of the dash, as I watched the clock get closer to our briefed engine start time. About ten seconds prior to start, I flipped on the anticollision lights, which we sometimes referred to as "smacks." The bright-white strobe lights on either side of the aircraft began flashing, alerting anyone watching that we were about to "turn blades." The crew chief, who had been seeking shelter from the sun under the wing, came out and stood just under the rotor disk on the left side of the aircraft to observe engine 1 as we started.

As the clock hit zero, I announced, "Starting 1" to my front-seater and the crew chief on the intercom. I pressed the start button and moved the power lever for engine 1 into the start position. The engine spooled up nicely, and after the starter dropped off-line, I heard the crew chief announce, "Doors closed," meaning that the air bypass doors on the bottom of the engine nacelle had closed like they were supposed to. Engine 2 started like a champ as well, and we went through the before-taxi checks like a well-oiled machine. When we were ready for taxi, I called, "One Three, Red One" over team internal, letting the other aircraft know we were ready to taxi. Several seconds later, they replied with "One Four, Red One." Immediately I replied, "Calling tower."

"Taji tower, Crazyhorse One Three, flight of two in parking, taxi for Alpha Key."

"Crazyhorse One Three, Taji tower, taxi to Alpha Key, winds three six zero at five gusting to fifteen, altimeter two niner, niner two, no other reported traffic."

With that, I increased collective and began to back out of the revetment. The crew chief cleared us back, giving us hand and arm signals. When we reached the centerline of the taxiway, he signaled us to turn and head out on our way. Before we began to move away, he gave us a sharp salute, which Capt. Daigle returned. As we taxied behind gun 2's parking space, I called them that we were clear, so they could start backing out.

We arrived at the Alpha keyhole (an area off the approach end of the runway where we could do our before-takeoff checks and boresights without getting in the way of landing traffic). After completing our checks, I made radio contact with the AWT we were replacing, while waiting for our departure time. The city had been quiet during their mission window, and there wasn't much going on, since many units weren't doing much during the holiday. We hoped it would stay that way.

A lot of guys would complain if they flew missions and nothing went on. The philosophy I had was that a day without enemy activity is a good thing, because it just might mean that things are finally getting better. I fully understood their desire to get out there and get bad guys, but boring was good.

Eventually our launch time arrived, and I called tower, "Taji tower, Crazyhorse one three, flight of two for takeoff, departure Alpha Tango."

"Crazyhorse one three, winds three six zero at seven, runway three five, cleared for takeoff, call Alpha Tango."

As soon as I heard the tower begin his clearance, I was already light on the wheels, so as soon as he finished, I relied with "Crazyhorse one three is on the go, will call Alpha."

I kept the takeoff low to help trail get on top of my rotor wash, which requires a lot of power (which we didn't have because of the heat), and additionally gave them the opportunity to try to make our departure "pretty." Because, as we all know, looks are everything. Trail called me soon after takeoff with the code word "Sausage," meaning we were linked up as a flight of two. I turned right off the runway, heading toward the Alpha sector and, beyond that, Baghdad. As we headed for the boundary of Camp Taji, I began the "fence check," which would get the aircraft ready for combat.

First I turned off the smacks, and then I informed Capt. Daigle that our weapons are "hot" as I tell him, "Aircraft's armed." I look at my symbology and see that he already has the tape going, since I see the message "RECORDING" on the bottom left of my screen. Then I turn on the CMWS and call trail with "Fence check complete." He replies with the same as they finish up theirs.

Before we make it to the Tango ring and frequency change with the tower, an inbound UH-60 pilot decides that today is a good day to flirt with the female tower operator.

"You're sounding pretty fine today, Taji tower."

She shuts him down immediately with "Thanks; I'll let my husband know."

We all got a good laugh at that pilot's expense. But things like that were the way a lot of folks chose to fight boredom. It also wasn't unusual to hear something called "the cat game" on the radio from time to time. "The cat game" was lifted directly from a movie called *Super Troopers*, which was extremely popular among a lot of us. In the movie, the game revolved around how many times during a highway patrol traffic stop could a state trooper use the word "meow" in place of another word like "now." In Iraq, the game was just getting the word "meow" wedged somehow into a radio call. For instance, a call using the "cat game" might go like this: "Baghdad Radio, Crazyhorse 11 is off Zone 9 for Taji time meow." It is important to understand that there were no points to be scored in the cat game, and there was no way to win it . . . kind of like being in Iraq.

Sometimes, the radio horseplay offended some of the listeners.

Such as on a day much like this, when there was nothing going on. A flight had just departed Taji and was making its initial check-in with Baghdad Radio. One of the pilots, a female warrant officer from our unit named Cindy, made the call: "Baghdad Radio, Crazyhorse zero one is off Taji en route to Zones nine and two four; will call arrival."

After Baghdad Radio acknowledged the call, an unidentified voice on the frequency said, "That Crazyhorse chick sounds HOT."

The voice on the radio was coming from the other aircraft in the flight. One of the other pilots was having some fun at Cindy's expense. She obviously knew who it was, but everyone else monitoring Baghdad Radio didn't.

A few minutes later, when they arrived in sector, she gave Baghdad Radio the call: "Crazyhorse zero one is arrival zone nine and two four will call the next three zero or departure."

Again, Baghdad Radio acknowledged the call, and again an unidentified voice said, "Don't stop talking, Crazyhorse; I'm almost done."

I heard about this because I had walked into the TOC soon after the acting battle captain, Capt. Daigle, answered the phone call from Baghdad Radio alerting the battalion that someone was harassing one of our pilots, and they were going to find out who that person was and make sure that they got what was coming to them. I don't know, exactly, how they thought they were going to track that person down, but it seemed they were pretty upset and could see their point.

Most of the pilots in the TOC had a good idea of who had done it, even without looking at the flight schedule to see who was on the mission. One of the other pilots on the flight had been friends with Cindy for a long time and was also known to be a bit of a jokester. As soon as the flight returned, Capt. Daigle told them about the phone call and said to them that they should probably cool the radio jokes for a while, to which he got the "I don't know what you're talking about" routine. Happily, though, the BN never got any more calls about airborne sexual harassment from Baghdad Radio. Our joker should be incredibly grateful that Capt. Daigle was the person who answered the phone, since it could have gotten very ugly. It's a strange, strange world we lived in.

Folks unfamiliar with the military might find this information either a shocking indication of how unprofessional we are or a comforting indication of our humanity. For me, I view it as a way that people dealt with the boredom and frustration of being away from home and family, and just a way to have a little laugh. Did some of it push up against the limits of acceptable behavior? Yep. The slower things were, actionwise, the more likely people were to clown around a little or cut up on the radio. That was one of those slow times. If you didn't manage to find a way to laugh every now and then, you'd probably go crazy around here.

So off we charged into possible battle. After our frequency change with the tower, we switched over to Baghdad Radio and I let trail know we were also switching to the ground unit. We would now be in contact with the unit that owned the ground we were flying over, and trail would be responsible for staying in contact with Attack Mike and keeping them advised of what we were doing and whom we were working with.

According to the paperwork we had been given, the first unit we were scheduled to work for had a patrol going out that we were supposed to support. I knew something was up as soon as we made the joining report and got the return call of "Stand by." This unit had a history of submitting AMRs as a placeholder. This meant they just made up a mission to ensure that we would be in the AO to fly around during a certain time period. They had just done that again.

This situation was rather aggravating to a lot of us, because it was like they didn't understand that every time we took off and crossed the fence of Camp Taji, there was someone down there who wanted to kill us and would do their best to make that happen. We would respond every time we were asked, and sacrifice everything for those guys if they really needed us, but when there was no actual mission, one couldn't help but have the feeling you were being used.

I had trail call Attack Mike and tell them what was going on. I'd let the battle captain get on the phone and deal with the ground unit. In the meantime, we would give these guys a bit of area recon and then move on to the next unit. Your punishment, if you lie to me, is that you certainly won't get the entire block of coverage you were asking for. There were plenty of units that didn't lie that were looking for support as well. That was the issue, after all; too many requests and not enough aircraft, and some of the units saw this technique as a way to get what they wanted.

So as the day went on, we went from unit to unit, "sharing the love" as it were. There was no significant activity, since the bad guys were also taking the day off. That wasn't all that unusual, since we were pretty much the only people in Iraq dumb enough to be out in the afternoon sun.

One of the last things we did, having completed all our requested tasks, was to perform CM2RI around Camp Taji until the end of our mission window. Usually during the mission brief, the S2 would give us points of interest to look at around Camp Taji if we had the time. Today we did.

During the mission brief, Lt. Haas had requested that I take a picture of his aircraft while he held up the flag of his alma mater: the University of North Dakota. So, on our way back to Camp Taji, we formed up, took a few photos, and then continued with the mission.

If you look closely at the picture, you can see part of Camp Taji in the background. If you look really, really closely, I'm sure you'll find a CSM harassing someone about something that really doesn't matter.

We hit all the points that our intel folks had given us, and then some. By the time that was over, trail had completed the BHO with the next team and we headed in at last light, to land, shut down, and, most importantly, get some chow. It had been a long day, and while we didn't get any bad guys, they didn't get any of ours either, so we would call it a wash. On short final, in honor of the holiday, I punched off a couple of flares—our fireworks to mark the birth of our nation, so many years ago. Happy birthday, 'Merica!

Happy Fourth of July. *Top, left to right:* CW2 Cole Moughon, 1Lt. Brian Haas; *bottom, left to right:* CW4 Dan McClinton, Capt. Paul Daigle. *Photo courtesy of the author*

1Lt. Haas and CW2 Moughon's aircraft fires off a couple of flares on July 4, 2007. Camp Taji is in the background. *Photo by author*

AN ENGAGEMENT CALLED "COLLATERAL MURDER": JULY 12, 2007

There is many a boy here today who looks on war as all glory, but, boys, it is all Hell. —William Tecumseh Sherman

On July 12, 2007, an attack weapons team (AWT) from 1-227 AVN responded to a TIC call issued by 2-16 Infantry in a section of Baghdad well known for enemy activity. Arriving at the scene, the team identified and subsequently engaged a group of people carrying weapons who were located within range of an American infantry unit nearby. This was one of thirty-seven separate engagements carried out by the 1st ACB during the month of July.

Almost three years after the engagement took place, a disgruntled private first class saw an edited portion of the gun camera tape on the classified computer network called SIPRNET, which disturbed him. He then decided not to go to his platoon sergeant, his commander, the inspector general's office, or even his elected representatives with his concerns of a "possible war crime." He decided to download, copy, and release this tape and thousands of unrelated documents to an outside entity, whose motivations weren't clearly known.

After they received the tape, a group calling themselves Wikileaks posted the gun camera tape online via their website, in a presentation titled "Collateral Murder." Of course, they did this after editing it enough to show only the things they wished to highlight. In this video, scenes can be seen where members of the crew are heard to say things that are frankly insensitive and unfeeling. Unfortunately, in combat, people do tend to lose some of their humanity. Urging a wounded enemy to pick up a weapon so you can finish him off may understandably revolt a person sitting in their easy chair, reading about it. To someone who witnessed the handiwork of those in the Mahdi army or AQI daily, a situation like that becomes an opportunity to keep one more bad guy from setting an IED, launching an RPG, or firing mortars ever again. While it might shock some people to hear this, I have been told many times over the radio to "kill that motherfucker" by soldiers on the ground. We all wish warfare were as clean and simple as killing a roach with a can of bug spray. War is, however, ugly, terrible, and messy. Because humans are fallible, things can rapidly get confused. People often say things in inartful and profane ways that if given the opportunity to reflect, they may not otherwise have done. It doesn't mean that they are criminals; it means that they are imperfect.

In the ensuing storm of comments and controversy, all sorts of people with varying levels of military experience and belief systems have come to condemn or praise the actions of the attack weapons team known as Crazyhorse 18 and 19 that morning in July, calling them war criminals and demanding that they be tried for war crimes, among other things.

I wasn't flying there that day, but I have been in situations that were similar to this one. Having talked with the crews and viewed their entire tape, I feel I have a good understanding of what happened. Nobody I have seen comment, pro or con, in a public forum has ever flown an Apache in combat. A fact that many people fail to realize is that the crew and the aircraft were constantly at risk. An AWT over Baghdad wasn't some hovering eye in the sky, impervious to the enemy entity. We were down there in it, at risk, and as a result, anytime a crew responded to a TIC situation there was often significant anxiety and stress involved. I say these things not as an excuse or disclaimer, but so the reader can have some idea of what, exactly, the situation is like for those who are flying attack helicopters.

I have been asked by others if I had been there that day, what would I have done—would I have done everything the same way as those crews did? The honest answer is I don't know. There are things about this engagement that are so clear that there is no doubt in my mind that any crew under that ROE would have done the same thing in the same situation. But every attack weapons team is different, and everyone reacts to situations differently. All I would ask from anyone is to try to read this with an open mind.

I know all the aviators who were involved that day, and they were and are men of courage and honor. They are men who are fathers, brothers, and sons. They are also quite human.

A short description of the day goes like this:

At 0953, local elements of 2-16 Infantry (call sign: Bushmaster) received enemy fire while conducting Operation Cure in Zone 30 in the Strike Brigade Area of Responsibility (southeast Baghdad) and requested aviation support. CZ 18/19, which was conducting CM2RI operations at the time, responded to the TIC call. The CZ team checked in with Bushmaster and was tasked to identify the source of the enemy fire. Initially after checking in on-station, CZ 18/19 sighted several individuals on the rooftops of buildings in the area. After determining that these were friendly forces, the AWT then spotted eight to ten individuals standing in the street, some of whom were believed to be armed with RPGs and small arms, and reported this to Bushmaster. At 1030, Bushmaster cleared the AWT to engage this group. CZ 18/19 engaged a group of individuals with thirty rounds of 30 mm. Soon after the engagement, a van arrived with three to four persons inside. The personnel in the van were observed attempting to evacuate the individuals and weapons from the street. CZ 18/19 received clearance to engage the van and engaged with 30 mm, destroying it. At 1040, ground forces cordoned the area and began to evaluate causalities, confirming eleven KIA. They also found one RPG launcher and small arms. At this time the ground forces reported two children had been WIA. Both children were removed from inside the van. They were evacuated to FOB Loyalty as "urgent surgical." At 1102, CZ 18/19 reported sighting three more individuals with AK-47s, and RPGs at another location. The AWT engaged the group with ten rounds of 30 mm cannon fire, resulting in no enemy casualties. At 1118 the ground unit attempted to conduct a cordon and search of a structure. The unit took sustained small-arms fire and requested destruction of the structure. CZ 18/19 then engaged the building with two N-model and a single K-model Hellfire missiles, causing an estimated eight to ten AIF killed. Bushmaster TOC cleared all fires.

As part of my duties as the battalion TACOPS officer, I viewed the videotape of the mission in question several times. Now I feel, several years down the road, that some people looked at this event either with expectations or presumptions, or when they heard language that shocked them, they immediately thought everything the crew(s) did was wrong or premeditated somehow. I can tell you that when the senior warrant officers in the battalion initially looked at the tape, we were concerned about the language they used, not because their actions were wrong, but because of the impression it gives. In fact, it was a constant fight to try to get some people (not just the crews involved in this event) to remain professional in their language, because we knew other people who weren't involved would see these tapes. That said, if you took the audio out of this and looked at the steps the crews took, they did them according to the rules of engagement at the time.

A TIC was the second-highest priority of any mission we could be tasked with, superseded only by a medevac. As a group, we took TICs very seriously because it meant our ground forces were under attack and required aviation support. That said, I would estimate that at least 75% of TICs became TWIC (troops were in contact) by the time an AWT arrived, either because the enemy heard the aircraft coming and decided to break contact or the ground forces defeated the threat before the aircraft arrived on station. Therefore, when an AWT arrived on station and a firefight was still ongoing and the friendly forces were still in contact, it was pretty much a given that the enemy was more motivated than usual, or things were really going badly for the friendly forces.

The primary task of an AWT prior to and immediately after arriving on station is to gain situational awareness as to the exact location of friendly and enemy forces in the area. Other information, such as previous events that are pertinent to the situation, is communicated in what is called a "fighter check-in." During the fighter check-in on July 12, the Crazyhorse AWT was informed that there had been enemy contact in the area, all morning, and that an unmanned aerial vehicle (UAV) had spotted a dark-colored vehicle dropping off supplies, sporadically, during the fighting. Shortly after the check-in, one of the AH-64s spotted a person looking around the corner of a building in the direction of friendly forces, holding what the crew thought to be an RPG (it was in fact a camera with a telephoto lens that was being used by a reporter from Reuters news agency). I feel it needs to be said that even if the crew had identified the object as a camera, they still would have proceeded as they did.

Anti-Iraqi Forces (AIF) were known to photograph and videotape attacks on US personnel for propaganda purposes. As the aircraft circled around the building, they spotted several armed individuals in a group at the same corner of the building as the photographer looking in the direction of friendly forces. At this point the AWT asked for and gained permission to fire.

I have heard it asked, "If they saw only three armed individuals in a group of ten, why did they shoot them all?" There was at least one RPG (actual) visible to the crews. One RPG could destroy a Bradley IFV if it struck the vehicle in the right place, and one RPG could also kill many people if used correctly. Those pilots were charged to protect 2-16 Infantry, and as such they were looking for any possible threats, which they would in turn attempt to eliminate in accordance with the rules of engagement. Many folks have preconceived notions about giving a warning shot or being fair. War is not fair. War is in fact ugly. That is why, when the shooting starts, it doesn't stop until all the threats are eliminated. We do this because the person who survives today may be the one who plants the IED that kills a soldier or innocent person tomorrow. Baghdad in 2007 was a city at war, and unfortunately bad things happen in war. We become the judge, jury, and executioner because that is the nature of combat. It isn't pretty, but it surely isn't a war crime. The fact of the matter is, if a reporter (or anyone else, for that matter) chooses to accompany armed enemy forces in the vicinity of a firefight with US forces, he or she is likely to get shot or killed.

Shortly after the first engagement, a dark-colored van arrived on the scene. As mentioned earlier, during the fighter check-in the pilots were told that a dark-colored vehicle had been dropping off supplies to the AIF fighters all morning. It had been my experience in this and past deployments that if a gunfight was going on, non-combatants stayed out of the way. In the thirty-seven months I spent in that country, I never once saw a vehicle randomly pull into the middle of a battle or even stop to render aid, like a passerby on the highway who witnesses an accident. I will grant you that there's a first time for everything, but it is difficult not to believe the person driving this vehicle was somehow involved with what was going on. One of the pilots reported seeing weapons being loaded into the van, but this is not seen on the video; the video records only what is being seen by one person in one aircraft through the soda straw view of our TADS. After the weapons sighting was reported, permission to engage was sought by the AWT and granted by the ground unit.

Unfortunately, two children were injured when the van was engaged with 30 mm cannon fire. I have read a lot of remarks about this part of the fight, and a lot of people have spent a lot of time poring over the aircraft videotape, spotting this and that, and saying the aircrew should have seen the children in the van. The fact is that they didn't see the children. Knowing them as I do, if they had seen the children, they would have held their fire. In fact, later that day when they spotted children in the engagement area, they withheld fire on a legitimate target.

There are more than a few people who are quick to blame the crews for firing on a van that contained children (whom they couldn't see), but I've never heard a peep from the same people about the guy who would drive a van with two kids in it into the middle of a gunfight. The same people who call those pilots war criminals have yet to condemn the enemy, who would strap bombs to the chests of mentally handicapped children and then send them to their remotely detonated deaths. The same people never once stop to mention that Iran was supplying the militias in east Baghdad, where this fight occurred, with arms and in some cases advisors, which just prolonged the conflict. Pilots saw the information available on a 6-by-6-inch screen in a moving and turning helicopter with multiple radios blaring, flying over an active firefight in the middle of an area where, in two weeks' time, we would lose a helicopter due to a surface-to-air missile. This was by no means a sterile environment. Everyone I know believes that the fact that those children were hurt is horrible. Nobody I know has ever launched on a mission looking to go out and just inflict damage upon random people, especially children. It was horrible that this happened. It was tragic, to be sure, but it was NOT a war crime.

Now I am quite certain that nothing I have written here is going to change the mind of someone who has convinced themselves that we were all a bunch of thuggish monsters, out to kill and destroy as much as we could get away with. It is unfortunate that there are people who believe this. For some reason, they want to believe that we are the true bad guys. That the United States of America and, by extension, its troops are the ones causing all the trouble in the world. Of course, the truth is a lot more complicated than that, but people are free to think and believe what they want.

What bothers me the most, though, are current or former soldiers who choose to comment about things they have never seen or done. Because these people are/were soldiers, their claims seem inoculated from serious scrutiny. I attempt to confine my remarks to things I absolutely know about, because either I was there or I have talked with the people who were there, and understand the processes involved. I can't say the same thing about people who profess to "know" what we did as attack helicopter crews on a daily basis. People who have never been to a single mission brief or visited the flight line, the FARP, or anywhere else pretend to know my business and what those guys were thinking. I fail to understand how people who never received the same rules of engagement (ROE), intel, or mission briefings that I did are able to say what we knew, what we didn't know, or what we did on a daily basis. It is quite easy to call people you don't know names and ascribe motives and actions to them, when they are just disembodied voices on a videotape. It is quite a different thing when you know those people to be husbands and fathers. Honorable men who were trying to do the best job that they could that day. I have flown beside every person who was on the mission that day, and would gladly do so again. They have put themselves, willingly, into harm's way time and again, sometimes literally placing themselves between the enemy's guns and their comrades on the ground to get the job done. Their valor has been well established to me and anyone who knows them. Yet, time after time, people who know them from a snippet of videotape, taken out of context, rise to attempt to sully their names and reputation.

Since this incident was revealed, a "documentary" called *Incident in New Baghdad* has been made, giving us the story of a man hurt by war, by what he saw and did on the streets of Baghdad. Anybody who comes back from war physically or mentally injured deserves to get all the help that they need, but when that person slanders other soldiers and tells untruths about the circumstances surrounding events he was involved in, that person has crossed the line. When the film came out, I had an extensive online conversation with the director of the film. I told him that people had a right to their opinion, and if someone was there, they had a right to communicate what they saw . . . they had earned that right. But the director owes the people watching his film more than just that person's viewpoint. Especially knowing that the individual in question could not have attained the specific knowledge of all the events he describes in the film, given the position he served in. It is unfortunate that such a one-sided film was nominated for the Academy Award for Best Documentary in 2012 (it didn't win, thankfully). The film presented only one point of view, a point of view that is clearly at odds with the facts regarding the attack helicopter engagements of July 12, 2007.

There were two official investigations accomplished regarding this engagement: one by our parent unit, the 1st Air Cavalry Brigade, and the other by the 2nd Brigade Combat Team (Strike). They are both included, in their entirety, in the appendix section of this book. What the reader may find enlightening, though, are the findings of the 1 ACB investigation:

a. The AWT was on a directed mission, conducted the appropriate check-in with ground elements in contact, and received an adequate situation report describing the current status and disposition of forces on the ground. At this point, the AWT began to develop the situation in concert with the ground element in contact and maintained positive identification of friendly locations throughout the supported period. As the situation developed, the AWT exercised sound judgment and discrimination during attempts to acquire insurgents or, moreover, to identify personnel engaged in hostile or threatening activities against our brothers on the ground.

b. The AWT accurately assessed that the criteria to find and terminate the threat to friendly forces were met in accordance with the law of armed conflict and rules of engagement. Fundamental to all engagements is the principle of military necessity. This was clearly established and supported by the friendly forces' inherent right to self-defense and the ground commander's obligation to ensure that all necessary means were employed to defend or protect his soldiers from hostile acts. In this case, the AWT was employed to destroy insurgents attempting to kill friendly forces. The attack weapons team

(1) positively identified the threat: The AWT, with reasonable certainty, identified military-aged males both in a location and with weapons consistent with reports of hostile acts conducted against friendly forces. While observing this group of individuals, the AWT satisfied all requirements to initiate an engagement.

(2) established hostile intent: Hostile intent was exhibited by armed insurgents peering around the comer of a home to monitor the movement or

activities of friendly forces and was confirmed by the presence of those personnel carrying an RPG and AK-47s. These weapons systems were reported in the initial check-in as the type used to engage friendly forces.

(3) conducted collateral damage assessment: The AWT accurately assessed that using the 30 mm cannon was proportionally appropriate to omit the threat while reducing the probability of excessive damage to surrounding structures, vehicles, and real property in the area.

(4) received clearance of fires: Having already identified through voice communications, physical markings, and, ultimately, visual recognition of friendly positions, the AWT again requested and received clearance from the ground unit that there were no friendly forces in the engagement area.

c. Only after an extensive review of the AWT's gun camera video and with the knowledge of the two missing media personnel is it reasonable to deduce that two of the individuals intermixed among the insurgents located in the engagement area may have been reporters. There was neither reason nor probability to assume that neutral media personnel were embedded with enemy forces. It is worth noting the fact that insurgent groups often video and photograph friendly activity and insurgent attacks against friendly forces for use in training videos and for use as propaganda to exploit or highlight their capabilities. The aircrews erroneously identified the cameras as weapons due to presentation (slung over shoulder, with the body of the object resting at the back, rear of the torso) and association (personnel collocated with others having RPGs and AK-47s). (Bold text in the original)

Of course, as I said previously, none of this is going to change the minds of those who would like to see us as murdering kill-bots who were bent on death and destruction, instead of imperfect human beings who are required to make split-second decisions on the field of battle. Because someone says things like "Look at all those dead bastards" or urges a wounded enemy with the words "Come on, buddy; just pick up the weapon" so we could legally engage him again doesn't mean we think this is a game, or find this particularly amusing. It means we are sick of seeing our fellow soldiers and innocents hurt and killed, and when you feel you have finally gotten one of the people who has been doing these things in your sights, forgive us if we don't show much sympathy or even professionalism, because by this point in the deployment, things had become very personal.

If you find these comments disgusting or particularly brutal, I can assure you that this is nothing compared to the things I have heard and seen on other deployments, when talking to people on the ground, or listening over their radio network. War is a brutal, ugly thing, and if you are offended by the language, that is unfortunate. The language is also a coping mechanism that people tend to use, to depersonalize the ugly, vicious things that we must sometimes do. I am also quite sure that infantrymen and tank crews are happy that their engagements aren't taped.

I think the pilots who were involved in this event would be the first ones to tell you that this was not a textbook example of how to conduct an engagement. I also feel safe in saying that if most of us in the unit were placed in this situation, every single one of us would have probably done it differently. The point being this: A TIC scenario is dynamic and changes by the second. Each TIC is different from the one before, and things happen in a hurry. This crew followed the rules of engagement that were in place at the time, and while it might not have been pretty and people said words or expressed feelings that you may not have wanted to hear, that is the reality of what happens. But it isn't a war crime.

If you have seen the video and were disturbed, I would first tell you that you should be, because those are human beings being killed. This is no game; this is what war is. Engagements are filmed to document what we do, and to improve our tactics, techniques, and procedures as well as to protect us from people who say we did one thing when in fact something else occurred. There are many, many different videos on YouTube and other video sites of AH-64 and other aircraft engaging the enemy since September 11, 2001. Some people refer to these videos as "war porn." They show some crews celebrating their success on the battlefield as one would after

Typical scene of a Baghdad neighborhood as seen from our operating altitude during daylight hours.
Photo by author

An AH-64 from B Company, 1-227th AVN, on patrol over Baghdad. Sadr City can be seen in the background. *Photo by author*

scoring a touchdown at a football game, while others are stoic and professional. That is their way of dealing with what they do. I don't expect you to understand, but would hope that people wouldn't be so quick to judge. Personally, I viewed my job as being like that of a person who has a rat infestation in their house. If I kill a rat, I don't go running through the house high-fiving the family; it's a nasty job that needed to be done. But every pilot had their own way of dealing with what they were required to do. I would suggest that you try to separate the verbal pronouncements made by the aircrews, and view the rules of engagement and what was actually done by them, and you'll see that while it was ugly and horrible, it was what they thought needed to be done at that moment in time on a battlefield in Iraq, and within what the rules of engagement were in place at that time.

THE MEDIA, A SOMETIMES LIKE/HATE RELATIONSHIP

I hate newspapermen. They come into camp and pick up their camp rumors and print them as facts. I regard them as spies, which, in truth, they are. —William Tecumseh Sherman

You might find it odd that I would choose to write about my distaste for the media and their coverage of military affairs and the Iraq war just after I described how my unit accidentally killed a couple of news reporters. I concede that many folks might say this proves that we or, more correctly, I don't care about what happened. I would counter with the fact that reporters who would willingly embed themselves with people who would strap bombs to children or lop the heads off prisoners are pretty much amoral persons, who would do just about anything. While I wouldn't go out of my way to track these people down and do them harm, I wouldn't be that enthusiastic about helping them out of a jam either. In the face of pure evil, they can't find it inside themselves to take a stand, or if they do, they stand opposite from me, and that I find reprehensible. The short version of all that is if you choose to walk alongside my enemy on the field of battle, you are no different than him.

I come by my dislike of most of the media honestly. I don't actually think it was a single event that made me dislike them, but a cumulative total of all the things I had seen and heard since I had deployed. Looking back now, the incident I am about to describe probably ended up being the straw that broke the camel's back.

I had just finished flying a mission and was watching the "news" in the DFAC early in the deployment. In DFAC #1, along the walls and down the center of the DFAC were TVs placed every 50 feet or so. If you wished, you could usually find a seat near a TV and catch up on sports back home (usually the TVs in the middle were tuned to ESPN or AFN Sports) or the news (TVs along the walls showed the news channels). I didn't really seek out a spot near the wall, but I ended up there most likely because someone I knew was already sitting there. We had just finished another four-plus hours of flying over Baghdad and had received our minimum daily requirement of war, so I wasn't really in the mood to hear from some talking head back in the States spout off about how bad the war was going. So, I was sitting there eating chili mac or some other equally nondescript entrée when something caught my attention on the TV overhead.

The graphic on the screen showed an outline of Iraq with a picture showing a soldier in his battle rattle, with the headline "5 killed in Baghdad as SURGE continues to go badly" . . . or words to that effect. Having been flying over Baghdad less than an hour before, I listened to the news report, which as far as it went was true enough. The trouble is that if you present reports only about the causalities suffered by coalition forces and nothing else, it sort of gives one a false impression of what is actually occurring . . . well, not sort of—it does.

While on leave, I lost count of the times I had to answer questions about what was actually occurring in Iraq, to hear the reply "Really? I didn't know that." Now why would that be? There were reporters from many various news agencies in Iraq. They were privy to pretty much the exact same information I was, minus certain operational details, yet they chose to focus on the personnel losses being suffered by mostly American forces.

When *Wall Street Journal* reporter Greg Jaffe reported on the actions of our troopers during the actions in Tarmiyah, the events would be used to represent how the war was doomed to failure. The article titled "At Lonely Iraq Outpost, GIs Stay as Hope Fades,"[5] published on the front page of the paper on May 3, 2007, focused on the hopelessness felt by the survivors of the attack. The report lacks both depth and perspective.

He states, "It's the best they can hope for under the new US 'surge strategy,' which some US officers in Iraq say does little more than chase insurgents from one part of the country to another."

He then goes on to write this: "The experience of the soldiers from the Second Battalion, Eighth Cavalry Regiment's Demon Company here is a window into what motivates troops in a war that an increasing number of Americans have concluded is a lost cause."

Tarmiyah had always been an enemy stronghold, going back as far as the initial invasion, but the reader of the piece wouldn't know that by reading the article. Do you think that the most objective source of our prospects of success in Iraq would be members of a unit who survived a difficult fight and continue to serve in an exceedingly difficult place? In May 2007, when this article was written, the Surge strategy had yet to even be fully implemented. Jaffe mentions some unnamed officers who were not very enthusiastic with the strategy, but common sense would tell you that there are always people who don't favor a certain course of action. Of course, there were Americans who felt the war was a lost cause, mainly from this type of reporting.

I wouldn't expect the press to be cheerleaders for our side, but I would expect that they be objective and add some perspective and information to broaden the overall understanding of the event being reported on. The news reported that the US Senate majority leader at that time said that "the surge has failed," and they reported that statement as fact. The real fact was that "the Surge" hadn't even begun. So as a result, the reporter becomes part and parcel to the agenda of that person, not an objective presenter of facts. Articles and reports such as this reinforce the opinions of some that reporters today are in the business of pursuing an agenda. In this situation, I saw them as giving aid and comfort to the enemy.

Every house, shack, and mud hut I flew over in Iraq seemed to have a satellite dish. Our enemy watched our news reports and surfed the internet to get every bit of information they could about us, there is no doubt of that. When they saw news networks report such things as this or read quotes like the ones made by Senator Harry Reid or then senator Barack Obama, who's to say that story didn't push them to decide to fight just one more day, to emplace one more IED, or to kill another American soldier, because that act might be the thing that makes us quit.

Telling a partial truth isn't a lie, but it isn't the entire story either, and it can cause one to reach a conclusion that is not totally based on reality. I have no problem with a media that would present both sides and present opinions as such and not try to make the viewer believe it is a fact. In the case of my war, reporting such as that was difficult to come by.

When I think of the actions at Tarmiyah in February 2007, I think of it as an exemplar of the fighting spirit of the American soldier. What Greg Jaffe saw was an opportunity to make it a symbol of the failure of the war effort as a whole.

Back home, when politicians—primarily for political purposes—declared the war lost, the Surge failed (before it even started), and our soldiers guilty of criminal acts, there was little pushback in questioning from the so-called objective reporters. While I hold the politicians who make such statements personally responsible, an objective reporter would question their assertions and might ask for examples rather than take those assertions at face value. But we wait in vain for such scrutiny of those who oppose or question our actions and intent. The only people who were getting tough questions were the guys giving the briefings at the Pentagon or President Bush, not anyone else. Especially anyone who thought that the war was lost or a lost cause. I only wish that they would attempt to be fair and impartial, but apparently that's asking too much.

For another example, I look to a 2008 article for the *Washington Post* by Ernesto Londono and Amit R. Paley.[6] A bumper sticker that I had made during the OIF 06-08 deployment, with the sarcastic statement "I [heart] Sadr City," made an appearance juxtaposed with statements being made by Iraqi citizens of Sadr City about how heartless and cowardly the American Apache pilots were in 2008 for having the bad taste to kill rocket and mortar teams with a Hellfire missile next to their homes. To me it appears as an attempt to make US forces look callous and trigger-happy.

The pilots sometimes scrawl messages on the 5-foot-long missiles (they're actually 6 feet long, but who's counting) strapped to their "birds." During a recent visit to the base, a reporter saw a missile addressed to "Haji," an honorific for people who have made the pilgrimage to Mecca. Many US soldiers use it to refer dismissively to Iraqis and Arabs in general. Someone wrote "rock this thang" on another.

The small white trailers adjacent to the airfield where the pilots do paperwork have Christmas lights strung from the ceiling. Two bumper stickers on windows say: "I [heart] Sadr City."

"It's not Hollywood and it's not 110 percent perfect," said Col. Timothy J. Edens, the commander of the 12th Combat Aviation Brigade, of the accuracy of his unit's strikes. "It is as precise as very hardworking soldiers and commanders can make it. These criminals do not operate in a clean battle space. It is occupied by civilians, law-abiding Iraqis."

Those civilians include people such as Zahara Fadhil, a ten-year-old girl with a tiny frame and long brown hair. Relatives said she was wounded by a missile on April 20 at approximately 8:00 p.m. in Baghdad's Shiite enclave of Sadr City. The US military said it fired a Hellfire missile in Zahara's neighborhood at that time, targeting men who were seen loading rockets into a sedan.

Her face drained of color and her legs scarred by shrapnel, Zahara spoke haltingly when asked what she thought of US troops.

"They kill people," she said. Lying in bed, she gasped for air before continuing. "They should leave Iraq now."

"The heart of this family has been ripped out," said Alaa Rahi Shaie, twenty-nine, another uncle, who was stoic in describing the death of his brother. "This is his blood," he said, indicating red splotches in front of his home. "And the remains of his head are over there."

I suppose this is what they think the balanced reporting I was just asking for looks like. To a certain extent they tried, but Leni Riefenstahl couldn't have done a better job if she tried with the image of a wounded little girl.

There is no mention in the article if the reporters stopped by the places where Sgt. William Brown (C Co 2-227 AVN) and SPC Zandra Walker (615th ASB) were killed during separate AIF rocket attacks on Camp Taji in 2007, during their search for bad words scribbled on missiles.

In the schools that I attended, I was taught the place in a newspaper for opinion was called the editorial page. Straight news stories were supposed to contain words such as "who," "what," "when," "where," and "why," not the reporter's opinions about things, but facts. Time and again I read or saw reports that contained the views of the "reporter" about the situation, not facts. Of course, there are those who will point out that the articles DID have facts. That is true as far as it goes, but when you present only the facts that support the position you are holding, you are an advocate, not an objective observer. Confirmation bias is a real thing.

It doesn't take seeing too many reports such as that one to drive you away . . . especially when you are knee deep in the situation they are reporting on. I just didn't need the aggravation about something I had no control over. To be fair, there were some reporters who did great work, who did their best to tell an honest story, but to my eyes they were far outnumbered by the reporters and editors who came to this fight with an ax to grind.

I would still watch the TV news when I would see Kiran Chetry show up on FOX News, but that was for reasons other than getting the news.

"War is an ugly thing, but not the ugliest of things. The decayed and degraded state of moral and patriotic feeling which thinks that nothing is worth war is much worse. The person who has nothing for which he is willing to fight, nothing which is more important than his own personal safety, is a miserable creature and has no chance of being free unless made and kept so by the exertions of better men than himself."
—John Stuart Mill

CAV HATS
AND COMBAT PATCHES

Given all that was going on in the summer of 2007, you might think that the chain of command would focus on more-pressing issues but suddenly it seemed that making sure soldiers wore the 1st CAV patch as their "combat patch" was extremely important to the 1st Air Cavalry Brigade.

The Army has a long tradition of wearing unit patches on the shoulder(s) of their uniforms. The left shoulder has the patch of the unit to which the soldier is currently assigned, and the right can have a patch of a unit a soldier has served in combat with. In accordance with Army regulation AR 670-1, if a soldier has served with more than one unit in combat, the choice of which patch to wear is up to the individual.

As you might imagine, with the war on terror starting in 2001, by 2007 there were many soldiers who had a choice of which unit's patch they wore as their "combat patch."

Several guys in our battalion had served previously with the 1st Infantry Division, which is also known as the Big Red One. They always seemed to be fighting with people in the chain of command about wearing their patch. It got to the point where one of the guys made a copy of the regulation regarding the wearing of combat patches and carried it around with him in order to show it to the people who wanted him to replace it with a CAV patch.

There were also a couple of guys who had served with the 101st Airborne Division, whose patch had a screaming eagle on it. One of them was the C Company commander CPT Patrick (Josh) Baker. His own troops, participating in some good-natured ribbing, concluded that the 101st eagle's name was in fact "Nancy." The rechristening of the eagle caused the young captain no small amount of emotional upset, which of course only egged them on.

As you might imagine, soldiers were and are proud of their service, and many wished to honor their previous deployments in other units by wearing the patches of those units. This was well within their rights as outlined by AR 670-1. Unfortunately, there were those in the chain of command who interpreted those actions as being somehow disloyal to their current unit of assignment, to the 1st Air Cavalry Brigade and the 1st Cavalry Division, and to the commander specifically.

It may seem obvious that you can't order or command someone to have pride in something, but this simple fact seemed beyond the grasp of many who wore eagles and stars on their uniforms.

It was interesting to me that some people in the chain of command were so clueless as to how to build esprit de corps. They couldn't understand that you can't order someone to wear a patch or write a song and then expect those soldiers to have positive feelings about those things. Deeply held attachment, pride, and emotional attachment come from shared experience and accomplishment, not a directive.

Some people thought you could walk into a TOC and order a soldier to write a battalion song, and THAT would provide some esprit de corps.

One slow day, the commander walked into the TOC and told CPT Daigle that he wanted him to write a song for the battalion, "like the one we had in 1-7 CAV." He then began clapping his hands together rhythmically and singing "Garryowen, Garryowen, Garryowen!"

I was standing in the back of the TOC and overheard the entire thing. I spoke up and told the commander, "Sir, I'm pretty sure you are singing "If You're Happy and You Know It." This is exactly what the tune sounded like, not the 7th CAV regimental song, Garryowen. The LTC gave me the skunk eye and went back into his workspace to, no doubt, write my next mediocre fitness report. I can't help it if he's a lousy musician.

For some reason, they couldn't or didn't want to grasp that the answer to their esprit de corps needs was right in front of their noses all along. The Stetson.

The Stetson cavalry hat, made famous in modern times by Robert Duval in the film *Apocalypse Now*, is controversial in the modern Army. The hat, first worn in the 1800s, was reintroduced in June 1965 at Fort Benning, Georgia, by the unit that was soon to be known as 1st Squadron, 9th US Cavalry. This tradition has persisted since then, despite those who would denigrate and dismiss it.

In my experience, the response to wearing the hat by those outside the military has been almost universally positive, and chicks dig it. The only negative reactions I have ever seen have come from within the military and from those with a desire to get rid of or regulate it.

So, if one desired to build esprit de corps, why wouldn't you take a symbol that is recognized and admired by many, and legitimize and encourage its wear? Who knows why they won't do it, but it's almost as if they are afraid of even the idea of it. The situation is quite confounding, especially for an institution that prides itself on traditions, because there is hardly a tradition in Army aviation that is older than this headgear.

If ever I am the king of the Army (and thank your lucky stars I won't be), you can rest assured that Stetsons will not only be approved but encouraged.

This whole situation was obviously a sideshow to what was going on every day on the battlefield, so it was equally confounding as to why so much time and effort was spent trying to get people to wear a particular patch or not wear a hat. The complexities of command and how this can be SO important have somehow escaped me during and after my service to this great nation. I guess some things we were never meant to understand.

I [HEART] SADR CITY! THE SHOOT-DOWN OF CRAZYHORSE 03, JULY 31, 2007

Sadr City, which lies on the far eastern side of Baghdad, was built in 1959 by the order of Iraqi prime minister Qassim, in response to housing shortages in Baghdad. At the time named Revolution City, it provided housing for Baghdad's urban poor. It quickly became a stronghold of the Iraqi Communist Party, and resistance to the Baathist-led coup of 1963 was strong there.

The district is one of the poorest in Baghdad, but that isn't saying a great deal. Unemployment is rampant. Homes are in disrepair. The population consists mostly of Shiite Muslims, who generally sympathize with and receive support from Iran, numbering over three million. It is also a haven for criminals released from Iraqi prisons by Saddam shortly before the start of Operation Iraqi Freedom.

Electrical services are intermittent. Parts of some streets in some neighborhoods are flooded with sewage from long-neglected pipes. Trash pickup stopped during the war, and residents started dumping their trash on the medians in the potholed streets.

Sadr City is also the home of Moqtada al Sadr (whom we sometimes referred to as Mookie) and the Mahdi army militia. Since the end of the invasion in 2003, we had been fighting off and on with Mookie and his merry band of militia, with varying degrees of intensity.

In the summer and fall of 2004, elements of the 1st CAV Division, led by LTC Gary Volesky's 2nd Battalion, 5th Cavalry (Lancer), conducted operations in order to destroy or remove the Mahdi army and Moqtada al Sadr from inside Sadr City. In late 2004, apparently tired of getting its ass kicked, the Mahdi army enacted a ceasefire with US troops and offered to help repair and rebuild the city's main infrastructure. There would be several ceasefires over the years, which became eerily reminiscent of the strategies employed by our Vietnamese opponents in the 1960–1970s, designed to gain time and breathing room.

During my OIF 2 deployment, I had many experiences flying in and around Sadr City, supporting Lancer. A lot of them included looking outside the aircraft and seeing things that reminded me of the attack on the "Death Star" scene in *Star Wars*. There was no doubt that a lot of bad people were in that particular section of Baghdad.

In November 2006, right after we arrived in country, one of our AWTs spotted rockets being fired at the Green Zone from a soccer field inside the city. They responded and killed the personnel who were manning these positions. In 2007, Sadr City was still a bad place. It wasn't unusual to look in its direction at night under NVGs and see aircraft stacked all the way up to outer space as one special-ops unit or another took out an HVT in there. The BDE placed Sadr City off limits to aircraft

Flying over Zone 9, looking north, with Sadr City in the background. *Photo by author*

unless you had a mission or requirement to be in there. Although not nearly as much as in OIF 2, the BN still often went into Sadr City, or Zone 21, as it was known. If you went there, the odds were rather good that you would be engaged by the enemy.

Believe it or not, as a gun pilot, sometimes being shot at was a good thing. At least you knew where some of the bad guys were, and it sort of simplified things, from the rules-of-engagement perspective. The bad thing was that by this time, we had pretty much killed off all the stupid or crazy AIF, and were now facing the more skilled or lucky ones.

This brings us to late July 2007. Ground units operating around Sadr City were being hit quite regularly by IEDs that were implanted regularly by persons who operated out of Sadr City. Rocket and mortar crews would dart into range of their targets (mostly the Green Zone), launch their weapons, and then scurry back to their holes before we could find and destroy them. Granted, we did have some success in interdicting some of this activity, but they were successful far more than we would have liked.

The unit (2 BCT, 2nd Infantry Division; call sign: STRIKE) operating in the sectors to the direct south of Sadr City (Zones 9 and 24) was particularly hard hit by IED strikes and was constantly requesting support from us. As a result, during every mission briefing we were reminded to go down to Zones 9 and 24 and support STRIKE as much as we possibly could.

Just due to our presence in those areas, enemy activity decreased. Because they didn't know what we could and couldn't actually see, the enemy would assume that we were watching them, and became a lot more reluctant to move about when an AWT was patrolling overhead. It is probably a prudent move on their part, since they had seen what we would do when we caught them in the open.

After several weeks of the BN spending most of our mission time in support of STRIKE, I expressed my concerns to the S3 about us setting a pattern that the enemy could take advantage of to shoot one of us down. The S3 responded that he couldn't very well tell the guys down at STRIKE that we weren't going to support them because we might lose an aircraft, when they were getting killed and maimed every day in IED and indirect weapons strikes. I replied that I didn't mean that we should stop supporting them; I meant that we needed to find a way to randomize coverage to the point where the enemy wouldn't know when and where we could appear. Fact of the matter was that we could never give constant coverage to any particular BCT. At that time, we were responsible for supporting four different combat teams, so the challenge was how to randomize our patrols.

With us being in the support business, it was exceedingly difficult for us to plan to BE randomly; we supported our customer (the ground units in our AO) when and where they needed it, to the best of our ability. As a result, I could have talked to our S3 till I was blue in the face, and nothing would have changed because we basically did what the folks we worked for wanted. I think it is our responsibility, as aviators, to explain to them the unintended possible consequences of their requests and to suggest alternatives, because, after all, if we are shot down or have to execute a precautionary landing, then they are the ones who will have to take their resources and secure the aircraft and the area around it for however long it takes to recover us and our stuff. But there existed a reluctance to do that because we (Army aviation in general) didn't want to be perceived as viewing ourselves as being more important than others, especially since the soldiers on the ground had it much worse than us most days. So, we were in a bit of a pickle in that regard.

I would like to point out that the reality of the situation is different. It doesn't matter what value we place on ourselves or others; it is what value the enemy and the rest of the world place on it that matters. It wasn't the dead Rangers that made President Clinton withdraw from Somalia; it was the pictures of dead aircrew members being dragged through the streets. Unfortunately, when a Humvee or Bradley gets blown up and the crew are killed or maimed, it doesn't make the front page, but if they shoot down a helicopter it's on every news station. I wish it weren't that way, but it is.

Are our aircraft more important strategically than our brothers on the ground? That is certainly not the way we employed ourselves, and we never felt ourselves to be more important. In fact, I regularly told pilots during briefings and just in regular conversations that the only reason we existed was to support that soldier on the ground. If we were told that someone was in trouble, there would be nothing that would stop us from getting there, and once we identified who the bad guy was, we were going to shoot him and we wouldn't stop until the threat was gone. Given all of that, we had to balance aggression with survivability. Even though our aircraft had a lot of armor and other things to help us survive on the battlefield, it was hard to make a living going toe to toe with heavy machine guns, RPGs, and MANPADS. So, in what was called survivability moves, we attempted to vary patterns, change altitudes, use standoff ranges, and other things so as not to present the same picture to the enemy over and over again. We had already found out several times, the hard way, that pattern setting was deadly.

It becomes impossible, however, to vary patterns and times when you are given a specific mission to carry out for a particular place at a certain time just about every day. All the warning signs were there. Several aircraft had already been engaged with MANPADS (that missed) in the Sadr City area in the past several weeks; it was just a matter of time until they got lucky.

On July 31, 2007, they got lucky, but also, in a way, so did we.

On the morning of the thirty-first, Crazyhorse 03 and 04 were conducting NAI reconnaissance in Zones 9 and 24. After conducting a route recon of RT Predators, the major east–west road separating Zones 9 and 24, the team moved east into the edge of Zone 77, attempting to locate any signs of enemy activity. Operating above a scud layer consisting of smoke and pollution that morning, finding anything with the Mark-1 eyeball was pretty much a losing proposition at best, so while flying they were also scanning roads and open areas, using their FLIR.

Just before 9:00 a.m., while moving through the scud on the edge of Zone 77, the pilot in command (PIC) of Crazyhorse 03 made a call over the team internal radio frequency that they were hit and going down. Later, listening to the recovered voice recording, one could hear a loud bang followed by the sounds of extreme vibration, the PIC telling his front-seater to make sure his seat belt was locked, and then, several seconds later, by the aircraft striking the ground. Crazyhorse 03 had been struck by a missile, which failed to detonate but still managed to break one of the four pitch change links, which control the angle of the rotor blades. Now the blade that was connected to the broken link was free to do whatever the laws of physics and aerodynamics compelled it to do, which, for now, meant causing a great deal of vibration. It caused so much vibration that the cockpit canopy shattered in several places. The crew, of course, had no idea of this. All they knew was that the aircraft was darn near uncontrollable and that they needed to find a place to land now.

They spotted a field just ahead and set up to make a running landing. Not knowing exactly what was wrong with the aircraft, the PIC didn't slow down too much and touched down at a fairly high rate of speed. While the aircraft was now on the ground, the challenge became that of getting it stopped. Normally we use a technique known as aerodynamic breaking, where we use the rotor system and thrust from it to help us stop. With the rotor system damaged, that technique wasn't going to work too well, so that left friction as the only option. Unfortunately, an earthen berm for an irrigation ditch was in the way of the speeding helicopter.

The aircraft, rapidly running out of energy, took the berm like the car "General Lee" on the TV show *Dukes of Hazard* and flew over the canal. But a slow broken rotor system does not a soft landing make, and when the helicopter struck the ground the landing gear bottomed out (exactly as designed), absorbing a lot of the impact forces. They had so much forward energy left, however, that a rocket pod, the 30 mm cannon, and several other items were ripped loose from the aircraft as it finally came to a rest.

Crazyhorse 04, flown by CW2 Micah Johnson and Capt. Laura Parunak, witnessed the entire landing sequence, and when 03 came to rest they swooped in to assess the situation and discourage anyone with ideas of approaching the aircraft. They fired two bursts of cannon fire in an open field nearby their wingman, to let anyone nearby know they were serious. Seeing an opportunity to possibly extract their wingman, CZ 04 landed nearby the broken carcass of CZ 03. The PIC and CPG of CZ 03 got out of their ruin of an aircraft and made their way to their wingman's aircraft and, after attaching themselves to the outside, were on their way back to Camp Taji.

Several minutes later another AWT arrived and secured the crash site, and eventually the downed-aircraft recovery team (DART) made it to the site to assess the situation and make the aircraft ready for recovery. Later that night, the aircraft, hanging beneath a CH-47, was brought back to Camp Taji.

The reports after the shoot-down were that the crew suffered minor injuries. Tell that to the PIC, CW4 Steve Hart—he suffered back injuries during this event, which eventually caused him to be medically retired. Not having been in combat like this with any other unit, it is hard for me to say what is normal, but I always found it a little strange how guys would return with aircraft shot to pieces, avoiding crash landing in dangerous territory or, in the worst cases, death, and be expected to jump into the spare aircraft and just go back out there. In this instance the crew of Crazyhorse 03, after being blown out of the sky and cheating death by shear dumb luck, were given a superficial exam, asked how they felt, and sent on their merry way, marked "return to duty."

Unfortunately, after this incident there were those in the brigade who would say things such as the aircraft hit wires because they were flying too low. The initial assessment by our S2 section was that the aircraft had been hit by an RPG. My opinion was that that possibility was extremely unlikely, given the speed and the altitude the aircraft was flying. It was almost as if there were people in denial that a MANPADS could even be involved in this. It wasn't until professionals from Fort Rucker arrived and gave their findings that people in our unit actually believed the truth about things. It was disappointing to me, personally, that my word wasn't even considered, especially given that it was my job to know about these kinds of things.

In the following weeks there were many more engagements by missiles in the vicinity of Sadr City; fortunately, we didn't lose any more aircraft during those exchanges. It was obvious that weapons were being supplied by someone (Iran) to the people fighting out of Sadr City. Given the history of Sadr City and the Mahdi army, it wasn't too difficult to figure out where these weapons were coming from. Unfortunately, at that time, little if anything was done about it, and we continued to hunt and peck around that cesspool for the rest of our time in Iraq.

While the policymakers and plan makers in the puzzle place in Washington and in the palace over by BIAP didn't owe me any explanations, it was very puzzling why this hive and scum and villainy continued to exist on the east side of Baghdad, being bothered only by raids conducted by special operators from time to time. The Mahdi army hung out; launched rockets, mortars, and missiles; planted IEDs; stockpiled smuggled weapons; and trained and plotted their operations in relative safety. It wasn't until after we rotated out that, in 2008, an operation was conducted to finally clean out Sadr City. In the meantime, how many soldiers lost their lives, innocent Iraqis were hurt and killed, and millions upon millions of dollars of equipment were lost because we didn't go in there and do what needed to be done before then?

"ALL THOSE PILOTS DO IS FLY AND PLAY XBOX!"

Even with the twenty-four-hours-a-day operation that was occurring, there was downtime available that most of us used to try to unwind a bit. There had to be. Nobody can operate continuously for fifteen months in an everlasting state of readiness. So, on the rare day or two someone had off, everyone had their own way that they used to try to relax. I passed the time by editing the photos I had taken, using my computer, or watching movies in the trailer. Some people worked out at the gym. Others played Xbox.

There were a small percentage of people in the BDE, mostly field-grade officers who couldn't stand the thought of soldiers with nothing to do. For some of those, this was simply an expression of envy that they didn't have a lot of downtime, and they hated that fact that others were "lying in the rack" when they had to work all the time. Others came to this feeling honestly, having seen firsthand that for some soldiers, the saying "Idle hands are the devil's workshop" is definitely true. The majority, however, had a more realistic view of things and knew that over a fifteen-month deployment, you HAD to give people time off or else they would wear themselves out.

In past wars the United States has fought, for better or worse the consumption of liquor was allowed. During OIF/OEF, to honor the beliefs of our Muslim hosts and to avoid all the associated issues involved with the consumption of alcohol, General Order #1 was written and posted. Also known as GO #1, the order forbids the consumption of alcoholic beverages (unless approved by somebody at the general officer level). It also bans items such as *Playboy* magazine that showed nudity, and other things such as soldiers having a romantic interlude or even public displays of affection. Oddly enough, even though we weren't supposed to have printed items that showed nudity, possessing "R-rated" films that had such things was tolerated. It was a order that was filled with contradictions and flew in the face of human nature, to be sure, but it was an order nonetheless. Some people obviously took it more seriously than others though.

The ban on alcohol in the field or on deployment was something that had been pretty much a constant since I had joined the Army in 1986, and I didn't drink much anyway, so that wasn't a big deal to me. On the other hand, for a place that was supposed to be dry, it was pretty easy to find a drink if one knew where to look.

There were all sorts of techniques that people used to get their booze sent to them. One of the favorites was to use a bottle of Listerine mouthwash, replacing the original contents with something a little stronger. For the most part these smuggling episodes went unnoticed and uncared about. Unfortunately, some people were caught imbibing or in possession of alcoholic beverages and had to face varying degrees of wrath from "the Man," according to your position in the food chain.

If anyone ever wonders why soldiers didn't respect or care about adherence to GO #1, all one has to do is look at the way it was enforced. If you were a PFC and you were caught with your favorite adult beverage, rest assured that you were more than likely going to receive an Article 15 (nonjudicial punishment, which could and often did include monetary penalties). If you were an NCO or junior officer, you could bet your bottom dollar your career just ended . . . oh, you can hang around and maybe even get another promotion or two, but you are effectively done. Then we have the field-grade officers. If you were in that position, especially if you were a commander of a battalion and caught doing something you weren't supposed to, you were allowed to quietly retire for the "good of the service."

I once remarked to the BDE assistant commander that if they really wanted to get the soldiers' attention about GO #1, when the next field-grade officer is caught in violation of the order, the chain of command should fully prosecute him and make all the details public. If you were a private and saw Lieutenant Colonel X get court-marshaled and run out of the Army, don't you think that would get your attention? Of course, they never did it. Partially because something like that would be very difficult to do, legally. I don't think anyone can deny the effect something like that might have though.

The other problem was sex. For obvious reasons, the military doesn't want its soldiers hooking up downrange. It doesn't take a vivid imagination to think of all the problems that can result from sexual entanglements in the workplace, much less in a combat environment. Nature does, however, take its course, regardless of any order or guidance from the chain of command. Some soldiers had relationships prior to deployment. Now, in the war zone, the Army said not only could you not have sex, you can't kiss your girlfriend goodnight or even hold her hand. The Army was, in essence, the Taliban. So what results from that is that some soldiers were sneaking around like a bunch of horned-up teenagers.

A not-inconsiderable amount of time and effort was spent by elements of the chain of command making sure soldiers weren't hooking up. A unit at Taji resorted to putting all their female soldiers in a single area and then surrounding it with barbed wire and guards to "protect" them. Despite that, we still had pregnancies in the unit.

The Army has a real challenge dealing with this issue, and they haven't done a very good job in that respect. There are apparently folks in the upper echelons who believe that you can trump hormones and human desire and turn everyone into warrior monks with several strokes on a keyboard. If one was to examine the pregnancy rates of deployed units, you will find this hasn't been 100% successful. Fighting human nature and biology is an exceedingly difficult proposition.

On top of that, you have the other issues of sexual harassment, and people in positions of authority using that to abuse their subordinates. I didn't hear of or see any of that, but it certainly existed then and now. It is certainly something that is unacceptable and, when found, is prosecuted to the fullest level possible.

But since we couldn't have sex, we could at least look at a good old nudie book, just like they did in Vietnam, right? Nope, you can't have any of that; you might make the people trying to kill you mad. But you CAN have AAFES porn!

AAFES porn, what is THAT? Since they couldn't sell *Playboy*, *Penthouse*, or any of the other popular "men's magazines," the Army & Air Force Exchange Service (AAFES), or what some people still refer to as the "PX," had alternative selections. With titles such as *Stuff*, *Maxim*, and *FHM*, these magazines featured a snarky editorial style, which is what passes for hip these days, and, most importantly to more than a few folks, photos of women in various stages of undress. What made them acceptable and gave them the name AAFES porn? Well, it was porn that really wasn't porn. Also, like a lot of stuff that AAFES sold, it was half-ass, and they never showed what "Monty Python's Flying Circus" called "naughty bits."

Anytime you would walk into the crew chief office down on the flight line, there would be a stack of these magazines about a foot high sitting on a desk, beckoning you to come and look. The interesting thing about those magazines was that unlike *Playboy*, popular actresses and models who would never think of posing nude had no problem appearing almost nude in the likes of *Maxim* and other similar publications. Some of them also liked to treat the readers with their thoughts about things, because they want to be seen as something other than just an object. It may be just me, but it is kind of difficult to take someone's opinion about Middle East peace seriously when I am looking at a picture of them in a garter belt and a G-string. Now, if I knew them personally, I might be more inclined to give them the benefit of the doubt about their views and ideas, but since I don't, I have some advice for them.

A MEMO TO SCANTILY CLAD ACTRESSES

This goes out as a public service to all the starlets or models who have or will in the future choose to pose in various stages of undress in magazines that those of us in the service call "AAFES porn."

When you do the little interview that they do with the photo spread, please don't mess with the fantasy. If you think about it for a moment or two, I'm sure you know what I mean.

On second thought, you obviously don't, so I will spell it out for you.

First, nobody wants to hear about your boyfriend, husband, or significant other. Honestly, I'm glad you're happy and everything, but I didn't just walk 2 miles through a dust storm and across a gravel pit in my body armor with my weapon, eye protection, and helmet to stand in line behind forty other Joes with the same magazine, an outrageously overpriced twelve-pack of Dr. Pepper, and a bag of stale Doritos at the checkout to walk the 2 miles back to my trailer to read about how happy you are to be shacked up with Maurice or whatever the name of your significant other might be. I have plenty of reality here in my world right now; just allow me the fantasy that you or someone like you is available, for once. Is that too much to ask?

Second, use *Playboy* magazine as an example; they learned long ago not to print that kind of information about their Playmates. Every reader of that magazine (except that deluded idiot in Tennessee [you know who you are]) knows that these women have lives, and most of them have boyfriends or even husbands, and this is nothing but the business of providing a fantasy for the reader.

Here's an example of what I mean about the WRONG way to do it: In a 2005 edition of *Maxim* magazine, actress Eva Longoria told everyone about her work in the 2004 election for the Democratic candidate for president, and her displeasure about how stupid some folks were who voted the way that they did. This statement was sandwiched in between the pictures of her in her underpants, so many folks may have missed that nugget.

It made me wonder; Eva, do you really think people picked up that magazine off the rack and said, "Wow, look, Eva Longoria is in *Maxim*—I wonder what she has to say about politics?" I don't know; this might have been in her agreement with the editors. Somebody might have thought that this would be a good place to show that this lady is more than a nice smile and a beautiful body. I get it, I really do, but in the immortal words of a senior aviation warrant officer acquaintance of mine: you have to "know your audience."

We get it; you have a brain or would like to give the impression that you do. That is great, but no one buys those magazines for their pithy political insight or social commentary, especially when it's coming from the girl featured on the cover of the magazine (no offense).

Maybe this rant should be directed at the dork who asked the question during the interview, but hell, all you had to say was "Are you stupid? I'm not answering that." I mean, you're smart, or at least you try to appear to be in a silly leftist kind of way . . . you have all these opinions and stuff, but you'd think you might, if you are actually as smart as you think you are, figure out that if you start running your yap about politics, you're going to piss off 50% of the population . . . that is, if they even read the stuff that you said. I guess that's what you might be counting on . . . hell, I don't know, write an editorial or something. But I think you get my point, or at least most people would if they put a couple of seconds of thought into it.

Finally, in the future, stick to how much you love puppies, the scent of lavender, and how you secretly fantasize about being ravaged on a bed of roses by some guy fresh off deployment. Because that's all most of us really cared about anyway. Well, not the dogs-and-lavender part.

Since booze, porn, and sex were technically out, a lot of folks resorted to Xbox and other video games to pass the time. For some reason this really seemed to piss a lot of senior officers off.

There was a trailer down on the flight line where crews who were on standby to launch could hang out while waiting; it improved their response time and kept them more or less in the same space. In the trailer were a TV and an Xbox system. A lot of pilots had no problem passing the time playing Madden football or Halo. Some, as you might imagine, were rather good at it. For some peculiar reason this seemed to anger some of the staff officers. I heard one major remark, "All those pilots do is fly and play Xbox." Most of these kinds of remarks can be chalked up to petty envy.

Most of the RLOs had duties other than flying, which took a lot of their time. They were at work more often and for a longer period than the junior warrant officer aviators. When they did fly, the RLOs still had to go back to work and do their "real jobs." This was also my situation, but having been a junior warrant officer at one time, I understood the situation. Some RLOs, out of spite or because they just couldn't stand to see someone who had it "better" than them (if "better" meant less pay or more overall exposure to danger), would complain and deride the pilots who were, in fact, doing their jobs.

In some ways it reminded me of an experience I had in the late 1990s. The unit I was assigned to was going to the field, at Fort Hood, for an exercise called an FTX. This is where we would live in a tent for two to three weeks and perform missions from the field. Normally in the field, when you aren't flying or planning, there is downtime, which is usually spent playing cards and reading magazines or books. This time, for some reason, the company commander decreed that there was to be no reading of non-military-issued publications or card playing. Despite some of us trying to explain that you can't be ON all of the time and you need some time to yourself, the captain insisted that his decree would stand. THAT was one of the most miserable times I ever spent in the US Army. If there was a reason for it, we were never told what it was. Most of us believed it was the commander exerting his will because he could, and not because there was a good reason for it. That struck at the heart of what the guys complaining about the Xboxes were all about, making people do things, and wanting something they couldn't have . . . off time. The result of all this was that they made a hard time even harder for everyone.

One of the brigade's senior warrant officers, CW5 Don Washabaugh, had a formula that he called the Three Rules of Company Command, which pretty much explained some of the unexplainable things we regularly encountered from RLOs, especially new company commanders:

The Three Rules of Company Command or How to Get Ahead, without Really Doing Anything

1. No matter how ergonomic the office environment is, as soon as you take command, move the furniture to prove you are in charge.

2. There is nothing you can do at any level until you are at least a battalion commander. You can't really give time off, can't give a raise, can't promote anyone, or can't implement own ideas without the approval of the battalion commander. About the only thing you can do is more PT, so always do more PT!

3. Read AR 670-1 and AR 385-40 and focus on something uniform or safety related weekly. For example: There have been no documented head injuries in accidents involving Gator vehicles, but make sure people wear the noncrashworthy Kevlar helmet designed for combat every time they drive a Gator, and ream their asses if they don't.

Always remember that it is about the illusion of control: aviators talk on four different radios, use two different night vision systems, and of course shoot crap from 5 miles away, but remind them that you can't even use a hands-free device while driving!

When all else fails, revert to rule 2 (more PT), and before you know it, your eighteen months are up and you will get two good OERs, be known as a mover and a shaker, and make it to the 93% of RLOs that make LTC!

I often wondered if I were at the beginning of my career rather than towards the end would I have resigned instead of putting up with some of the ridiculous things that I saw. Some of these things were done out of pure spite, just because the person in charge didn't like something or thought they knew better than you about something. It is amazing to me that for some people, getting the job done wasn't enough. Fighting a war every day wasn't enough for some of them. They needed MORE out of you to consider you a worthwhile officer and aviator. In some ways, I think that says more about those people than it does about the guys who were going out and flying every day and just wanted to relax by playing a little Xbox during their off time.

COP CAVALIER, AUGUST 23, 2007: "HOLY SHITE!"

It was a typical hot summer afternoon when our AWT CZ 18/19 took off from Taji to begin our assigned mission. We were conducting CM2RI just west of Camp Taji, along one of the roads where there had been some incidents of AFI activity recently, and were looking for signs of digging, where the road had been melted, or other shenanigans. I was in CZ19, with the newly promoted Capt. Griggs as my CPG. CZ18 was being flown by CW4 Bill Ham and his CPG, Capt. Mike Hutson. We had barely established ourselves on station when I heard Bill on team internal say, "Holy shite!" Looking back to the east, I could see exactly what he was talking about: a dark, boiling mushroom cloud from an explosion of some kind was rising rapidly into the afternoon sky. We would soon find out that this was the result of a VBID detonation at COP Cavalier.

Without saying another word, Bill turned and accelerated, flying directly toward the site of the explosion. While lead attempted to contact the ground unit (2-8 CAV) that had control of this area, I had Capt. Griggs contact Attack Mike and tell them the situation.

It was a short distance to the site of the explosion, and as we got closer we could easily see that the explosion had occurred just outside COP Cavalier. We were in the process of setting up an orbit, to establish security, when there was a second detonation. I felt it as much as saw it. I could literally feel the heat from the blast through the canopy, and we watched an orange fireball, truck parts, and other debris fly through the air, well exceeding the altitude of our aircraft, as another VBID detonated at the northern security point to the small combat outpost. It was 1943 hrs local time.

It was immediately obvious to all of us that they were going to try to overrun the COP.

There was a flurry of radio calls on the 2-8 CAV frequency as people attempted to assess the situation at the COP. I asked Capt. Griggs to call Attack Mike and tell them to get in touch with 2nd Batt and tell them they were going to have medevac business shortly, and that we'd call back with specific information when we got it. As we assumed a protective orbit around the COP, I spotted the blackened, smoking wreckage of what used to be an Iraqi army BMP at the north gate.

Within minutes of the explosion, as we circled around, I saw rounds exploding just outside the perimeter of the COP. I called this to the flight over internal, and initially I misidentified the rounds as incoming. They were, in fact, outgoing. The rounds were from an M-2 Bradley fighting vehicle inside the perimeter; he was directing his 25 mm cannon fire down a path that led from a village toward the COP.

The COP was taking fire from the little village named Hor Al Bash on the other side of the road, to the west side of the outpost. They requested that we direct our fires to suppress the incoming rounds. Annihilator 6 (the ground commander) reported that they were taking heavy fire from west and southwest of the COP. The enemy was well concealed as we circled, desperately trying to find the source of the fires. In the meantime, we requested permission to place fires in an empty field just outside the village, in an attempt to suppress by intimidation. Our request was granted, and we placed forty rounds of 30 mm in a field to try to get the bad guy's attention. During the entire process, we continued the futile effort to spot the AIF that were firing at the COP. Evidently they went to ground, their plan foiled as the firing at the COP eventually ceased.

At 2003 we got a report from Annihilator that there were ten individuals requiring medical evacuation (four Urgent, four Surgical Urgent, and two Priority); we relayed this information back to Attack Mike and requested that they relay the info to the medevac guys (call sign: BANDAGE) down the hall in the TOC.

About ten minutes later, we got a call from Attack Mike telling us they had information about a possible ADA ambush in the vicinity of the COP. I passed that info off to flight lead, wondering what good that did us. The reality was that unless you can give me specifics, that warning wouldn't do us much good. Besides, I always assumed that somebody was out there trying to shoot us down. A few minutes later we called Attack Mike and let them know we were switching to the medevac freq for the duration of that operation.

Soon after that, Annihilator let us know where the LZ for the medevac would be, and we set up security and got ready to give Bandage a Cherry/Ice call. I asked Capt. Griggs the rhetorical question "Where the hell is the medevac?," mainly to vent my frustration, because he had no more of a clue about the answer than I did. This COP was maybe five minutes' flying time from the ramp of Camp Taji to wheels down, here. We called them almost as soon as the bomb(s) went off, and now it was nearly thirty minutes later—where were they? I came to find out later that they couldn't launch on my word alone. The request had to go up through the medevac request chain and then back down to the unit. There would be no jumping of the chain. If I had known that before, it still would not have eased the frustration. This was taking entirely too long. Time was dragging.

So, we circled, waited, and looked for the ambush we'd been warned about. We changed patterns and tried to avoid circling in one area for too long. Occasionally, we pushed out to the west (the most likely avenue of approach for someone wishing to do us harm), looking for any incoming traffic. I listened to Taji Tower on the VHF and eventually heard Bandage call to taxi. At about 2030, the last UH-60 lifted off from the LZ, with the wounded en route to the CASH. It had taken only forty-five minutes from the time we called the first explosion into our TOC, but it seemed like it had taken a lot longer. This was the second time I had been in a flight that called for medevac within sight of the ramp at Taji, and it had taken what I felt was an inordinate amount of time to get the job done. I couldn't help but think that there had to be a better way.

While the medevac operation was occurring, several ground convoys converged on the COP to reinforce Annihilator and to posture for follow-on operations. We continued to provide security in the vicinity of the COP until we did a battle handover with CZ 16/17 at 2051 LCL, so we could hit the FARP and get some gas at Taji.

We got to the FARP quickly, and once we were down and had an engine pulled back, I was able to loosen the seat belts, get some circulation going back in my butt, and take a drink of Gatorade from the bottle I had brought with me in the cockpit. While we sat on the refuel pad, I watched the last orange go from the sky to the west. It was full-on dark now. While I was waiting for the aircraft to get its gas, out of boredom I brought up an image file on my TSD of a Playboy Playmate, just to have one thing of beauty in this nasty place. After a few minutes contemplating the visage of the beautiful model, a depressing thought crossed my mind. I didn't have a relationship with anyone, much less know anyone who looked like her, and I probably wouldn't, at least as long as I kept doing this business of deploying for a year to fifteen months, redeploying only to train up to go again ad infinitum. I didn't need those particular thoughts floating around in my head right then, so I decided to put the girl back in her image folder and look at the pretty colors on the aircraft fuel page instead.

The fueling was going really slow that night. In fact, I think I could have sucked fuel into the aircraft with a straw faster than it was flowing through the hose from the fuel truck. In the meantime, I started reoptimizing my FLIR to get the best picture I could. I managed, in five minutes of playing with the contrast and gain knobs, not to screw the picture up any more than it already was. Finally the tanks were full, and I gave the POL guy the cut sign. I told the pad chief thanks as he unplugged his headset from the wing, and we waited for them to get clear before we pulled in the required power to ensure that everything was functioning correctly, in a process called a "bubble burn." We hurried to get up to REDCON 1 because, personally, I didn't want to be the guy holding up the flight. As we finished the before-takeoff checks, I turned on my landing light and called lead over internal, saying "One nine is RED 1," signaling that we were ready to go. A few seconds later Bill replied with "Calling tower."

"Taji Tower, Crazyhorse one eight, flight of two at the FARP, request departure Tango Delta."

"Crazyhorse, Charlie and Delta are closed."

"Roger, tower; we are players." Apparently in the ten minutes we were in the FARP, they forgot we were just out there.

"Crazyhorse one eight, FARP is not observable from the tower, winds three six zero at six, cleared for takeoff, call established Delta."

"Tower, one eight is on the go."

Almost as soon as the words were out of his mouth, Bill's aircraft began to lift off the ground and accelerate toward the Hesco barrier wall about 100 feet away. The first time in that FARP, it was kind of unnerving to blast off and head straight toward a wall in a heavy helicopter, trusting that the laws of aerodynamics would kick in and you would be able to climb over it . . . but it always seemed to work out. As Bill cleared the wall, I lifted off. We were still eating some of his rotor wash, and until we got into clean air the aircraft didn't really want to climb too much. As Bill turned west to head back to the COP, I extended a bit to the north and, upon reaching cleaner air, turned west and climbed to get above lead in our standard formation. We climbed out, heading for the fence. Being on the north side of lead, I was looking for the Taji JLENS balloon, which was in the northeast corner of the camp. We were clear of the balloon, and as we approached the perimeter to Camp Taji, I started cleaning up the aircraft for combat: landing light off, anticollision lights off, and CMWS and weapons armed, and Capt. Griggs started the videotape. "One nine, fence check complete, we're saddled," I called as we crossed the wire. Since we were so close to the COP, Capt. Griggs completed the BHO while we were on the ground in the FARP, and as soon as 16 and 17 saw us take off, they started moving away to the south, allowing us to retake the fight, while they headed back to Taji, looking forward to landing and calling it a day.

Since we were now back on station, I had responsibility for the flight, following calls with tower. "Tower, Crazyhorse one eight, one nine established Delta at one and one point five. I'll call you next three zero or departure." Meanwhile, Capt. Griggs called Attack Mike and told them that we were off the FARP and back on station with Annihilator. Up in the lead, they called the ground unit to get any updates and let them know we were back on station, updating our "playtime" and weapons status.

Shortly after arriving back on station, Stallion 3A (the 2-8 CAV assistant operations officer) told us that they were preparing a plan for a hasty air assault operation. Intelligence assets have located the position of the individuals behind the VBIED attack, and they intended to take them down tonight. Additionally, he told us that they had also intercepted conversations about trying to shoot down a helicopter. This was nice-to-know data, to be sure, but once again no other information that we could use to prevent or avoid the attack. More than anything else it caused me to wonder what they expected us to do with that information. I don't know about anyone else, but I'm always looking for signs that someone is preparing to shoot me down. It's now around 2100 hrs.

Around 2200 we were given a WARNO for the air assault and given the coordinates for the LZ. The ground unit call sign would be ROCK 6. The LZ was located a few kilometers north of COP Cavalier, near a small cluster of buildings, where the target was located, and H hour was to be around 2300 hrs.

For the next hour we moved between the COP location and the area around the planned LZ. We were able to gain observation and, we hoped, avoid making anyone there aware that something was about to occur. We generally tried to remain downwind from the target and avoided hard maneuvering, which causes the rotor blades to make a growling noise and can be heard at a greater distance than the noise generated by straight and level flight. Darkness is our friend, and we took full advantage of it, using our FLIR to observe and report any activity on or near the planned landing zone and target. As the time of the Cherry/Ice call approached, we climbed up and stacked, allowing the UH-60s to go underneath us as we observed the target area. At 2315 we made the call "ICE," and the Hawks deposited the troops on the LZ and departed back to Taji. We remained on station, contacting ROCK 6 as they maneuvered to the target.

Everything went smoothly, since ROCK 6 hit the objective. We were now in an orbit around the target, looking for "squirters." By the time we did a BHO with CZ 20/21 at 2355, ROCK6 was still working the objective, so we never found out if they got a "jackpot." Once the BHO was complete, I called the TOC and let them know we were inbound to Taji, mission complete. Of course, it couldn't be that easy. They had one more thing for us to do.

I don't know how they came by this information, but we were told by Attack Mike to go check out a possible IR strobe located in Zone 110, west of Taji. "Sweet," I thought to myself. They kept warning us about intercepted transmissions and people wanting to shoot us down, and now they wanted us to go check out a reported "IR strobe" in an area of known enemy activity . . . this just didn't seem right. I thought about asking the TOC if they were sure about this, but I elected not to.

The location of the "suspected IR strobe" was near what we called "the Grand Canal." So off we went in pursuit of the phantom IR strobe people. We flew south and picked up the road that ran east–west on the north side of the canal, and flew out toward the grid coordinate. Sure enough, when we arrived near the area and looked through NVGs, there was, in fact, an IR strobe going. We kept our distance and looked at that grid and the area around it with the TADS. There were no dismounts or movement in the area. It could have easily been dropped by a solider on a patrol; it also could have been a lure to get us into an ambush. We knew there weren't any friendlies in the area at the time, so after not seeing any other activity in the area, we decided to call it a day. We started back toward Taji and gave them the negative spot report in such a manner as to discourage them from having us do anything else.

"Attack Mike, Crazyhorse 19 confirms there is an IR strobe at the grid, negative activity at that site; we are RTB at this time."

Thankfully, they didn't ask us to do anything else. I think they may have realized that we were just about at the flight time limit for a combination day/night system mission (without getting an extension from the commander), so they left us alone. You always kind of held your breath when you announced to the TOC over the radio that you were RTB, because far too often they found just one more thing for you to do. As much as we wanted to help folks who needed it, there is a limit to our endurance and, to be honest, sharpness as a crew and team.

We touched down back at Taji and rolled into parking without any trouble. I already had the APU running as we pulled into our revetment, so as soon as we set the brakes, I pulled the power levers to idle. We went through the shutdown checks and, after a two-minute cooldown, killed the engines. Seconds later I shut down the

APU, and a quiet settled in over the flight line; 5.8 hours after we left, we were back in the same spot.

The crew chief was there, waiting on us to get out of his aircraft. I handed down my helmet, pubs bag, and rifle, and he set them next to my helmet bag that he's pulled out of the survival kit bay. I thanked him as I climbed out, and he handed me the cover for the infrared jammer, which I put in its rightful spot, to protect the mechanism from possible flying debris.

Doing the postflight inspection, I opened the engine cowling and gave the #2 engine a close look, using my flashlight that I usually wore around my neck. The engine was still popping and crackling as it cooled down after the flight. Everything looked OK with the engine itself. Nothing was leaking and the fluid levels were where they were supposed to be. Looking over the rest of the aircraft, I was pleased to see that there weren't any holes that weren't supposed to be there. After Capt. Griggs and I finished the postflight, we put our flight gear in the shed and headed back to the company CP to fill out the aircraft logbook. During the walk back we linked up with Bill and Capt. Hutson and compared notes. We informed Capt. Hutson that he had drawn the imaginary short straw, so he got to fill out the debrief paperwork over at the TOC. After making sure Capt. Griggs had all my info to fill out the logbook, I left with Capt. Hutson for the TOC, since I still had to do the ACO and ARTY ROZ sheets for tomorrow.

When we got to the TOC, we turned in the PCMICAs and gave our videotapes over to the S2. They knew about the VBIED and were anxious to download the video for a briefing or some product the S3 or commander had dreamed up.

Somebody had thoughtfully gone to the DFAC and gotten us some sandwiches, which were sitting on the briefing table next to the computer. I grabbed one and realized just how hungry I was, since this tasted like the greatest sandwich in the history of the world . . . even though in the back of my mind I knew it didn't even approach the quality of a day-old sandwich from Jimmy Johns. After all, it IS the thought that counts, that and I was starving. The folks who worked in the TOC always took care of us, in that regard, and we never really thanked them enough for doing things like that.

As CPT Hutson got to work on the debrief paperwork, I excused myself to go to the back and work on my daily TACOPS tasks. I hoped that tonight there wouldn't be any SPINS compromises that would add to my workload.

On the way to the back of the building, I ran into CW3 Dana Dreeke, who was a UH-60 pilot and the 2nd Batt TACOPS officer. In one of those weird coincidences that always seem to occur in the Army if you stay in long enough, Dana had been my crew chief when I flew UH-1Hs in the 6th Cavalry Brigade back in the 1990s. We talked for a few minutes and exchanged some nonprofessional opinions about the way things were being run around "this place." It was sort of comforting to find out that your unit wasn't the only one facing "challenges."

Matt Silverman, from 4th Batt, was still hanging around at his desk, which had now "magically" moved its way into what, at first, was my part of the room. In an event that I choose to call "the 4th Battalion Sooner land grab of 2007," they decided, one day, to build an office in the back of the plans area for their mission video-editing crew. This left no room for Matt, their TACOPS officer, so he moved into "my" area. If someone had let me know this was about to happen, I might not have been so upset about it, but it just happened. One day I came into work and saw all of Matt's stuff piled onto a desk in what was previously considered my space. To top it off, when I had asked their S3 about it several weeks prior, he told me that they wouldn't move into my area. I don't really enjoy being lied to . . . I mean, I had been lied to by a major before, but usually they don't do it directly to your face. Kudos to them for being up-front about being lying sacks of shit.

In the grand scheme of things, I had more than enough room to get my work done, and it was more of an annoyance than anything else, but these are the kinds of things that really begin to grate on your nerves during a deployment. It was, after all, the principle of the thing that bothered me.

For those who have never been deployed and can't imagine why something like this would be such a big deal, imagine all the little things you find aggravating about your job, then imagine that there was no escape from those things. No days off. No family. No real recreation. Now you have a just a little bit of understanding of what being deployed is like.

I said hello to Matt and engaged in some small talk, grabbed some cheese peanut butter crackers from my goody box and a Dr. Pepper from the fridge, and sat down behind the computer on my dusty desk and went to work on the airspace control and active artillery zone products. By the time they were printed and posted to their correct places, I got out of there around 0130 or so.

The walk back to my trailer wasn't too bad, since I didn't have any interaction with CSMs jumping up out of the shadows to challenge me about the kind of eyewear I may or may not have. The thought momentarily crossed my mind that if we hadn't been extended, that would have probably been one of my last flights in country, since we would have been wrapping up our tour just about now. But it ended up being just one more day done during a long deployment, with a bunch more left to go.

. . . AND BANGO
WAS HIS NAME-O!

Military working dogs are nothing new. Dogs have been on the battlefield as long as people have been fighting one another. In Iraq, military working dogs were especially important. Given the enemy's penchant of using explosive booby traps, explosive-detection animals were invaluable to soldiers, given the task to search and clear buildings daily. One of these dogs was named "Bango."

Bango and his handler first showed up at our TOC when we picked up the mission to support snap air assaults into HVT locations, as derived by different intelligence sources. The ground forces would position themselves every night in the BDE briefing room, which was just down the hall from our TOC, waiting for

"And Bango was his name-o." CW2 Geoff Horvath poses with military working dog "Bango" in the First Attack TOC. *Photo by author*

the word to launch. Because these missions were on call, there were a lot of nights where nothing happened. During this downtime, Bango and his handler made the rounds and visited some of the TOCs of the units that were standing by.

Like most people, I had little to no interaction with military working dogs during my service in the Army, and my impressions of them were from demonstrations I had seen where they tried to rip the balls off some guy in a padded suit. So, the first time I met Bango it was somewhat of a shock to find out that he was a lot like any other dog I had ever come into contact with in my life. A big black dog that appeared to be a shepherd/Lab mix, Bango loved to play fetch, and he quickly became a friend to many of us who worked in and around the TOC area.

Aside from being a friend to those in and around the TOC, Bango did his job and did it well. Because we covered many operations he was working on, we had video of him rushing forward into battle. We had been told that Iraqis, for the most part, were not keen on interacting with a big black dog, and I can only imagine what that would be like in the middle of the night to have him bearing down on you. So, for the purpose he was sent to Iraq to do, Bango succeeded in spades. What also was of value was the secondary effect he achieved in morale support.

The thing about having Bango around that I found the most interesting, and something I think the Army would be wise to investigate, was the therapeutic value of having a dog or other pet around while deployed. Obviously, there would be an issue of veterinary support in theater and other issues I probably haven't considered, but I think, overall, it might be worth investigating. It was amazing to me to see the transformation of the soldiers in the TOC when Bango arrived.

When that dog came through the door of the TOC, hardened soldiers became kids again. You could see the joy on their faces as they played with a dog. To me the transformation was amazing and a much-needed thing. The mood in the TOC was significantly lightened every time Bango was around, of that there was no doubt. He obviously wasn't there for therapy; he was in Iraq to do a specific job, and from all reports he did it very well. But the joy he gave was a secondary mission that he accomplished well beyond what anybody might have expected.

Of course, there are people who don't like dogs or are allergic to them, and I understand that. In fact, I understand that the unit that replaced us had banned Bango from the TOC. So maybe this idea isn't for everyone.

I know it wasn't for our S2 OIC. She either didn't like dogs or enjoyed the idea of playing keep-away and hiding the ball from a dog that loved to play fetch so much that it frustrated him to the point where he wanted revenge. Dogs tend to be quite the judge of character sometimes, and after being jerked around by the S2, he took a dislike to her. Please don't misunderstand—he was a very well-behaved dog until one day, when he saw the opportunity for payback and took it.

It was at the very end of our deployment, and the S2 had folded up a comforter and had given it to the assistant S2 to put in the shipping container for their personal gear. The blanket was in a bag sitting next to the wall in the briefing area when Bango arrived to make his nightly rounds.

The first thing Bango usually did, when he arrived, was to head to the front of the TOC to look for his girlfriends, Flight Ops Specialists Thomas and Hernandez. They were always lavishing attention on Bango when he was around, and he obviously loved them back. Tonight, however, there was a particular scent that caught his attention. It was the scent of retribution for all those times he hadn't been given the ball he desperately wanted.

Before his handler could stop him, and before anyone could grab the blanket, he was on it and ripped it to shreds faster than it took you to read these words. Justice was swift and brutal when administered by Bango, whether you were Al Qaeda in Iraq or the S2.

In the end, though, I'd say the presence of this animal provided relief and a much-needed morale boost for the vast majority of those who came into contact with Bango. If it meant losing a few blankets in the deal, then I am cool with that. Fortunately for those who would lose blankets in the deal, I am not in charge. Unfortunately, the Army currently doesn't allow pets, mascots, or animals other than those like Bango in combat theaters, for obvious health and other reasons. But part of me wishes it could be so. The value of his presence was obvious for anyone willing to look.

Maybe all those old guys in wars fought way back when were on to something with their unit mascots and stuff.

FIGHT AT THE CROSSROADS: SEPTEMBER 29, 2007

As the days ticked by and our deployment rapidly drew to a close, the number and intensity of engagements decreased dramatically.

It is easy to lose track of the big picture when you are always looking at the ground-level detail of things. To remedy this situation, during the mission briefs the S2 section began to put up slides showing the significant actions (SIGACTS) from the year before, contrasted with the SIGACTS of today. The contrast was stark; things were getting better in that regard. But it didn't mean that the enemy had left the battlefield. There still were some days when we were able to exact a toll on an increasingly hard-to-find foe. A lot of our successes were intelligence driven. Through various means, our military intelligence sections across Iraq were able to predict the location of targetable concentrations of Anti Iraqi Forces on a consistent basis.

During the late-morning mission briefing, the crew members of CZ 14 and 15 were told by our S2 that there might be a meeting of several members of an insurgent organization just west of Camp Taji, in the vicinity of Route Redlegs. That area was the responsibility of 2nd Battalion, 6th US Cavalry (call sign: Stallion). Coincidentally, we also had a standing requirement to conduct CM2RI around the boundary of Camp

Taji, which fell into this area. So, during the team brief, it was decided to investigate the area for any suspicious activity as part of their mission set for that day.

Shortly after departing Camp Taji, one of the aircraft began to give indications of a possible tail rotor malfunction. The team returned to the airfield and landed in Taji FARP, where they assessed the condition of Crazyhorse 14. After determining that the aircraft was flyable, they made the decision that they could continue the mission. The aircraft then ran back up and, after completing some systems checks, reentered the battlefield. Taking off from the FARP, they headed west into 2-8 CAV's AO.

After working the area for ten minutes or so, the team turned northwest along Route Redlegs. In the lead, CZ 14's pilot in command, CW3 Terry Eldridge, spotted four white bongo trucks gathered at a four-way intersection about 2 kilometers away. After alerting his front-seater, air mission commander Capt. Thomas Louix, they also noted a group of individuals, numbering around fifteen, moving between several single-story buildings and the vehicles. This type of activity was unusual for that area, so the team immediately dropped down below 150 feet in altitude and proceeded inbound to assess the situation.

As the aircraft closed on the location, they began to take fire from machine guns mounted on the backs of the pickup trucks they had spotted. Seeing the fire directed at them, CW3 Eldridge alerted the flight that they were taking fire, and flew even lower to the ground after suppressing the incoming rounds with several rockets. The aircraft were flying so low that one of the buildings the trucks were parked next to blocked the enemy's line of fire, providing some temporary protection for the team. At the same time, CW3 Kyle Kittleson and CW2 Cole Moughon in CZ 15 lay down suppressive fire from their 30 mm cannon. After the initial enemy contact, CW2 Moughon had contacted Attack Mike and apprised them of the situation. Attack Mike then ordered a second AWT to move toward the battle.

Unfortunately, due to the way CW3 Eldridge in CZ 14 had set up the aircraft weapons selection page, earlier—during the start and run-up sequence—the rockets they fired initially were illumination rounds, which lack high-explosive warheads, but they did their job and got the enemy's heads down for a second or two, allowing the team to momentarily disengage and prepare for a reattack.

But the enemy didn't stay down for very long. While CZ 14 was turning the flight away and preparing to reengage, a 7.62 round sliced through its rear cockpit, narrowly (by inches) missing Eldridge's face.

Now back inbound, with machine gun and RPG fire all around them, CZ 14 engaged and damaged one of the pickup trucks mounting a machine gun in the back. CZ 15, attacking from a different direction, engaged and damaged a second vehicle. During that pass, Moughon, in CZ 15, had a round from one of the enemy's weapons pass through his cockpit as well.

As the swirling and turning fight ensued over the next several minutes, the team engaged targets, coordinating their movements with each other and then returning to reengage as more threats presented themselves. It was about that time when two black sedans bolted from the village, attempting to escape the carnage at a high rate of speed.

As the vehicles bounced and swerved down the dirt road, CZ 14 flew in pursuit, angling to cut off their escape. In a scene right out of Hollywood, CZ 14 fired their 30 mm cannon, shredding one of the vehicles and causing it to explode and flip several times, ending up in a ditch beside the road. They also shot the second vehicle, disabling it. One of its occupants was killed when he tried to flee, but another escaped in a field of reeds nearby. CZ 14 then returned to the intersection to assist his wingman in cleaning up what was left of enemy opposition there.

Arriving overhead about that time was the team of CZ 16/17, led by Capt. Lee Robinson, the A Company commander, with his CPG, Capt. Aaron Smead, along with CW4 Kimo Hansen and CW3 Al Davison in Crazyhorse 17 on their wing. After coordinating with the first AWT on scene, they stacked above CZ 14/15, separating the two teams by altitude. When CZ 14 returned to the four-way intersection, they assumed responsibility for the site where the two black sedans were, looking for survivors and providing area security for the overall fight.

Back at the intersection, the fight had pretty much ended and the team of CZ 14/15 went about "cleaning up." Using their 30 mm cannons, they disabled or destroyed the remaining vehicles and their associated weapons systems.

Eighteen minutes after the first shots were fired, CZ 14/15 declared "Winchester" and gave the fight over to CZ 16/17. During the engagement, they had fired seven Hellfire missiles, sixty-one rockets, and over eight hundred rounds of 30 mm cannon ammunition. They had destroyed three bongo trucks, two sedans, and six AIF. Later that day, an air assault was conducted by 2-8 CAV to conduct sensitive site exploitation. Arriving there, they discovered and destroyed three 14.5 mm heavy machine guns, four PKCs (Russian-made 7.62 mm machine guns), four AK-47s, and three thousand rounds of mixed ammunition.

After the fight we reviewed the tapes, just like after every other engagement in the battalion. Some of the missile shots during this engagement were fired so close to the target that they looked like torpedoes fired from a World War II PT boat. While they did a great job and were eventually commended appropriately, a lot of people in the aviation standards community tend to be "glass half empty" kind of folks and had a few things to say about their shooting technique in particular.

Our master gunner (the guy responsible for the unit's helicopter gunnery proficiency) and SIP were always wound up about poor firing technique and the tendency (mentioned earlier) of crews to press in on the target in the heat of the battle. There's a ton of legitimacy to that criticism. Crews would expose themselves to needless danger getting in range of the enemy's weapons, when the better choice would be to stand off and use our advantages better. Obviously, sometimes you don't have a choice and have to make the best of the crappy situation you have been handed. I always believed the key was being flexible and to react as the situation dictated. Unfortunately, this isn't the way that we train, for the most part.

I feel that most of the problems we had with gunnery technique and accuracy were a direct result of the way that we had trained and how crews had learned to shoot.

We had trained pretty much the same way that attack helicopter units had trained since before the war started, with only minor variations. There were some (CW4 Steve Kilgore being one) who saw, from their combat experience, that the way we trained to conduct helicopter gunnery wasn't cutting it. On the one hand, we were constrained by Army requirements for gunnery qualification tables that were based on concepts that aren't germane to the current situation on the battlefield. On the other, the commander of a unit had significant leeway to prepare his unit for combat. Unfortunately, it was usually a lot easier to take the course of least resistance and do things the way we always had.

When the Army first came up with the idea and started fielding attack helicopters back in the 1960s and 1970s, one of the things that had to be done was come up with a way to allow aviators to "qualify" with their weapon (the helicopter). Qualifying with your weapon usually meant firing at a target at a given distance, counting the number of hits, and then determining a score, which showed whether you passed or failed. Nobody ever wants to reinvent the wheel, so it was decided by someone that it would be a good idea to take a tank gunnery table and adapt that for aviation use. In some respects, the process isn't that bad, but there's one thing it surely isn't, and that's flexible.

For instance, in Iraq a lot of our engagements occurred from an orbit. We would circle a suspected target and then engage after going through the appropriate procedures. Most gunnery ranges in the Army are linear. Let's say our range is oriented north to south. For range safety we want the barrel of the weapon pointed downrange (south), within a range fan of 170 to 190 degrees. So anytime the weapon is outside those constraints, it should be "safe" and unable to fire. This obviously is not how we were fighting. So the question is this: Does our training prepare our aircrews to fight properly? Once we are in combat, it is difficult if not impossible to fix these issues, but this gunnery thing (our reason for being) seemed to be an ongoing issue that always appeared to be something we were working on.

The process of gunnery training and qualification consists of several events called "tables."

To attempt to understand the process, I present the following, which is a synopsis of the *Army Field Manual FM 1-140: Helicopter Gunnery*:

TRAINING STRATEGY

The helicopter gunnery program begins with individual qualification on aircraft weapon systems and progresses through crew qualification to unit collective training. The unit-training strategy must build on the skills learned by individual crew members during the aircraft qualification course. The unit gunnery program must be progressive and continuous. It must emphasize training that allows integration of new personnel while maintaining qualified crews. This program is focused on building warfighting [*sic*] units that can engage and destroy the enemy.

Helicopter gunnery range training is a training event where individuals, crews, teams, and companies show proficiency and validate the operational readiness of the helicopter weapon systems. Crew qualification on table VIII is the cornerstone of this gunnery program. Table VIII qualification is a live-fire event and an annual requirement. Once crews qualify, units can begin work on the advanced tables that focus on collective training.

The unit's mission-essential task list and mission training plan enable the commander to focus helicopter gunnery training on the unit's primary mission. This procedure allows the commander to exercise command, control, and communication functions while conducting gunnery. Commanders can use training devices like the MILES/AGES (an electronic device than resembles laser tag) to enhance the collective training program so that the unit can train as it fights. Commanders tailor the advanced tables (tables IX through XII) to meet their particular unit's mission and training requirements.

GUNNERY STANDARDS
The goal of Army training is a combat-ready force that can deploy on short notice, fight, and win. To achieve this goal, commanders must have a common set of weapons and weapon systems qualification standards. They also must have an objective way to judge those standards. Army aviation's gunnery program standards are discussed below.

The Aerial Weapon Scoring System is the standard for objective scoring of cannon and rocket fires with no subjective upgrades.

A target hit within the effective range of the system is the standard for cannon and machine gun engagements.

A target hit also is the standard for the AGM-114 Hellfire missile.

Target neutralization is the standard for rocket engagements. Because rockets are most effective when fired in mass, the rocket-training strategy is to train crews for neutralization engagements.

Target neutralization is an engagement that causes 10 percent casualties and/or destruction of materiel in the target effect area. It should be a deliberate engagement in which the crew fires a minimum of two pairs of adjustment rockets, senses the impacts, makes adjustments, and fires at least five pairs of rockets for effect.

During the conduct of basic and intermediate gunnery tables, crews will train and show proficiency in adjusting rockets onto a target without completing a fire for effect.

GUNNERY TABLES
The gunnery tables are designed to train and evaluate the crew's ability to engage targets with the helicopter's weapon systems at short, medium, and long ranges. These gunnery tables are progressive; they must be fired in order. Except for tables III and IV, these tables cannot be accomplished in a compatible

simulator. Commanders may modify the engagement sequences, conditions, and target arrays within the tables to meet mission training requirements or to fit resource constraints such as range layout. Because modifications to tables are temporary, commanders must work with installation or regional range authorities to upgrade and improve helicopter gunnery ranges so the unit can fire the tables as stated in this manual.

Basic Tables.
Tables I and II are used for initial weapons qualification. These are done at Fort Rucker during initial training in the aircraft.

Tables III and IV are used for prequalification training and the commander's evaluation of newly assigned crew members. Units may use these tables to evaluate unit trainers or to conduct refresher training for qualified aviators. Tables III and IV are individual tables evaluated by a unit instructor pilot.

Intermediate Tables.
Table V is the commander's pregunnery assessment of unit helicopter gunnery readiness. This table allows evaluation of the crew's knowledge and gunnery skills before the crew progresses to live-fire gunnery. Table V is a gate to live-fire training; crews must complete this table before attempting live-fire gunnery.

Table VI is the calibration and verification table. This table includes ammunition for units to calibrate and test-fire weapon systems before qualification range training. An aircraft must meet the table VI standards before it can be used for qualification on tables VII and VIII.

Table VII is a training table. Table VIII is a crew qualification table and is a gate to the advanced tables.

Advanced Tables.
Tables IX through XII are the advanced tables. These tables orient on tactical scenarios and multihelicopter employment. They allow the commander to focus the unit on collective live-fire training. The unit (mission, personnel, and equipment) will dictate tactical scenarios, task organization, and weapons mix.

One can plainly see that helicopter gunnery qualification is neither quick nor easy. Also please keep in mind that tables VII and VIII are done both day and night. As a result, gunnery is a yearly or sometimes twice-a-year process that is organized and dealt with as a major event, taking all a unit's focus for several weeks until it's done, and then we shall never speak of gunnery again until the next time we have to do it . . . and therein lies the problem.

To be proficient with any kind of weapon, gunnery needs to be accomplished with live rounds as much as possible. Unfortunately, most installations in the Army are configured in such a way that it precludes the ability to use the ranges to fire more often, even if the units were inclined to do so. For example, on Fort Hood, if

I want to fire a Hellfire missile, there are one or two locations available to use. Additionally, I must be directly over the firing point at a hover, with the aircraft facing in a range fan of so many degrees, and fire at a target array at X location . . . so unless I just want to do this for the experience of firing a missile, what is the training value of that? I understand that some of the constraints are safety based, and that is understandable and mostly logical. But units become hamstrung in their ability to create realistic training scenarios, which involve live-fire training, due to range and ammo constraints. Even during table VIII qualifications, firing aircraft are restricted to certain azimuths, altitudes, and airspeeds to engage targets. While understandable from a safety point of view, this is not the way we fight. Given that tables VII and VIII are the ONLY live-fire training most crews receive before deploying, is it surprising that the same crews might face challenges when engaging a live reactive target in a rapidly changing urban environment?

Contrast this with the way USAF A-10 pilots train. They fire their gun or drop ordnance much, much more often than their Army counterparts. It is no exaggeration to say that almost every training flight they conduct involves some type of weapons engagement. Often, this is done with live rounds or training ordnance designed to be dropped or fired from the aircraft. This contrasts with actual combat, where Army aviation was engaging the enemy at a much-higher rate and in much-closer proximity than our USAF brothers and sisters.

I have had numerous discussions about this subject with my contemporaries, and I try to put it into terms that are easily understood, so when I present this concept to West Pointers, they don't feel so overwhelmed. If you have a difficult time understanding why helicopter gunnery should be a task that we work on every time we fly, I will use Major League Baseball and their pregame rituals to illustrate my point. Every team takes batting practice before every game. They also take practice fielding grounders and fly balls. They don't do this because they aren't proficient (well, maybe the Yankees do); they do it because they want it to be second nature when it actually means something. We should do the same thing regarding gunnery techniques.

While an AH-64 has a training mode that allows for some training without using actual ammunition, and it is possible to use the laser and simulate engaging targets with the practice version of the Hellfire missile, the former doesn't give any feedback on whether or not the rounds would have struck the "target," and the latter can be done only from preapproved laser-firing points, usually on a military base.

The ability to train realistically is just not there in the amount that it should be. As a result, when a unit arrives in theater, there is a learning period. Because it is combat, the learning is pretty much self-taught. Some people never get there. This is, in my opinion, a major shortcoming of our attack helicopter operations. We could be much more effective (once again, in my opinion) if we changed the way we train and evaluate gunnery to something that approaches "real" combat conditions. Obviously, this would be something an order of magnitude more difficult than what we currently do, and there would certainly be failures to qualify. Currently, a failure to qualify is viewed as unacceptable, so to prevent failure, crews are allowed to memorize the range tables before firing them, which is obviously not what happens in "real life" combat.

Now I know there are people out there who read the portion of the FM that I quoted who are saying to themselves, "What about tables IX through XII; shouldn't those be the tables that are focused on what you are referring to?" In an ideal world you would be correct. Unfortunately, money, time, lack of imagination, or any portion of the above often conspire to limit the ability of units to complete what are known as advance tables. Earlier in the book, you will remember, I described my participation in some advanced tables. The sad truth is that those opportunities are often not given to all the pilots in a unit, or even the ones who need the training most.

Given all of that, it is amazing to me what our attack helicopter crews were able to accomplish and the things they continue to do every day. Of course, no matter how well trained someone is, there is always room for improvement; unfortunately, the focus on training back in the States isn't always on combat skills. So what ends up happening is that limited training time is often frittered away on things such as motorcycle safety, Native American Heritage Month, and scolding sessions regarding cell phone usage on post or while driving. That's not meant to imply that safety or Native American heritage isn't important. We lose more soldiers to accidents and suicide than we do to combat, so those briefings do have their place. The Army exists to fight our nation's wars. So, one might think that the primary focus would be on preparing for the combat operations that we KNOW will occur. However, often it seemed that it was anything but the priority.

Even in Iraq, now that the end of our tour was approaching, we were required to attend classes often referred to as "annual training" on such things as sexual harassment and driving safety. So in between flying missions, packing, and writing after-action reviews, we now had to go to the chapel, which was in a muddy field behind the dining facility, to hear lectures on suicide prevention and other things that we either had little to no interest in or sailed over the heads of those who needed the guidance/training the most.

My last flight in Iraq . . . this time, November 26, 2007.
Photo courtesy of the author

It was classic "check the block" training. Everybody attended the class; who really cares if it meets their intended purpose or not. The important thing is that everyone attended, and a box can now be checked off.

In a stroke of "genius," we were doing these things now, so we wouldn't have to do them when we got home . . . but the joke was on us, because in less than six months we did them all AGAIN.

Another thing that people were doing was the annually required (except while you were deployed to combat . . . hey, wait a second—tell me why we are doing this again) Army physical fitness tests. We were still getting rocketed and mortared occasionally, but I guess it was OK to have a PT test, where soldiers would do push-ups, sit-ups, and 2-mile runs, all the while sucking in lungs full of that nasty garbage, burn-pile, smoke-filled Taji air, hoping they don't end up in the wrong place at the wrong time. Fortunately, nobody was injured (at least by shrapnel) while doing this. I would imagine that it is tough enough to have to write a letter to a loved one telling them their soldier had been killed in combat, but could you imagine what it would be like if you had to write one telling the family that their soldier was killed during a mortar attack while he or she was out running, doing a PT test that wasn't really required? Of course, they wouldn't write that; they would say something about what a great person that soldier was, but they would never admit something like that. Fortunately they didn't have to, but it wasn't for lack of trying.

On November 26, 2007, I flew my last combat mission in Iraq for OIF 06-08. I don't recall anything about it other than it was at night. I didn't write anything down about it in my notes, so I'm assuming nothing significant happened. The only way I'm sure that was the date is that I had someone take a photo of me. It was par for the course for the last month or so, since all the units that were rotating out and scaling back their operations, and "SIGACTS" were way down for the division.

All I knew was that I was happy that this thing was coming to an end. In the back of my mind, I knew we would be back here or in some other garden spot in about a year, but for now it was a good feeling to know that we had done a good job and would be going home.

CHAPTER 8

CAMP TAJI, IRAQ, DECEMBER 2007: "GOODBYE, CRAZYHORSE! GOOD . . . BYE!"

Eventually our replacements arrived. This twelve-month deployment that had turned into fifteen, that seemed like a decade, was finally coming to an end.

Like the guys we had replaced, we were more than happy to see them. Personally, I was sick of moving. Packing, unpacking, filling out customs forms, and having someone rifle through all of your stuff on the hunt for war trophies and all manner of banned items . . . all the while knowing that we would be back here in a year or so, doing the same thing all over again. It sucked, but at least for now we were going home.

I was taken aback by some of the attempts by our replacements to get a bargain though.

I had a 36-inch color TV and DVD player that I had obtained from someone in the 4th Infantry Division when I arrived in country. Fifteen months before, I had paid $75 for both. Now, since I had used them pretty much every day the entire time we had been there, I was asking $25 for the pair. I considered that a damn good bargain, since they were in good working order, and I certainly wasn't making any money on the deal. A guy from the incoming unit had other ideas and had the nerve to offer me $10 for the combo. I told him in the most dramatic fashion I could muster, "Before I take $10 for a TV and a DVD player, I will take a baseball bat and break them into little pieces right in front of you." He eventually coughed up the $25 . . . I guess some people always must be the "winner" in a deal.

While we all looked forward to getting back to the USA, there were those of us who were rather unsettled in what it was we would be returning to.

The Army expends considerable time and energy in making sure its families are taken care of and informed about their loved one who is in harm's way. Single enlisted soldiers who live in the barracks are taken care of and informed where they will be going when the unit returns from deployment and what their living arrangements will be. For people like myself, a single officer, there were no such assurances, and I was on my own to find suitable quarters for myself. Of course, if I had said anything,

I would have been offered a space in the barracks . . . which is about all they could have done anyway. But the situation was a bit difficult, nonetheless. I spent more than a little bit of time online, attempting to find an apartment to lease so I wouldn't end up in a hotel for an extended period of time. It was just one more thing to add to the list of things that needed to get done prior to redeployment.

There was, of course, route and mission planning to be done for the flight back to Kuwait. A month or so before, I had planned the route for the aircraft headed south for redeployment, and I had that stored on my AMPS. Now we had to print out strip maps, load mission cards, and do all the other stuff that is involved with flying a bunch of aircraft across a war zone.

The commander, S3, or somebody up at BDE had convinced themselves that we had to get our aircraft to Kuwait to be waiting for the wash rack to open on the very first day it was available for redeployment. To accomplish this, it would mean that we would have to launch aircraft starting around 0300, with a second wave leaving around 0430 or so.

December is, of course, winter, and it's also the rainy season in Iraq. Looking at weather trends, especially down toward Kuwait, it didn't look like the smartest thing for us to try to fly across a desert where there are no lights from human activity at night. There was a good possibility that there would be rain, high winds, and embedded thundershowers, which our FLIR or NVGs cannot see through. Other units had lost aircraft in that area, flying at night through bad weather, and I had some concern about our transit. I took my concerns to the S3, who told me that we HAD to be on the wash rack at first light or we would lose our spot. Well, that pretty much settled that. We HAD to be there. I didn't ask what would happen if we couldn't launch due to weather. There's always a way; some people just don't want to find it.

With apologies to the post office, neither rain, cold, heat, nor gloom of night will stop First Attack from its appointment to wash helicopters. So, on the appointed day and time, we got up short of sleep (since we had all been working on the day shift), loaded the last of our belongings into our aircraft, and launched into the darkness, headed south to Kuwait. As we cleared Taji airspace for the last time, we radioed the tower: "Taji Tower, Crazyhorse 01 is clear to the south, frequency change, negative ETR [estimated time of return, meaning we weren't coming back]."

The tower threw the wet blanket of reality on the festivities, saying, "Roger; see you here next year."

For a while it looked as though we were going to make it to our refuel stop at Tallil Airbase without encountering the rain showers that had been predicted, but just south of our alternate refueling stop, we started running into a hellacious headwind, which was followed shortly thereafter by the beginning of the rain. The headwind began to cause us some concern, since our ground speed had dropped to the point where we started to doubt whether we could make our fuel stop. I was in Gun 2, and we were doing fuel checks every few minutes. It was looking like if the wind didn't get any worse, we would be OK fuelwise. Then the rain really started coming down.

I was on NVGs in the front seat, and one of our maintenance pilots, CW4 Chris Elkins, was on the FLIR in the back. You know when it gets kind of dicey in a flight when all chatter on the radio ceases, and it suddenly becomes noticeably quiet on the net. I was having trouble seeing lead as the rain began to get heavier, and then a voice from the back seat asks me if I can see lead. I reply, "Yeah, barely."

Chris then says, "You have the controls; I've lost them."

Now I'm on the controls, trying to keep the flight in sight, thinking to myself it would really suck to die after surviving fifteen months of combat by flying this thing into the ground during a rainstorm. But here I was. Looking out in front, all I can see ahead is blackness and the flashing light of lead's IR strobe light. Off to our right I can see the lights of a small town, and I suggest to flight lead that we divert a bit in that direction because it seems that the rain is a bit lighter over there. For what seems like hours but was only about fifteen or twenty minutes, we dodge and weave around rain showers, and then out of the blackness came the most beautiful sight I had seen in quite some time—the approach lights of Tallil. A rabbit trail of flashing lights beckoning to a passing aviator. These lights were a flashing welcome sign in the darkness. The lights say to me, "Come on in; we have fuel and snacks." Why yes, I think I will.

I let out a huge sigh as we taxi in to refuel, since the worst is over. Capt. Morton announces over team internal that we'll wait till sunrise to fly the hour to Kuwait. He probably just took his career in his own hands. We shut down on the ramp and wait for the sun to come up.

When old Sol makes its appearance, it's in an overcast, low-lying, scud-filled sky. We take off flying over the barren desert of southern Iraq, crossing the border with Kuwait and landing at the same place we left from fifteen long months ago, Camp Buehring, an hour later.

After we taxi into our parking spaces and shut down, our armament techs appear and begin to de-arm the aircraft, removing the ordnance we brought with us on the trip south.

After we stretched our legs a bit, the unpacking of the aircraft began in earnest. After that, we would unpanel and start washing. Oh, yeah, that's right . . . we didn't wash the aircraft till the next day . . . so much for getting down here at dawn so we could wash the aircraft. Glad we nearly killed ourselves getting here.

Meanwhile, back at Camp Taji, those who weren't fortunate enough to have an aircraft to fly out on were gathered at the Camp Taji passenger terminal, waiting for their flight north to Balad, to ultimately catch a ride from the USAF south to Kuwait.

The commander was there as well, slapping backs and shaking hands. As the soldiers filed out to get on the aircraft that would carry them north, Attack 6 said, "Goodbye, Crazyhorse!" One soldier replied with a weak "Hooah."

When the story was described to me later, I could almost imagine the scene as played out in melodramatic Hollywood style. The commander standing at attention on the ramp, the wind from the rotors tearing at his uniform, a single tear runs down his cheek as he salutes his soldiers as they file past, and finally, in an almost inaudible

Flying toward Kuwait at first light, December 5, 2007. *Photo by author*

whisper, he says goodbye to his troops and in essence his command . . . "Goodbye, Crazyhorse; goodbye." He would change command in a month or two after our return.

For the rest of us, soon after we finished washing aircraft and then flying them down to the port, where they would be placed on a ship for their return to the USA, we went through the grueling, annoying, and aggravating process that is required to go home. After our bags were unpacked, scanned, and searched, we were placed in a holding area to await our flight back to Fort Hood.

We spent nearly an entire day in the holding pen. The only thing to do in there was sleep, watch TV, and eat prepackaged meals or order a Pizza Hut delivery. They never tell you how long you are going to be there, exactly, so you (or at least I do) have this anxiety hanging over your head that if you doze off or go to the restroom, you'll miss something . . . you won't, because they hold formations at random intervals, to make sure nobody is enjoying themselves and to fool you into believing that you will actually be leaving soon.

Eventually, they figure they can't keep us any longer because there are more people coming behind us. Here's hoping that the folks crewing our airliner have had their mandatory downtime and done whatever it is they need to do while laying over in Kuwait.

We get on buses that take us to Kuwait International Airport, and go through the kabuki dick dance that ensues whenever a military unit gets on a charter aircraft to go anywhere. It's not like we didn't know they were going to need a baggage detail—why did you wait till now to pick/appoint one? Yes, let's have another roll call. Someone might have magically showed up in the last five minutes. Get on the bus. Get off the bus.

Finally, we get to board the plane. We get the silly briefing about weapons on the plane . . . like someone would hijack us, to where? Shut up; rules are the rules. "You can't say 'bomb' on an airplane."

On the way home we stop in Shannon, Ireland, to get gas. Everyone is sternly reminded before we are allowed off the plane that GO #1 is still in effect, which means don't go to the duty-free store and buy some Irish whiskey to mix with your free Coke in the back of the plane. And you, yes you, stay away from the airport bar selling Guinness by the draft!

Finally, we get back to Texas. Before we can get off the plane, we have to wait for some customs agent to come on and give a briefing we all have heard before, and nobody is listening right now anyway. I look out the window and it's raining. The 1st CAV band is standing out in the cold December rain, on the tarmac, waiting for this guy and us to get on with it. There's some general out there as well, at the bottom of the stairs . . . waiting.

Eventually, we were allowed to deplane and begin the reintegration process. The band played "Garryowen," and we all saluted and shook the general's hand and left to go stand in line to turn in our weapons. We were then given a welcome packet that I finally got around to reading about six months later . . . eventually we got on another bus, the last bus.

The bus carried us to the 1st Cavalry Division headquarters. The street out front was blocked off, there were guys on horses, the band had somehow made it over there now, and families were in bleachers cheering. It was an awesome sight.

The buses pulled up next to the curb and parked so we would exit away from the families in the stands, with the vehicles blocking their view. Everyone got off their bus and scrambled into a massive formation. When we were all set, the buses pulled away to reveal us standing there in front of the crowd.

People were cheering, horses neighed, and the band played "Garryowen." We marched forward in what had to be the worst display of drill and ceremony in the history of the military, but nobody cared. Some officer stood at a podium and said something (at least it was short), and then we were dismissed. Bedlam erupted and kids, wives, family, and significant others rushed into the ranks. I made my way to one side of the mass of people and eventually spotted my old aviation photography buddy from North Texas, Keith Snyder, who had the keys to my Mustang that he had been storing for me while I was downrange. I went over, shook his hand, grabbed my bags, and then left to go get my car, eat a steak dinner, and find a place to live.

What an odd feeling it is, after fifteen months of deployment, to walk to a car, jump in, and just drive off, with nothing to do for the next several days. I hoped I could remember how to drive a stick.

Sixteen months later, the battalion would be back in Iraq to do the whole thing all over again. ATTACK!

AFTER-ACTION REVIEW

So, what had we accomplished during those fifteen months in Iraq? The following is taken from the packet the BN submitted for its nomination for the Ellis D. Parker award for the top attack battalion in the United States Army for FY 2007, which was compiled in September 2007. While not a complete record, it does give the reader an idea of some of the things the battalion accomplished, and the vast number of enemy engagements and ammo expended during our time in Iraq:

> 1-227th Aviation Regiment's Apaches and Aircrews [were] the key kinetic enablers for Multi-National Division—Baghdad. During the pre-Surge period, First Attack solely provided around-the-clock area security and reconnaissance, overwatch, and responsive fires for eight Brigade Combat Teams. The battalion was completely integrated with each BCT as their formations executed intense clear and control operations as part of the overall Baghdad Security Plan, Operation Fardh al Qanoon. The operational environment consisted of the City of Baghdad, a densely populated urban terrain, and Taji and Mada'in regions, dangerous rural areas lying on the periphery of the city. The battalion led the way in developing actionable intelligence by organizing the first fires and intelligence cell, an internal effort to make intelligence and operations complementary. [After] the start of the "Surge," 1-227th AVN REGT . . .

collapsed its coverage to two BCTs operating in and around Sadr City, and to two battalions in the Taji area. Tremendously lethal and agile, First Attack is a respected and proven combat multiplier to each soldier in and outside the wire in Baghdad. Our OIF call-sign, Crazy Horse, has become synonymous to the 12th man of an infantry squad who has the power to tip the scales in favor of the coalition during any engagement.

To date [September 2007], 1-227th AVN REGT has flown in excess of 22,000 flight hours in support of MND-B. First Attack is the most tasked attack battalion in theater; so far the battalion has received, processed, and executed 4,243 air mission requests. Twenty-four hours a day and 7 days a week, the attack weapons teams provide general support and periodic direct support to either a BCT element, special operations force, or Multi-National Corps-Iraq elements. First Attack aircrews have consistently demonstrated the most astute situational understanding, which has led to unmatched air-ground integration with our ground brethren conducting ground convoys, raids, searches, or patrols. Since the beginning of the "Surge," our AWT's have become an essential component of over 61 air assault operations aimed at capturing radical insurgent leaders that threaten the security condition in Baghdad from the Taji and Mada'in regions: 23 High Value Targets have been detained, 42 weapons confiscated, and 4 large weapons caches destroyed. During the course of clearing neighborhoods, or muhallas, in Baghdad, our crews have been routinely injected into extremely chaotic and complex situations and they incessantly and rapidly develop the situation for the on-scene commander and provide confidence for the troopers on the ground to press on knowing that overwhelming combat power is literally over-their-shoulder.

Always ready, First Attack has responded to an unprecedented total of 819 troops-in-contact events thus far. We have answered the preponderance of BCT-requested TIC's in seven minutes or less. The warrior ethos of our attack crews is exemplary and was made obvious during five separate downed[-] aircraft situations in which our crews responded first to take charge and secure the area for casualty and aircraft recovery. As stated earlier, the operational environment of Baghdad is extremely complicated for the Soldiers on the ground and for the aircrews. The insurgents clearly use busy streets, local nationals, and narrow urban canyons to cover and conceal their sinister actions. The standard of exceptional care to avoid collateral damage and judicious application of ROE is characteristic of our well-disciplined and professional aviators. The First Attack standard has led to 275 successful separate engagements against the enemy and/or enemy materiel. Over the course of OIF 06-08, the 1-227th AVN REGT, Crazy Horse, has earned the respect and confidence from our US and coalition counterparts not due to a total enemy body count, but rather by the responsiveness, precision, and lethal effects we provide.

The battalion has been well out-front of the other aviation units in achieving meaningful analysis of the operational environment, insurgent groups, and their ever-evolving tactics, techniques, and procedures. Prior to deployment, we organized many available officers and NCOs to become a dedicated fires and intelligence cell (FIC). The FIC increased our capability to pull relevant intelligence from our ground counterparts, analyze it, brief, and create products that aided the aviators in finding, fixing, and finishing many insurgents in zone. This robust intelligence section allowed First Attack to maintain an offensive mindset and to be proactive in the battle space. Additionally, our aviator's [sic] situational understanding has been exponentially enhanced through frequent briefs by the FIC. The 1-227th AVN REGT developed a weekly targeting process that helped to identify new enemy patterns and vulnerabilities, as well as provide focus for our staff and aviators on how best to disrupt the insurgent group's strategy. Each weekly targeting meeting produces well-developed terrain targets that become our reconnaissance focus which complements well the efforts of the BCTs.

1-227th AVN REGT was the first in the 1st Air Cavalry Brigade to successfully team with BCT ISR assets. First Attack prosecuted 19 insurgent targets during engagements that were made possible by the effective and increasingly efficient use of ISR assets teamed with our AH-64D Longbows. The battalion always assures that each event was reviewed to gain information on how to improve effectiveness. Lessons learned are typically always shared at all levels throughout MND-B. Our Intelligence Reconnaissance Surveillance efforts in the battalion have matured as well. The relevance and quality of our reports after detailed reconnaissance is recognized by many of the ground units we support. We have observed a noticeable effort by our ground counterparts to send patrols to confirm or deny our reports. On several occasions, ground raids and air assault operations have been executed based on the intelligence gained by thorough reconnaissance by our aircrews. Now in the twelfth month, the aviators and staff execute an aggressive, laser-focused reconnaissance plan that incorporates dedicated tactical and echelons-above-division ISR assets.

As a key member of the "Surge," the 1-227th AVN REGT looks at ways to continue improvement and enhancement of our effectiveness in support of the ground tactical plan. A learning and adaptive organization, First Attack will become increasingly agile and supportive in the next phase of MND-B COIN operations[,] which has already shown progress in reconciliation with local nationals that are now empowered to fight alongside the coalition due the improved security situation in Baghdad. With the aim to fully accomplish our mission and bring all our troopers home, the First Attack leaders will continue to work to keep all Soldiers focused on all tasks and especially attentive to the volatile environment of Baghdad, Iraq.

I just wanted to thank your organization for flying cover for us yesterday. . . . We did not have a single "Ranger" injured yesterday in a fight that lasted almost 8 hours for us and a large portion can be attributed to your pilots. Thanks again.

—Maj. David Goetze, S3, 2-16th Infantry

1st Battalion, 227th Aviation Regiment has been an outstanding enabler for the Strike Brigade Combat Team during our deployment in support of Operation Iraqi Freedom 06-08. For the past ten months, their extensive support has included hundreds of missions including reconnaissance, security, and close combat attack missions. First Attack's responsiveness and courage under fire is a testament to their skill and valor, and on many occasions their combat power has been the difference between failure and success on the streets [of] Baghdad and throughout AO Strike.

The men and women of the Strike Team are emboldened by the mere presence of the fine aviators of First Attack. Their fearlessness and aggressive nature have proven to deter the enemy from attacking our Soldiers and saved many lives as a result. Whether it be a kinetic strike against the enemies of Iraq or providing security for a logistical patrol, the pilots of First Attack have displayed an amazing balance of lethality and tactical patience. When the call for their support goes out from our headquarters, we are never let down. Even in the face of an extremely dangerous surface to air threat, these men and women from 1-227th Aviation Regiment will not hesitate to come to our aid. They are the essence of selfless service.

—Col. Jeffery Bannister, commander, 2nd BCT, 2ID

1st Battalion, 227th Aviation Regiment has provided continuous support for the IRONHORSE Brigade Combat Team during our deployment in support of OPERATION IRAQI FREEDOM 06-08. For the past eleven months, this extensive support has included hundreds of missions including reconnaissance, convoy security and close combat attack missions. FIRST ATTACK'S responsiveness and courage under fire is a testament to their skill and valor, and on many occasions their combat power has been the difference between failure and success on the streets [of] Taji and throughout AO IRONHORSE.

When elements of the IRONHORSE Brigade Combat Team were ambushed in northeast Taji, FIRST ATTACK aviators put themselves between the enemy and the small combat outpost. The FIRST ATTACK pilots' heroic actions enabled my Troopers to break contact by forcing the enemy to redirect their fires onto their own aircraft, during which they suffered bodily and heavy aircraft damage. This act is an accurate depiction of the dedication FIRST ATTACK has for the IRONHORSE Brigade. When we need security, FIRST ATTACK is there. The pilots of 1-227th Aviation Regiment are totally fearless and have never failed to support us—no matter what the conditions.

—Col. Paul Funk, commander, 1st BCT 1st CAV

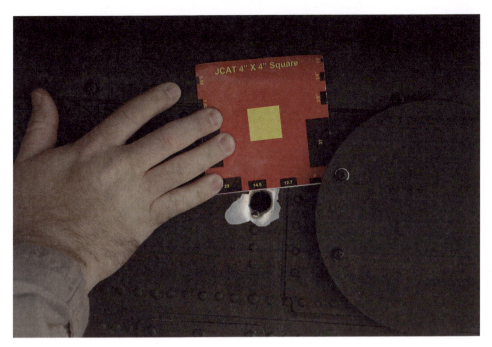

Battle damage from a 14.5 mm round that occurred on August 25, 2007. Damage like this occurred fairly often. *Photo by author*

Battle damage on the pilot's blast shield from August 25. *Photo by author*

A crew chief salutes his ship and crew as his aircraft departs. Apache crew chiefs get grief from their Black Hawk counterparts for doing this, but for some this is the last time they will see their aircraft and crew. *Photo by author*

An Apache taxis out for another mission at Camp Taji. *Photo by author*

An Apache flying over southern Baghdad near the monument aircrews referred to as "the Blue Tulip"

Flying over a typical Baghdad neighborhood. As the war went on, flying at these altitudes was frowned upon, primarily because of the way it upset the population of Baghdad. *Photo by author*

A murky day over Baghdad. There was always a lot of particulate matter in the air. Some days were worse than others. *Photo by author*

Up at dawn, flying just about the haze level over Baghdad. *Photo by author*

An Apache flying near what we referred to as the "Disco Mosque" in downtown Baghdad. This was because at night this mosque was lit up with bright, multicolored lights. *Photo by author*

Flying over eastern Baghdad at last light. My aircraft was hit by small-arms fire sometime during this mission, although I didn't realize it until conducting the postflight inspection. *Photo by author*

My wingman flying the flag. Aircrew often did this for a person back home to thank them for their support. *Photo by author*

Flying south toward Zones 9 and 24. The Blue Tulip is off the nose and Sadr City is out my left door. Something is on fire, which wasn't terribly unusual. *Photo by author*

Flying over the farmland just east of Camp Taji. *Photo by author*

Doing CM2RI just north of Camp Taji. *Photo by author*

Headed back to Camp Taji. This was taken in the area between Baghdad and the camp. *Photo by author*

A team returns to Taji at the end of its mission window. *Photo by author*

Returning to parking. *Photo by author*

Returning to base at the end of a crappy weather day. *Photo by author*

Sunset of Baghdad as the sand blows in from the west. *Photo by author*

CHAPTER 9

AWARDS AND DECORATIONS: AN AVIATOR'S PERSPECTIVE

Give me enough medals and I'll win you any war.

—Napoleon Bonaparte, *Napoleon's Art of War*

When I was a kid, I remember remarking about the bravery of Audie Murphy to my father (a World War II veteran) after watching the film *To Hell and Back*. I recall my father telling me that for every Audie Murphy who received the Medal of Honor, there were ten others whom nobody knew about, except the people who were there. At the time I thought he was wrong. I thought, why would the Army not recognize someone for doing heroic things on the battlefield? It just seemed counterintuitive and wrong. But like so many other things that I foolishly thought I knew better than he, I now know that Dad was right.

I was privileged to serve among and for heroes during my three deployments to war in support of Operation Iraqi Freedom. Many were, in fact, honored for what they did on the field of battle. The 1-227 AVN, during OIF 06-08, had among its ranks soldiers who earned the Distinguished Service Medal, Distinguished Flying Cross, Air Medal with Valor, and Bronze Star. Even with this stellar record, there were many more who were denied recognition for reasons that ranged from bureaucratic bungling to envy and outright stupidity.

As you may have noticed, I took care not to mention anything about awards that were presented, downgraded, or denied to the people participating in the events described previously in this book. I did that for a reason. First, I wanted the reader to judge the events on the facts, and try to present enough information so they could fully understand what occurred during those eventful days. Most importantly, though, I feel that identifying the award (even if there was one at all) that these brave men and women were presented might distract from the overall story. I feel it is insulting, in the extreme, how little value the 1st Cavalry Division chain of command during OIF 06-08 gave to the efforts that were put forth by often-heroic soldiers on the field of battle.

A special place in hell awaits those officers who, while sitting in the former palace of a tyrant, dining on prime rib and lobster every night, parceled out trinkets to the plebeians as if there were a quota or rank structure regarding bravery, valor, service, or sacrifice. There are some people who held positions of authority in MND-B during OIF 06-08 whom if I saw them on the street today, I would punch them right in the running lights, not for any award that was denied me per se, but for the petty, capricious nature by which they doled out accolades that denied recognition to those not only in my unit but elsewhere in the division. I hope someone saved the eight-sided die they used to decide the level of and denial or approval of awards, so it can be placed in a museum sometime in the future.

I know soldiers who were in the same aircraft during the same engagement who got different awards, or one got an award and the other—who was the pilot in command of the aircraft—received nothing. I have heard it explained to people that they weren't going to receive an award because they had one (Air Medal) already. I have seen the note on an award recommendation being returned to the submitter, written by a man who never flew a second in combat, that read "'standard' TIC (troops in contact); no valor involved." A platoon leader was told that his award for placing his aircraft between the enemy and a combat outpost about to be overrun was not getting a statement of charges for the damage done to the aircraft. All these years after OIF 06-08, this kind of thing still occurs, far too often. I have been told, by those who had firsthand knowledge, of an aviation brigade commander in OEF who told his subordinates that unless there had been damage to the aircraft or someone had been wounded, he didn't want to see any submissions for an award with a Valor device. If I didn't know better, I would think that some of these folks had to pay for the cost of these awards out of their own pockets.

As an example of the awards system in action, for the mission I flew on January 28, 2007, in support of a downed AH-64, the members of my AWT were submitted for an Air Medal with Valor, which was subsequently downgraded by the approval authority to an Air Medal only. During the same mission, the pilot of an Air Force F-16 dropped a laser-guided bomb from 14,000 feet on the same target we were working. For these actions, the pilot later received a Distinguished Flying Cross. We were engaging the enemy with direct fire, before and long after that F-16 left to go back to whatever airbase he came from that day. We were well within range of enemy weapon systems that had already brought down one AH-64 and damaged another, but those actions required no valor on our part, according to Maj. Gen. Fil, who (as the approval authority) downgraded my flight's awards while offering no comment as to why they needed to be downgraded.

Perhaps there is a misunderstanding among the officers in our Army of just what VALOR is. The Army awards regulation AR 600-8-22 defines "valor" as "heroism performed under combat conditions." HEROISM is defined by the same publication as "extreme courage demonstrated in attaining a noble end. Varying levels of documented heroic actions are necessary to substantiate recommendations for the Bronze Star Medal with 'V,' Air Medal with 'V,' and the Army Commendation Medal with 'V,' in connection with military operations against an armed enemy. This phrase covers all military operations, including combat, support, and supply, that have a direct bearing on the outcome of an engagement or engagements against armed opposition. To perform duty or to accomplish an act or achievement in connection with military operations against an armed enemy, the individual must have been subjected to either personal hazard as a result of direct enemy action or the imminence of such action or must have had the conditions under which his or her duty or accomplishment took place complicated by enemy action or the imminence of enemy action." COURAGE isn't defined in AR 600-8-22, but *Webster's Dictionary* defines it as "mental or moral strength to venture, persevere, and withstand danger, fear, or difficulty."

Life isn't fair, and neither is the awards system. I understand that it has always been that way, as illustrated by the remarks of my father. But it seems from anecdotal evidence that there doesn't exist a common standard with which commanders and their staffs judge these things they are charged to recognize. This, of course, does nothing to diminish what has been accomplished by those who didn't receive the awards they were put in for, or those who were never even submitted for an award in the first place. I have told others who have talked to me about the subject that those who were there know who did what, and they remember who the heroes really were, whether they received a medal for it or not. Of course, that fact does nothing for you if you are facing a competitive promotion board and that decoration might just make the difference between getting promoted or not.

With anything subjective, it is next to impossible to enforce a standard, but it does seem that some units and services are more inclined to reward their troops than others. A case in point is the award of the Air Medal. For my service, which included flying over 250 missions in combat while deployed fifteen months during OIF 06-08, I received a single Air Medal. For purposes of comparison, I am including (*below*) the US Navy standards for the awarding of the Air Medal in the OIF/OEF theaters of combat that were in effect in 2007:

Qualification Requirements. The award of the Air Medal on a Strike/Flight basis requires 20 points.
(1) (U) 10 strikes (1 strike = 2 points), or
(2) (U) 20 flights (1 flight = 1 point), or
(3) 50 missions (1 mission = .4 points), or
(4) 250 flight hours in direct combat support missions that do not encounter enemy opposition (25 hours = 2 points) or
(5) A combination of these, using the appropriate ratios:
3 strikes = 6 points
8 flights = 8 points
10 missions = 4 points
25 hours = 2 points

The USAF also employs a similar formula for the awarding of the Air Medal, regarding service in a combat zone. Almost every single pilot in 1-227th AVN received a single air medal for his or her flying during OIF 06-08, regardless of the number of missions they flew. Some, myself included, received awards for actions taken while flying missions, but that is a different award animal.

Of course, Army Regulation 600-8-22 specifically prohibits the use of hours regarding awarding the Air Medal, so we have a cross-services disagreement in why and how we give an award that is, in theory, the same. What I would boldly recommend is that for future conflicts, someone in a position of responsibility develop either a Department of Defense (DOD) or operational theater standard for what is supposed to represent the same thing: aviation achievement. A DOD standard would also address the issue of nonstandard presentation of this award across Army formations. I fully recognize that this issue is probably the least of our problems as far as the Army and DOD are concerned, but in some respects this is quite the opposite.

While I've spent a considerable amount of space discussing the perceived failures of the chain of command in making sure superior performance on the battlefield is rewarded, there is another side to this: the responsibility of the submitter and aircrews. Anyone who has ever been downrange knows that the last thing you really want to do after a mission is more paperwork. As a result, some of the paperwork that we do for things that are well deserved end up being rushed or incomplete or fail to tell the entire story of what happened. I know from reading my own sworn statements, written immediately after missions, that they are bare bones and dry and do nothing to give a reader who is unfamiliar with the events a complete picture of what occurred. It is imperative that soldiers know they must completely describe the events as if talking to an idiot, because, after all, most of the people who will be reading the recommendation above the brigade level will have little to no knowledge of what is required to fly a helicopter against an armed enemy in combat.

I don't know anyone who does this job for awards, and if I did I'd worry about their sanity. But the failure to reward outstanding performance in a consistent and fair manner not only is wrong on the face of it but ultimately has an adverse effect on morale and retention. No matter what we do, the awards process is never going to be completely fair. Everyone involved needs to do more in the future to ensure that soldiers are properly recognized for their actions on the field of battle, and that their place in history is secured.

As of this writing, my former unit is the only battalion within the 1st ACB that has yet to receive a unit award in recognition of its service during OIF 06-08. I can't speak for all the people who were above my level and were responsible to get this done and failed miserably, but I can say that this is absolutely and totally wrong. If the division band, which I am sure did an incredible job during OIF 06-08, gets a Meritorious Unit Award, then why would a battalion that flew in excess of 25,000 hours, responded to over 800 troops in contact calls, engaged the enemy with direct fire more than 300 times, and fulfilled over 450 mission requests get nothing? Is it apathy or just incompetence? I don't know and I really don't care, but what I do know is that it is an affront to the memory of those who fought and died with this unit that it is not justly recognized.

It is a symptom of the problem with awards that is Army wide. A person decides that getting someone or a unit an award is either too difficult to do, or they simply don't care. There is no accountability. Perhaps our military education system would benefit from a little more education about the value and place for awards and decorations and how they relate to history and esprit de corps, and should spend a little less time on commanders' sensing sessions, and reflective PT belts.

Unfortunately, a lot of soldiers who went above and beyond the call of duty haven't been adequately recognized by the Army or their nation for the outstanding manner in which they went about their duty. They didn't do these things for recognition or awards, but they damn well deserve them.

AFTERWORD

As I write this portion of the book fifteen years after the events I've just described, it is only human nature to think back on the things that happened, the billions of dollars that were spent, and the lives that were ruined or lost and ask if all of that was worth it. Certainly, a case has been made by some that all our efforts were in vain and were the result of outright lies and deceit by our national leadership. It would be easy for me and others who spent considerable time over there to become bitter and feel that we had been let down by those we trusted to make certain that the armed forces of the United States are not something to be used casually, and that our lives would be placed in harm's way only when it was absolutely necessary. Since I had almost no control over any of that when I was serving in the Army, I chose to concentrate on being ready to carry out my assigned tasks to the upmost of my abilities and to be there when it counted for my fellow soldiers. In that, for twenty-four-plus years I feel I was mostly successful. As for that deployment that began in 2006 and ended fifteen months later, I feel that the members of the 1st Battalion, 227th Aviation Regiment (First Attack), have nothing to hang our heads about. Our courage and aggressiveness were legendary. Most notably, the legacy of what was forged by those crews over and around Baghdad has been passed down to the next generation. It was never about us; it was always about the people we supported. We did whatever we could to protect them and make sure that they were able to return home safely. For that, I am proud of my fellow soldiers, and I always will be.

ATTACK!

APPENDIX A

"FIDDLERS' GREEN," "THE ARMY VALUES," "THE WARRIOR ETHOS"

The first printed appearance of the poem "Fiddlers' Green" was in a 1923 edition of the *Cavalry Journal*. The author is unknown. According to the article, the poem was inspired by a story told by a Capt. "Sammy" Pearson at a campfire in the Medicine Bow Mountains in Wyoming. The poem is used today to memorialize our cavalry brothers and sisters who have departed to the other side.

"FIDDLERS' GREEN"

Halfway down the trail to Hell,
In a shady meadow green
Are the Souls of all dead troopers camped,
Near a good old-time canteen.
And this eternal resting place
Is known as Fiddlers' Green.
Marching past, straight through to Hell
The Infantry are seen.
Accompanied by the Engineers,
Artillery and Marines,
For none but the shades of Cavalrymen
Dismount at Fiddlers' Green.
Though some go curving down the trail
To seek a warmer scene.
No trooper ever gets to Hell
Ere he's emptied his canteen.
And so rides back to drink again
With friends at Fiddlers' Green.
And so when man and horse go down
Beneath a saber keen,
Or in a roaring charge of fierce melee
You stop a bullet clean,
And the hostiles come to get your scalp,
Just empty your canteen,
And put your pistol to your head,
And go to Fiddlers' Green.

"THE ARMY VALUES"

Sometime in the 1990s, the United States Army decided that they would give every soldier a card that featured the "Army Values." At the time I can vividly remember that I felt quite insulted, because when I read the card, I felt I already had these values, and I certainly didn't need a stinking card to tell me that I should have something that I had even before I came into the Army.

Upon further review, I still feel I don't need the stinking card, but I suppose it isn't a bad thing to present at basic training to let NEW soldiers know just what is expected of them. Additionally, after thinking about it for a while, it's probably not a bad idea for some OLD soldiers to review as well.

Loyalty

Bear true faith and allegiance to the US Constitution, the Army, your unit, and other Soldiers. Bearing true faith and allegiance is a matter of believing in and devoting yourself to something or someone. A loyal Soldier is one who supports the leadership and stands up for fellow Soldiers. By wearing the uniform of the US Army you are expressing your loyalty. And by doing your share, you show your loyalty to your unit.

Duty

Fulfill your obligations. Doing your duty means more than carrying out your assigned tasks. Duty means being able to accomplish tasks as part of a team. The work of the US Army is a complex combination of missions, tasks, and responsibilities—all in constant motion. Our work entails building one assignment onto another. You fulfill your obligations as a part of your unit every time you resist the temptation to take "shortcuts" that might undermine the integrity of the final product.

Respect

Treat people as they should be treated. In the Soldier's Code, we pledge to "treat others with dignity and respect while expecting others to do the same." Respect is what allows us to appreciate the best in other people. Respect is trusting that all people have done their jobs and fulfilled their duty. And self-respect is a vital ingredient with the Army value of respect, which results from knowing you have put forth your best effort. The Army is one team and each of us has something to contribute.

Selfless Service

Put the welfare of the nation, the Army, and your subordinates before your own. Selfless service is larger than just one person. In serving your country, you are doing your duty loyally without thought of recognition or gain. The basic building block of selfless service is the commitment of each team member to go a little further, endure a little longer, and look a little closer to see how he or she can add to the effort.

Honor
Live up to Army values. The nation's highest military award is the Medal of Honor. This award goes to Soldiers who make honor a matter of daily living—Soldiers who develop the habit of being honorable and solidify that habit with every value choice they make. Honor is a matter of carrying out, acting, and living the values of respect, duty, loyalty, selfless service, integrity, and personal courage in everything you do.

Integrity
Do what's right, legally and morally. Integrity is a quality you develop by adhering to moral principles. It requires that you do and say nothing that deceives others. As your integrity grows, so does the trust others place in you. The more choices you make based on integrity, the more this highly prized value will affect your relationships with family and friends, and, finally, the fundamental acceptance of yourself.

Personal Courage
Face fear, danger, or adversity (physical or moral). Personal courage has long been associated with our Army. With physical courage, it is a matter of enduring physical duress and at times risking personal safety. Facing moral fear or adversity may be a long, slow process of continuing forward on the right path, especially if taking those actions is not popular with others. You can build your personal courage by daily standing up for and acting upon the things that you know are honorable.

"THE WARRIOR ETHOS"

I will always place the mission first.
I will never accept defeat.
I will never quit.
I will never leave a fallen comrade.

APPENDIX B

15-6 REPORTS

TABLE OF CONTENTS

Memorandum – Subject: Legal Review of AR 15-6 Investigation into Conditions Surrounding the Possible Death of Two Reuters Reporters during an Engagement on 12 July 2007 by Crazyhorse 18 and 19 in the New Baghdad District of Baghdad, Iraq (Zone 30); dated 20 July 2007

Memorandum – Subject: Appointment as Investigating Officer under AR 15-6; dated 13 July 2007

Memorandum – Subject: Findings and Recommendations Pursuant to AR 15-6 Investigation into Conditions Surrounding the Possible Death of Two Reuters Reporters during an Engagement on 12 July 2007 by Crazyhorse 18 and 19 in the New Baghdad District of Baghdad, Iraq (Zone 30); dated 19 July 2007

DA Form 1574 – Report of Proceedings by Investigating Officer/Board of Officers

Exhibit A – Sworn Statements

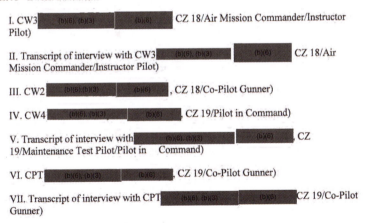

1ACB_ENGAGEMENT (REUTERS)_12 JUL 07

TABLE OF CONTENTS

1ACB_ENGAGEMENT (REUTERS)_12 JUL 07

CRAZYHORSE

REPLY TO
ATTENTION OF

AFVA-1ACB-JA

20 July 2007

MEMORANDUM FOR Commander, Headquarters and Headquarters Company, 1st Air Cavalry Brigade, 1st Cavalry Division, Camp Taji, Iraq APO AE 09378

SUBJECT: Legal Review, AR 15-6 Investigation, Finding and Recommendations of the Conditions Surrounding the Possible Death of Two Reuters Reporters during an Engagement on 12 July 2007 by Crazyhorse 18 and 19, 1st Battalion, 227th Aviation Regiment, in the New Baghdad District of Baghdad, Iraq (Zone 30).

1. In accordance with AR 15-6, paragraph 2-3, I have reviewed the AR 15-6 investigation into the Finding and Recommendations of the Conditions Surrounding the Possible Death of Two Reuters Reporters during an Engagement on 12 July 2007 by Crazyhorse 18 and 19, 1st Battalion, 227th Aviation Regiment, in the New Baghdad District of Baghdad, Iraq (Zone 30), investigated by LTC ██████ (b)(6), (b)(3) ██████, Headquarters and Headquarters Company, 1st Air Cavalry Brigade, 1st Cavalry Division. I make the following determinations:

    a. The proceedings comply with legal requirements.

    b. Errors in the proceedings, if any, do not have a material adverse effect on any individual's substantial rights.

    c. Sufficient evidence supports the findings.

    d. The recommendations are consistent with the findings.

2. The investigation is legally sufficient. The approval authority for the investigation is the Commanding General.

3. The point of contact is the undersigned at VOIP ████ (b)(6) ████

CPT, JA
Command Judge Advocate

DEPARTMENT OF THE ARMY
Headquarters, 1st Air Cavalry Brigade
Multi-National Division (Baghdad)
APO AE 09378

AFVA-1ACB-ADJ   13 July 2007

MEMORANDUM FOR LTC ░(b)(6), (b)(3)░ HHC, 1st Air Cavalry Brigade, Multi-National
Division (Baghdad), APO AE 09378

SUBJECT: Appointment as 15-6 Investigating Officer

1. You are appointed as an Investigating Officer pursuant to AR 15-6, in order to conduct an
informal investigation into the conditions surrounding the possible death of two Reuters reporters
during an engagement on 12 July 2007 by 1-227th ARB aircraft, Crazy horse 18 and 19, in the
New Baghdad district of Baghdad, Iraq (Zone 30).

2. Conduct your investigation using the informal procedures contained in AR 15-6. You must
obtain sworn statements from all witnesses.

3. Contact the Office of the Command Judge Advocate, CPT ░(b)(6), (b)(3)░ at VOIP ░(b)(6)░
before beginning your investigation.

4. Submit your findings and recommendations in memorandum format to COL ░(b)(6), (b)(3)░ no later
than 23 July 2007.

5. POC for this memorandum is the undersigned at VOIP ░(b)(6)░

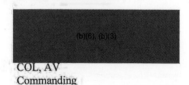

COL, AV
Commanding

1ACB_ENGAGEMENT (REUTERS)_12 JUL 07

For use of this form, see AR 15-6; the proponent agency is OTJAG.

IF MORE SPACE IS REQUIRED IN FILLING OUT ANY PORTION OF THIS FORM, ATTACH ADDITIONAL SHEETS

SECTION I - APPOINTMENT

Appointed by _____ (b)(6), (b)(3) COL, AV, Commanding _____
(Appointing authority)

on ___13 July 2007___ *(Attach inclosure 1: Letter of appointment or summary of oral appointment data.) (See para 3-15, AR 15-6.)*
(Date)

SECTION II - SESSIONS

The *(investigation) (board)* commenced at ___Forward Operating Base (FOB) Taji, Taji, Iraq___ at ___2000 hours___
(Place) *(Time)*

on ___13 July 2007___ *(If a formal board met for more than one session, check here [ ]. Indicate in an inclosure the time each session began and*
(Date)
ended, the place, persons present and absent, and explanation of absences, if any.)* The following persons *(members, respondents, counsel)* were
present: *(After each name, indicate capacity, e.g., President, Recorder, Member, Legal Advisor.)*

The following persons *(members, respondents, counsel)* were absent: *(Include brief explanation of each absence.) (See paras 5-2 and 5-8a, AR 15-6.)*

The *(investigating officer) (board)* finished gathering/hearing evidence at ___1720 hours___ on ___18 July 2007___
(Time) *(Date)*

and completed findings and recommendations at ___2300 hours___ on ___19 July 2007___
(Time) *(Date)*

SECTION III - CHECKLIST FOR PROCEEDINGS

A. COMPLETE IN ALL CASES	YES	NO 1/	NA 2/
Inclosures *(para 3-15, AR 15-6)*			
Are the following inclosed and numbered consecutively with Roman numerals: *(Attached in order listed)*			
a. The letter of appointment or a summary of oral appointment data?	X		
b. Copy of notice to respondent, if any?*(See item 9, below)*			X
c. Other correspondence with respondent or counsel, if any?			X
d. All other written communications to or from the appointing authority?			X
e. Privacy Act Statements *(Certificate, if statement provided orally)?*			X
f. Explanation by the investigating officer or board of any unusual delays, difficulties, irregularities, or other problems encountered *(e.g., absence of material witnesses)?*			X
g. Information as to sessions of a formal board not included on page 1 of this report?			X
h. Any other significant papers *(other than evidence)* relating to administrative aspects of the investigation or board?			X

FOOTNOTES: 1/ *Explain all negative answers on an attached sheet.*
2/ *Use of the N/A column constitutes a positive representation that the circumstances described in the question did not occur in this investigation or board.*

DA FORM 1574, MAR 1983   EDITION OF NOV 77 IS OBSOLETE.   Page 1 of 4 pages   APD PE v1.30

1ACB_ENGAGEMENT (REUTERS)_12 JUL 07

		YES	NO.1/	NA
2	Exhibits *(para 3-16, AR 15-6)*			
	a. Are all items offered *(whether or not received)* or considered as evidence individually numbered or lettered as exhibits and attached to this report?	X		
	b. Is an index of all exhibits offered to or considered by investigating officer or board attached before the first exhibit?	X		
	c. Has the testimony/statement of each witness been recorded verbatim or been reduced to written form and attached as an exhibit?	X		
	d. Are copies, descriptions, or depictions *(if substituted for real or documentary evidence)* properly authenticated and is the location of the original evidence indicated?	X		
	e. Are descriptions or diagrams included of locations visited by the investigating officer or board *(para 3-6b, AR 15-6)?*	X		
	f. Is each written stipulation attached as an exhibit and is each oral stipulation either reduced to writing and made an exhibit or recorded in a verbatim record?			X
	g. If official notice of any matter was taken over the objection of a respondent or counsel, is a statement of the matter of which official notice was taken attached as an exhibit *(para 3-16d, AR 15-6)?*			X
3	Was a quorum present when the board voted on findings and recommendations *(paras 4-1 and 5-2b, AR 15-6)?*			X
B.	**COMPLETE ONLY FOR FORMAL BOARD PROCEEDINGS** *(Chapter 5, AR 15-6)*			
4	At the initial session, did the recorder read, or determine that all participants had read, the letter of appointment *(para 5-3b, AR 15-6)?*			
5	Was a quorum present at every session of the board *(para 5-2b, AR 15-6)?*			
6	Was each absence of any member properly excused *(para 5-2a, AR 15-6)?*			
7	Were members, witnesses, reporter, and interpreter sworn, if required *(para 3-1, AR 15-6)?*			
8	If any members who voted on findings or recommendations were not present when the board received some evidence, does the inclosure describe how they familiarized themselves with that evidence *(para 5-2d, AR 15-6)?*			
C.	**COMPLETE ONLY IF RESPONDENT WAS DESIGNATED** *(Section II, Chapter 5, AR 15-6)*			
9	Notice to respondents *(para 5-5, AR 15-6):*			
	a. Is the method and date of delivery to the respondent indicated on each letter of notification?			
	b. Was the date of delivery at least five working days prior to the first session of the board?			
	c. Does each letter of notification indicate —			
	(1) the date, hour, and place of the first session of the board concerning that respondent?			
	(2) the matter to be investigated, including specific allegations against the respondent, if any?			
	(3) the respondent's rights with regard to counsel?			
	(4) the name and address of each witness expected to be called by the recorder?			
	(5) the respondent's rights to be present, present evidence, and call witnesses?			
	d. Was the respondent provided a copy of all unclassified documents in the case file?			
	e. If there were relevant classified materials, were the respondent and his counsel given access and an opportunity to examine them?			
10	If any respondent was designated after the proceedings began *(or otherwise was absent during part of the proceedings):*			
	a. Was he properly notified *(para 5-5, AR 15-6)?*			
	b. Was record of proceedings and evidence received in his absence made available for examination by him and his counsel *(para 5-4c, AR 15-6)?*			
11	Counsel *(para 5-6, AR 15-6):*			
	a. Was each respondent represented by counsel?			
	Name and business address of counsel:			
	(If counsel is a lawyer, check here [ ])			
	b. Was respondent's counsel present at all open sessions of the board relating to that respondent?			
	c. If military counsel was requested but not made available, is a copy *(or, if oral, a summary)* of the request and the action taken on it included in the report *(para 5-6b, AR 15-6)?*			
12	If the respondent challenged the legal advisor or any voting member for lack of impartiality *(para 5-7, AR 15-6):*			
	a. Was the challenge properly denied and by the appropriate officer?			
	b. Did each member successfully challenged cease to participate in the proceedings?			
13	Was the respondent given an opportunity to *(para 5-8a, AR 15-6):*			
	a. Be present with his counsel at all open sessions of the board which deal with any matter which concerns that respondent?			
	b. Examine and object to the introduction of real and documentary evidence, including written statements?			
	c. Object to the testimony of witnesses and cross-examine witnesses other than his own?			
	d. Call witnesses and otherwise introduce evidence?			
	e. Testify as a witness?			
	f. Make or have his counsel make a final statement or argument *(para 5-9, AR 15-6)?*			
14	If requested, did the recorder assist the respondent in obtaining evidence in possession of the Government and in arranging for the presence of witnesses *(para 5-8b, AR 15-6)?*			
15	Are all of the respondent's requests and objections which were denied indicated in the report of proceedings or in an inclosure or exhibit to it *(para 5-11, AR 15-6)?*			

FOOTNOTES: 1/ Explain all negative answers on an attached sheet.
2/ Use of the N/A column constitutes a positive representation that the circumstances described in the question did not occur in this investigation or board.

Page 2 of 4 pages, DA Form 1574, Mar 1983

APD PE v1.30

1ACB_ENGAGEMENT (REUTERS)_12 JUL 07

he *(investigating officer) (board)* , having carefully considered the evidence, finds:

ee Attached Memorandum, Findings and Recommendations to AR 15-6 Investigation into Conditions Surrounding the Possible Death of
wo Reuters Reporters during an Engagement on 12 July 2007 by Crazyhorse 18 and 19, 1st Battalion, 227th Aviation Regiment, in the
Jew Baghdad District of Baghdad, Iraq (Zone 30), dated 19 July 2007.

SECTION V - RECOMMENDATIONS   *(para 3-11, AR 15-6)*

n view of the above findings, the *(investigating officer) (board)* recommends:

See Attached Memorandum, Findings and Recommendations to AR 15-6 Investigation into Conditions Surrounding the Possible Death of
Two Reuters Reporters during an Engagement on 12 July 2007 by Crazyhorse 18 and 19, 1st Battalion, 227th Aviation Regiment, in the
New Baghdad District of Baghdad, Iraq (Zone 30), dated 19 July 2007.

HEADQUARTERS, 1ST AIR CAVALRY BRIGADE
MULTI-NATIONAL DIVISION (BAGHDAD)
CAMP TAJI, IRAQ, APO AE 09378

AFVA-1ACB-DBC   19 July 2007

MEMORANDUM FOR Commander, 1st Air Cavalry Brigade, 1st Cavalry Division (Multi-National Division – Baghdad), Camp Taji, Iraq, APO AE 09378

SUBJECT: Findings and Recommendations Pursuant to AR 15-6 Investigation into Conditions Surrounding the Possible Death of Two Reuters Reporters during an Engagement on 12 July 2007 by Crazyhorse 18 and 19 in the New Baghdad District of Baghdad, Iraq (Zone 30)

1. Purpose. The purpose of this memorandum is to outline findings and recommendations pursuant to the aforementioned investigation with emphasis on decision making between aircrew members and communications between the attack weapons team (AWT) and the 2-2 ID (Strike) unit in contact.

2. Summary.

   a. On 12 July 2007, the AWT, call sign Crazyhorse 18 and 19, began their mission window at 0630 hours. Tasked to conduct escort, armed reconnaissance patrols, counter-IED and counter mortar operations over Baghdad from 0930 through 1330 hours, the team departed Camp Taji at 0924 hours and began conducting task in accordance with their planned scheme of maneuver. After escorting a team of UH-60s to COP Callahan and harmonizing their 30mm cannons in Zone 101, the AWT was redirected to support troops in contact in Baghdad Security Zone 30. Soldiers from 2-16 IN were conducting operations in support of OPERATION ILAAJ (CURE) in the Mualameen Muhallah of Tisa Nisan District, East Baghdad. At 0953 hours, the AWT arrived on station and began operations in support of B/1-26 IN.

   b. Upon arriving on station, sporadic attacks on friendly forces continued. The AWT conducted local security operations and initiated a reconnaissance effort to find, report, and destroy hostile forces engaging our brothers on the ground. At 1019 hours, Crazyhorse 19 (trail aircraft) identified personnel with weapons (AK-47s and a RPG), both held and slung over the shoulder, in the vicinity of an open area East of the friendly unit's position and approximately one city block away. Having positively identified personnel with weapons, the AWT initiated an engagement sequence.

   c. Maintaining contact with the threat and knowledgeable of friendly locations, the AWT maneuvered to engage. On the downwind leg of a racetrack pattern, Crazyhorse 18's copilot/gunner (lead aircraft – front seat) perceived an escalation of the immediate threat to our ground troops after observing an individual peering around a building, preparing to fire an RPG at a friendly HMMWV positioned at the end of the block. Crazyhorse 18's pilot (lead aircraft – back seat) viewed the copilot/gunner's TADS imagery and confirmed his assessment after quickly looking outside the aircraft and acquiring the threat without optics. Seconds later,

AFVA-1ACB-DBC
SUBJECT: Findings and Recommendations Pursuant to AR 15-6 Investigation into Conditions Surrounding the Possible Death of Two Reuters Reporters during an Engagement on 12 July 2007 by Crazyhorse 18 and 19 in the New Baghdad District of Baghdad, Iraq (Zone 30)

Crazyhorse 19 (trail aircraft) observed the same individual. At this point, the individual was in a crouched, firing position with his weapon pointed towards friendly troops. Having observed a hostile act, the team continued to transition for the attack. At 1021 hours, the AWT engaged approximately 8 military-age-males eliminating the immediate threat to friendly ground forces less than 200 meters away.

d. Following the engagement, Crazyhorse 18 and 19 remained on station overwatching the engagement area and conducting reconnaissance along the ground patrol's ingress route. At 1026 hours and along with the ground patrol's entry into the engagement area, a black van arrived to retrieve one of the wounded insurgents. Crazyhorse 18 requested immediate clearance to engage the van, received it, and completely disabled the vehicle within seconds. The B/1-26 IN patrol continued to the engagement area to assess and exploit the scene and immediately established a cordon. The AWT remained on station conducting reconnaissance in search of insurgents still firing on friendly ground forces.

3. Findings.

a. *The AWT was on a directed mission; conducted the appropriate check-in with ground elements in contact; and received an adequate situation report describing the current status and disposition of forces on the ground.* At this point, the AWT began to develop the situation in concert with the ground element in contact and maintained positive identification of friendly locations throughout the supported period. As the situation developed, the AWT exercised sound judgment and discrimination during attempts to acquire insurgents, or moreover, to identify personnel engaged in hostile or threatening activities against our brothers on the ground.

b. *The AWT accurately assessed that the criteria to find and terminate the threat to friendly forces were met in accordance with the law of armed conflict and rules of engagement.* Fundamental to all engagements is the principle of military necessity. This was clearly established and supported by the friendly forces inherent right to self defense and the ground commander's obligation to ensure all necessary means were employed to defend or protect his Soldiers from hostile acts. In this case, the AWT was employed to destroy insurgents attempting to kill friendly forces. The attack weapons team:

(1). *Positively Identified the Treat:* The AWT, with reasonable certainty, identified military aged males both in a location and with weapons consistent with reports of hostile acts conducted against friendly forces. While observing this group of individuals, the AWT satisfied all requirements to initiate an engagement.

(2). *Established hostile intent:* Hostile intent was exhibited by armed insurgents peering around the corner of a home to monitor the movement or activities of friendly forces and

2

AFVA-1ACB-DBC
SUBJECT: Findings and Recommendations Pursuant to AR 15-6 Investigation into Conditions Surrounding the Possible Death of Two Reuters Reporters during an Engagement on 12 July 2007 by Crazyhorse 18 and 19 in the New Baghdad District of Baghdad, Iraq (Zone 30)

confirmed by the presence of those personnel carrying an RPG and AK-47s. These weapon systems were reported in the initial check-in as the type used to engage friendly forces.

(3). _Conducted collateral damage assessment:_ The AWT accurately assessed that using the 30mm cannon was proportionally appropriate to omit the threat while reducing the probability of excessive damage to surrounding structures, vehicles and real property in the area.

(4). _Received clearance of fires:_ Having already identified through voice communications, physical markings and ultimately visual recognition of friendly positions, the AWT again requested and received clearance from the ground unit that there were no friendly forces in the engagement area.

c. *Only after an extensive review of the AWT's gun-camera video and with knowledge of the two missing media personnel, is it reasonable to deduce that two of the individuals intermixed among the insurgents located in the engagement area may have been reporters.* There was neither reason nor probability to assume that neutral media personnel were embedded with enemy forces. It is worth noting the fact that insurgent groups often video and photograph friendly activity and insurgent attacks against friendly forces for use in training videos and for use as propaganda to exploit or highlight their capabilities. The aircrews erroneously identified the cameras as weapons due to presentation (slung over shoulder with the body of the object resting at the back, rear of the torso) and association (personnel colocated with others having RPGs and AK-47s).

4. Recommendations.

(b)(5)

3

AFVA-1ACB-DBC
SUBJECT: Findings and Recommendations Pursuant to AR 15-6 Investigation into Conditions Surrounding the Possible Death of Two Reuters Reporters during an Engagement on 12 July 2007 by Crazyhorse 18 and 19 in the New Baghdad District of Baghdad, Iraq (Zone 30)

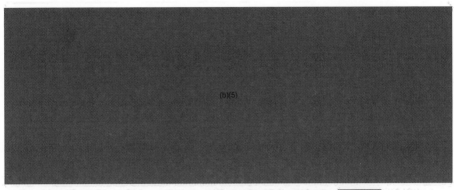

5. The point of contact for this investigation is the undersigned at: Phone – (b3)(b6) (SVOIP) or (b)(2) High DSN); email – (b)(2)High or

(b)(2)High

(b)(6), (b)(3)

LTC, AV
Deputy Brigade Commander

4

THIS REPORT OF PROCEEDINGS IS COMPLETE AND ACCURATE. *(If any voting member or the recorder fails to sign here or in Section VII below, indicate the reason in the space where his signature should appear.)*

(b)(3), (b)(6)

LTC   (b3)(b6)

_____   _____
        (Recorder)   (Investigating Officer) (President)

_____   _____
        (Member)   (Member)

_____   _____
        (Member)   (Member)

SECTION VII - MINORITY REPORT (para 3-13, AR 15-6)

To the extent indicated in inclosure _____ , the undersigned do(es) not concur in the findings and recommendations of the board.

(In the inclosure, identify by number each finding and/or recommendation in which the dissenting member(s) do(es) not concur. State the reasons for disagreement. Additional/substitute findings and/or recommendations may be included in the inclosure.)

_____   _____
        (Member)   (Member)

SECTION VIII - ACTION BY APPOINTING AUTHORITY (para 2-3, AR 15-6)

The findings and recommendations of the *(investigating officer)* ~~(board)~~ are *(approved)* ~~(disapproved)~~ ~~(approved with following exceptions/ substitutions)~~. *(If the appointing authority returns the proceedings to the investigating officer or board for further proceedings or corrective action, attach that correspondence (or a summary, if oral) as a numbered inclosure.)*

ACTION BY APPROVAL AUTHORITY:

I ratify the appointment of the investigating officer, LTC (b)(6), (b)(3)

I approve the "Summary" and "Findings."

The recommendation that:

-[1] 1ACB include this engagement in ROE training is (approved) ~~(disapproved)~~ (b)(6) (remanded to the Bde Cdr).

-[2] 1ACB enforce prohibitions on photographing aircraft is (~~approved~~) ~~(disapproved)~~ (b)(6) (remanded to the Bde Cdr).

-[3] 1ACB Master Gunner compile gun-camera footage for training purposes is (approved) ~~(disapproved)~~ (b)(6) ~~(remanded to the Bde Cdr)~~.

-[4] Reporters undergo "hazardous duty training" is ~~(approved)~~ (disapproved) (b)(6) ~~(remanded to the Bde Cdr)~~.

I remand the matter to the Bde Cdr for appropriate action.

VINCENT K. BROOKS
Brigadier General, USA   **21 JUL 2007**
Commanding

(b)(6), (b)(3)   Col 20 July 2007

COL   (b)(6), (b)(3)   Commanding

1ACB_ENGAGEMENT (REUTERS)_12 JUL 07

INVESTIGATION INTO CIVILIAN CASUALTIES RESULTING FROM AN ENGAGEMENT ON 12 JULY 2007 IN THE NEW BAGHDAD DISTRICT OF BAGHDAD, IRAQ

Report of Investigation UP AR 15-6
MAJ (b)(6), (b)(3) , Investigating Officer
2ND BRIGADE COMBAT TEAM
2ND INFANTRY DIVISION (MND-B)

2-2 ID_Civ Death in Cbt Ops (Reuters Employees) 12JUL07 IO MAJ (6), (b)(

DEPARTMENT OF THE ARMY
Headquarters, 2nd Brigade Combat Team
2nd Infantry Division (MND-B)
Forward Operating Base Loyalty, Baghdad, Iraq 09390

REPLY TO
ATTENTION OF

[JUL 1 7 2007

AFZC-B-CDR

MEMORANDUM FOR Commander, MND-B and 1st Cavalry Division

SUBJECT: Legal Review of AR 15-6 – Investigation into Civilian Casualties Resulting from an Engagement on 12 July 2007 in the New Baghdad District Of Baghdad, Iraq

I have reviewed the investigation and recommend you approve the findings and recommendations.

(b)(8),(b)(3)

COL, IN
Commanding

2-2 ID_Civ Death in Cbt Ops (Reuters Employees) 12JUL07 IO MAJ (b),(b)

TABLE OF CONTENTS

2-2 ID_Civ Death in Cbt Ops (Reuters Employees) 12JUL07 IO MAJ(6), (b)

DEPARTMENT OF THE ARMY
Headquarters, 2nd Brigade Combat Team
2nd Infantry Division (MND-B)
Forward Operating Base Loyalty, Baghdad, Iraq 09390

REPLY TO
ATTENTION OF

AFZC-B-JA

JUL 1 7 2007

MEMORANDUM FOR Commander, 2BCT/2ID (MND-B)

SUBJECT: Legal Review of AR 15-6 – Investigation into Civilian Casualties Resulting from an Engagement on 12 July 2007 in the New Baghdad District Of Baghdad, Iraq

1. In accordance with AR 15-6, paragraph 2-3, I reviewed the AR 15-6 investigation into the facts surrounding the death and injuries to apparent civilians resulting from the engagement by Apache helicopters on 12 July 2007 in the New Baghdad District of Baghdad, Iraq. This investigation complies with the Commanding General's directive to investigate the death or injury of apparent civilian non-combatants contained in FRAGO 352 to MNC-I OPORD 05-03 (17 Apr 06).

2. The investigation is legally sufficient. The investigation finds by a preponderance of evidence that affiliates of Reuters, Mr. Namir Noor-Eldeen and Mr. Saeed Chmagh, were killed and that two children were injured during the engagement. I make the following determinations:

   a. The proceedings comply with the legal requirements under AR 15-6 and contain no material errors or violate any individual's substantial rights.

   b. Sufficient evidence supports the findings.

   c. The recommendations are consistent with the findings.

3. The approval authority for the investigation is the Commanding General.

4. Point of contact for this legal review is the undersigned at ⬛⬛⬛⬛ (b)(6), (b)(3) or VOIP ⬛ (b)(6)

(b)(6), (b)(3)

(b)(6), (b MAJ, JA
Brigade Judge Advocate

2-2 ID_Civ Death in Cbt Ops (Reuters Employees) 12JUL07 IO MAJ (b)(6), (b)

DEPARTMENT OF THE ARMY
HEADQUARTERS, 2ND BRIGADE COMBAT TEAM
2ND INFANTRY DIVISION
MULTI-NATIONAL DIVISION–BAGHDAD
CAMP LOYALTY, IRAQ APO AE 09390

REPLY TO
ATTENTION OF:

AFZC-B-CDR

JUL 1 3 2007

MEMORANDUM FOR MAJ ████ (b)(6), (b)(3) ████ 2nd Brigade Combat Team, 2nd Infantry Division, Multi-National Division–Baghdad, FOB Loyalty, Iraq APO AE 09390

SUBJECT: Appointment as Investigating Officer under AR 15-6

1. You are hereby appointed as an Investigating Officer pursuant to *AR 15-6, Procedures for Investigating Officers and Boards of Officers*, to conduct an investigation into the facts and circumstances surrounding the civilian loss of life during a military engagement by the 1st Air Cavalry Brigade vicinity grid ████ (b)(2)High ████ on 12 July 2007.

2. You will investigate the injuries caused to any apparent civilian noncombatants resulting from the enemy engagement by aviation in the vicinity of Zone 30 in order to comply with FRAGO 352 to MNC-I OPORD 05-03 task 10 (17 Apr 06). Provide a brief narrative description of the events that occurred on or about 0950 hours 12 July 2007. You will limit the areas of your inquiry to—

   a. Describe the nature of the injuries of two local national children discovered by 2-16th Infantry Battalion. Make a recommendation whether any condolence or claims payment is warranted.

   b. Assess whether Mr. Namir Noor-Eldeen or Mr. Saeed Chmagh was killed during the hostile fire engagement based on all available evidence. Make a finding, if possible, as to their involvement in the engagement.

   c. Include in your investigation any photos or operational graphics that are relevant to your findings and recommendations.

3. Your legal advisor is MAJ ████ (b)(6), (b)(3) ████ 2nd Brigade Operational Law Team, VOIP ████ (b6) ████ who will give you an in-brief before you begin your investigation and be available to assist you during the investigation.

4. You may speak with any and all individuals that you believe have information pertinent to your investigation. You will obtain guidance from your legal advisor if in the course of your investigation you determine that completion thereof requires examining the conduct or performance of, or may result in Findings and Recommendations adverse to any person.

5. All witness statements will be sworn and, if possible, submitted on DA Form 2823. If circumstances preclude you from obtaining a sworn statement, or if you obtain a statement

2-2 ID_Civ Death in Cbt Ops (Reuters Employees) 12JUL07 IO MAJ ██(6), (b)██

AFZC-B-CDR
SUBJECT: Appointment as Investigating Officer under AR 15-6

telephonically or through an interpreter, you will summarize such a statement in a Memorandum for Record and swear to the accuracy of your summary.

6. Your report will be submitted to this office on DA Form 1574 together with all evidence marked as Exhibits, and an Index to said Exhibits. Your Findings must be based on the evidence you include as Exhibits and your Recommendations must be based on your Findings.

7. You are directed to begin your investigation upon receipt of these unsigned orders from your legal advisor. Your complete report will be submitted to this office no later than 19 July 2007. Requests for delays should be made to your legal advisor.

COL, IN
Commanding

2

REPORT OF PROCEEDINGS BY INVESTIGATING OFFICER/BOARD OF OFFICERS

For use of this form, see AR 15-6; the proponent agency is OTJAG.

IF MORE SPACE IS REQUIRED IN FILLING OUT ANY PORTION OF THIS FORM, ATTACH ADDITIONAL SHEETS

SECTION I - APPOINTMENT

Appointed by   (b)(6), (b)(3)   COL, IN, Commanding

(Appointing authority)

on   13 July 2007   *(Attach inclosure 1: Letter of appointment or summary of oral appointment data.) (See para 3-15, AR 15-6.)*

(Date)

SECTION II - SESSIONS

The *(investigation) (board)* commenced at FOB RUSTAMIYAH, Baghdad, Iraq   at   2000

(Place)   *(Time)*

on   13 July 2007   *(If a formal board met for more than one session, check here ☐. Indicate in an inclosure the time each session began and*

(Date)

ended, the place, persons present and absent, and explanation of absences, if any.) The following persons *(members, respondents, counsel)* were present: *(After each name, indicate capacity, e.g., President, Recorder, Member, Legal Advisor.)*

The following persons *(members, respondents, counsel)* were absent: *(Include brief explanation of each absence.) (See paras 5-2 and 5-8a, AR 15-6.)*

The *(investigating officer) (board)* finished gathering/hearing evidence at   2000   on   13 July 2007

(Time)   *(Date)*

and completed findings and recommendations at   2300   on   17 July 2007

(Time)   *(Date)*

SECTION III - CHECKLIST FOR PROCEEDINGS

A. COMPLETE IN ALL CASES	YES	NO[1]	NA[2]
1 Inclosures *(para 3-15, AR 15-6)*			
Are the following inclosed and numbered consecutively with Roman numerals: *(Attached in order listed)*			
a. The letter of appointment or a summary of oral appointment data?	☒		
b. Copy of notice to respondent, if any?*(See item 9, below)*			☒
c. Other correspondence with respondent or counsel, if any?			☒
d. All other written communications to or from the appointing authority?			☒
e. Privacy Act Statements *(Certificate, if statement provided orally)?*			☒
f. Explanation by the investigating officer or board of any unusual delays, difficulties, irregularities, or other problems encountered *(e.g., absence of material witnesses)?*			☒
g. Information as to sessions of a formal board not included on page 1 of this report?			☒
h. Any other significant papers *(other than evidence)* relating to administrative aspects of the investigation or board?			☒

FOOTNOTES: 1/ *Explain all negative answers on an attached sheet.*
2/ *Use of the N/A column constitutes a positive representation that the circumstances described in the question did not occur in this investigation or board.*

DA FORM 1574, MAR 1983   EDITION OF NOV 77 IS OBSOLETE.   Page 1 of 4 pages   APD PE v1.20

2-2 ID_Civ Death in Cbt Ops (Reuters Employees) 12JUL07 IO MAJ (b), (b)

		YES	NO[1]	NA[2]
2	Exhibits *(para 3-16, AR 15-6)*			
	a. Are all items offered *(whether or not received)* or considered as evidence individually numbered or lettered as exhibits and attached to this report?	☒	☐	☐
	b. Is an index of all exhibits offered to or considered by investigating officer or board attached before the first exhibit?	☒	☐	☐
	c. Has the testimony/statement of each witness been recorded verbatim or been reduced to written form and attached as an exhibit?	☒	☐	☐
	d. Are copies, descriptions, or depictions *(if substituted for real or documentary evidence)* properly authenticated and is the location of the original evidence indicated?	☒	☐	☐
	e. Are descriptions or diagrams included of locations visited by the investigating officer or board *(para 3-6b, AR 15-6)?*	☒	☐	☒
	f. Is each written stipulation attached as an exhibit and is each oral stipulation either reduced to writing and made an exhibit or recorded in a verbatim record?	☐	☐	☒
	g. If official notice of any matter was taken over the objection of a respondent or counsel, is a statement of the matter of which official notice was taken attached as an exhibit *(para 3-16d, AR 15-6)?*	☐	☐	☒
3	Was a quorum present when the board voted on findings and recommendations *(paras 4-1 and 5-2b, AR 15-6)?*	☐	☐	☒
B.	COMPLETE ONLY FOR FORMAL BOARD PROCEEDINGS *(Chapter 5, AR 15-6)*			
4	At the initial session, did the recorder read, or determine that all participants had read, the letter of appointment *(para 5-3b, AR 15-6)?*	☐	☐	
5	Was a quorum present at every session of the board *(para 5-2b, AR 15-6)?*	☐	☐	
6	Was each absence of any member properly excused *(para 5-2a, AR 15-6)?*	☐	☐	
7	Were members, witnesses, reporter, and interpreter sworn, if required *(para 3-1, AR 15-6)?*	☐	☐	
8	If any members who voted on findings or recommendations were not present when the board received some evidence, does the inclosure describe how they familiarized themselves with that evidence *(para 5-2d, AR 15-6)?*	☐	☐	
C.	COMPLETE ONLY IF RESPONDENT WAS DESIGNATED *(Section II, Chapter 5, AR 15-6)*			
9	Notice to respondents *(para 5-5, AR 15-6)*:			
	a. Is the method and date of delivery to the respondent indicated on each letter of notification?	☐	☐	
	b. Was the date of delivery at least five working days prior to the first session of the board?	☐	☐	
	c. Does each letter of notification indicate —			
	(1) the date, hour, and place of the first session of the board concerning that respondent?	☐	☐	
	(2) the matter to be investigated, including specific allegations against the respondent, if any?	☐	☐	
	(3) the respondent's rights with regard to counsel?	☐	☐	
	(4) the name and address of each witness expected to be called by the recorder?	☐	☐	
	(5) the respondent's rights to be present, present evidence, and call witnesses?	☐	☐	
	d. Was the respondent provided a copy of all unclassified documents in the case file?	☐	☐	
	e. If there were relevant classified materials, were the respondent and his counsel given access and an opportunity to examine them?	☐	☐	☐
10	If any respondent was designated after the proceedings began *(or otherwise was absent during part of the proceedings)*:			
	a. Was he properly notified *(para 5-5, AR 15-6)?*	☐	☐	
	b. Was record of proceedings and evidence received in his absence made available for examination by him and his counsel *(para 5-4c, AR 15-6)?*	☐	☐	
11	Counsel *(para 5-6, AR 15-6)*:			
	a. Was each respondent represented by counsel?	☐	☐	
	Name and business address of counsel:			
	(If counsel is a lawyer, check here ☐)			
	b. Was respondent's counsel present at all open sessions of the board relating to that respondent?	☐	☐	
	c. If military counsel was requested but not made available, is a copy *(or, if oral, a summary)* of the request and the action taken on it included in the report *(para 5-6b, AR 15-6)?*	☐	☐	☐
12	If the respondent challenged the legal advisor or any voting member for lack of impartiality *(para 5-7, AR 15-6)*:			
	a. Was the challenge properly denied and by the appropriate officer?	☐	☐	☐
	b. Did each member successfully challenged cease to participate in the proceedings?	☐	☐	☐
13	Was the respondent given an opportunity to *(para 5-8a, AR 15-6)*:			
	a. Be present with his counsel at all open sessions of the board which deal with any matter which concerns that respondent?	☐	☐	
	b. Examine and object to the introduction of real and documentary evidence, including written statements?	☐	☐	
	c. Object to the testimony of witnesses and cross-examine witnesses other than his own?	☐	☐	
	d. Call witnesses and otherwise introduce evidence?	☐	☐	
	e. Testify as a witness?	☐	☐	
	f. Make or have his counsel make a final statement or argument *(para 5-9, AR 15-6)?*	☐	☐	
14	If requested, did the recorder assist the respondent in obtaining evidence in possession of the Government and in arranging for the presence of witnesses *(para 5-8b, AR 15-6)?*	☐	☐	☐
15	Are all of the respondent's requests and objections which were denied indicated in the report of proceedings or in an inclosure or exhibit to it *(para 5-11, AR 15-6)?*	☐	☐	☐

FOOTNOTES: 1/ Explain all negative answers on an attached sheet.
2/ Use of the N/A column constitutes a positive representation that the circumstances described in the question did not occur in this investigation or board.

APD PE v1.2

2-2 ID_Civ Death in Cbt Ops (Reuters Employees) 12JUL07 IO MAJ (6), (b)

CRAZYHORSE

The *(investigating officer) (board)* , having carefully considered the evidence, finds:

See attached memorandum.

In view of the above findings, the *(investigating officer) (board)* recommends:

See attached memorandum.

2-2 ID_Civ Death in Cbt Ops (Reuters Employees) 12JUL07 IO MAJ (b), (b)

THIS REPORT OF PROCEEDINGS IS COMPLETE AND ACCURATE. *(If any voting member or the recorder fails to sign here or in Section VII below, indicate the reason in the space where his signature should appear.)*

(b)(6), (b)(3) (b)(6), (b)(3)

MAJ (b)(6), (b)(3)

_____   _____
(Recorder)   *(Investigating Officer) (President)*

_____   _____
(Member)   *(Member)*

_____   _____
(Member)   *(Member)*

SECTION VII - MINORITY REPORT   *(para 3-13, AR 15-6)*

To the extent indicated in Inclosure _____ , the undersigned do(es) not concur in the findings and recommendations of the board.

(In the inclosure, identify by number each finding and/or recommendation in which the dissenting member(s) do(es) not concur. State the reasons for disagreement. Additional/substitute findings and/or recommendations may be included in the inclosure.)

_____   _____
(Member)   *(Member)*

APPROVAL

SECTION VIII - ACTION BY APPOINTING AUTHORITY   *(para 2-3, AR 15-6)*

The findings and recommendations of the *(investigating officer) (board)* are *(approved) (disapproved) (approved with following exceptions/ substitutions)*. *(If the appointing authority returns the proceedings to the investigating officer or board for further proceedings or corrective action, attach that correspondence (or a summary, if oral) as a numbered inclosure.)*

I ratify the appointment of the investigating officer, MAJ (6), (b)(

The recommendation that:

-(10a) Members of the press be encouraged or required to wear identifying vests or distinctive body armor within the MND-B AOR is (approved) (disapproved) (remanded to the BCT Cdr).

-(10b) Coalition Forces be notified when members of the press are operating in their AORs is (approved) (disapproved) (remanded to the BCT Cdr).

-(10c) Condolence payments be made to families of the two children wounded in this engagement is (approved) (disapproved) (remanded to the BCT Cdr).

I remand the matter to the 2/2ID Cdr for appropriate action.

VINCENT K. BROOKS
Brigadier General, USA
Deputy Commanding General(Maneuver)

2-2 ID_Civ Death in Cbt Ops (Reuters Employees) 12JUL07 IO MAJ

DEPARTMENT OF THE ARMY
HEADQUARTERS, 2D BRIGADE COMBAT TEAM (2ID)
MULTINATIONAL DIVISION--BAGHDAD
FOB LOYALTY, IRAQ APO AE 09390

REPLY TO
ATTENTION OF

AFZC-B-IO   17 July 2007

MEMORANDUM FOR Commander, 2nd Infantry Brigade Combat Team, 2nd Infantry Division
(MND-B), Baghdad, Iraq

SUBJECT: 15-6 Investigation of Civilian Casualties Resulting from an Engagement on 12 July
2007 in the New Baghdad District of Baghdad, Iraq

1. The purpose of this memorandum is to detail the findings and recommendations of my 15-6
investigation into the presence of noncombatants during an engagement that occurred on the
morning of 12 July, 2007 in Zone 30, Mualameen Muhallah, of Tisa Nisan District, East
Baghdad, as part of OPERATION ILAAJ (CURE).

2. The appointing authority (Colonel ████ (b)(6), (b)(3) ████ 2BCT Commander) directed me to issue
findings and recommendations covering the following areas of inquiry:

   a. Describe the nature of the injuries of two local national children discovered by 2-16th
Infantry Battalion. Make a recommendation whether any condolence or claims payment is
warranted.

   b. Assess whether Mr. Namir Noor-Eldeen or Mr. Saeed Chmagh (Employees of Reuters
News Corporation), were killed during the hostile fire engagement based on all available
evidence.

   c. Assess any relevant issues, including the use of force, by members of 2nd Brigade Combat
Team. If you come into any evidence concerning the conduct of other individuals, refer the
matter to your legal advisor.

3. I began the investigation by contacting MAJ ██(b)(6), (b)(3)██(2-16 IN S3) and arranging to interview
the Bravo Company, 2-16 Infantry soldiers who first arrived at the scene at the engagement after
the helicopter engagment. Once these interviews were completed, I reviewed the gun-camera
tapes from the 1st Cavalry Division's Apache Helicopters that were in direct support of the
ground maneuver elements for OPERATION ILAAJ, the clearance of Zone 30 in the
Mualameen Muhallah of Tisa Nisan (New Baghdad).

4. From the witness statements and the Apache gun-camera film (Screen Print Exhibit A), I
determined that the engagement in which the Iraqi children were injured and the two Reuters
News employees were killed began at 1020 hours (local Baghdad time, Zulu +4), at grid
coordinates ████ (b)(2)High ████. The Bravo Company 2-16 soldiers were within 100 meters of
the location of a group of armed insurgents and two individuals carrying cameras when Apache
helicopters engaged the insurgents with 30mm gunfire. The engagement concluded with the
evacuation of casualties at 1041 hours.

2-2 ID_Civ Death in Cbt Ops (Reuters Employees) 12JUL07 IO MAJ██(6), (b)██

5. Bravo Company 2-16 Infantry had been under sporadic small arms and rocket-propelled grenade fire since OPERATION ILAAJ began at dawn on the morning of the 12th of July. The company had the mission of clearing their sector and looking for weapons caches. Two Apache helicopters from the 1st Cavalry Division's Aviation Brigade (call signs "Crazyhorse 18" and "Crazyhorse 19") were in direct support to the ground maneuver force and were monitoring the Bravo Company radio frequency.

6. The following sequence of events is derived from a review of the gun-camera film. The gun camera film was a video burned onto a compact disc which I received from my legal advisor. The video provided me an accurate timeline of events and allowed me to corroborate or deny other eye witness testimony received into evidence. However, it must be noted that details which are readily apparent when viewed on a large video monitor are not necessarily apparent to the Apache pilots during a live-fire engagement. First of all, the pilots are viewing the scene on a much smaller screen than I had for my review. Secondly, a pilot's primary concern is with flying his helicopter and the safety of his aircraft. Third, the pilots are continuously tracking the movement of friendly forces in order to prevent fratricide. Fourth, since Bravo Company had been in near continuous contact since dawn, the pilots were looking primarily for armed insurgents. Lastly, there was no information leading anyone to believe or even suspect that noncombatants were in the area. Although useful, an analysis of the engagement captured on the video is beyond the scope of my investigation and the subject of a collateral investigation. The digits appearing before the exhibit are the time derived from the Apache video footage. 0619:37 is 0600 hours, 19 minutes, and 37 seconds, Greenwich Mean or ZULU Time. Baghdad local time is 4 hours later.

a. 0619:37 Z (Exhibit A Photo). As the Apaches orbit counterclockwise, eleven military-aged males dressed in Western-style pants and shirts, are seen walking northward toward a wall vic ▮▮▮(b)(2)High▮▮▮ Two individuals can be seen carrying cameras with large telephoto lenses slung from their right shoulders. While two other males can be seen carrying an RPG launcher and an AKM. The cameras could be easily mistaken for slung AK-47 or AKM rifles, especially since neither cameraman is wearing anything that identifies him as media or press.

b. 0620:07 Z (Exhibit B Photo). Two individuals are seen openly displaying an RPG and an AKM, while a third individual carries what appears to be an RPG round. The rest of the military-aged males are obscured by the building in the foreground.

c. 0620:34 Z (Exhibit C Photo). One of the cameramen is seen peering from behind the wall looking west toward the approaching Bravo Company soldiers. The voice on the gun tape mistakenly identifies the long telephoto lens as an RPG.

d. 0620:38 Z (Exhibit D). The cameraman raises the camera to sight through the viewfinder and his action appears prompts one of the pilots to remark "He's getting ready to fire." Photos later recovered from the camera show a US Army HMMWV sitting at an intersection, less than 100 meters away from the camera. The digital time/date stamp on the photo indicates that these photos were the ones taken as the cameraman peered from behind the wall (Exhibit R). Due to the furtive nature of his movements, the cameraman gave every appearance of preparing to fire an RPG on US soldiers.

2

e. 0621:07 Z (Exhibit E Photo). As the Apache continues his orbit and clears the buildings he gains a clear view of the insurgents. Both cameramen are visible within a very tight circle of armed insurgents. An RPG launcher and an AKM are also visible at this point and all military-aged males are clustered within a two-meter radius. The Apache engages seconds later, apparently killing eight of the nine military-aged males.

f. 0626:03 Z (Exhibit F Photo). As ground forces approach the engagement area, A black van with white paint on the roof (erroneously reported as both a white van and a bongo truck) arrives. Two military-aged males and the vehicle's driver then attempt to load one of the wounded insurgents into the van. The Apache pilot requests permission to engage the van in order to prevent the escape of the insurgents. Bushmaster 7 responds "This is Bushmaster 7, Roger, engage." The Apaches engage disabling the van seconds later.

g. 0631:53 Z (Exhibit G Photo). The first elements of Bravo Company, 2-16 Infantry arrive on scene and begin to secure the area. They discover two RPGs and an AK-47 or AKM among the group of insurgents clustered near the wall. They also discovered two Canon EOS digital cameras with large telephoto lenses attached in the immediate vicinity of the bodies. The Soldiers gathered the two Canon digital cameras at the site as evidence for analysis. Two of the Military-aged males are still alive and the soldiers on scene render first aid and call for a medic.

h. 0639:44 Z (Exhibit H Photo). Bravo Company soldiers searching the van find an Iraqi girl approximately four years old with penetrating wounds to her torso, and evacuate her to FOB LOYALTY.

i. 0641:11 Z (Exhibit I Photo). Another Bravo Company soldier finds that an Iraqi male approximately eight years old is still alive after sustaining several penetrating wounds to various parts of his body, and evacuates that child as well. Both children were evacuated to FOB LOYALTY and then to 28th CSH on 12 July. Both children were then transferred to Medical City, an Iraqi controlled treatment facility, on 13 July 2007.

j. (Exhibits J-P Statements). As Bravo Company secured the scene, they continued to take small arms fire and were not able to conduct a detailed sensitive site exploitation of the engagement area. Pictures taken at the time (Exhibit P), reveal one of the digital cameras with a sand-colored telephoto lens attached as well as an AK/AKM and an additional RPG launcher with a loaded round still in it. The body lying closest to the camera had an RPG round underneath it (later destroyed by EOD). Not one of the soldiers present recalled seeing any indications of either media/press badges or photographers' vests to indicate that noncombatants were on scene. Bravo Company soldiers remained on scene until Iraqi Security Forces arrived to take charge of the bodies and weapons. The two digital cameras were turned in for analysis when Bravo Company elements returned to FOB RUSIMYAH later that afternoon.

k. By the late afternoon of 12 July, Iraqi Security Forces had recovered the press identification badges from the bodies of the Reuters employees and returned them to Reuters. I was unable to determine exactly where and when the identification was returned, and inquiries to Reuters have not yet been answered. By the afternoon of July 12th, Reuters was running the

3

2-2 ID_Civ Death in Cbt Ops (Reuters Employees) 12JUL07 IO MAJ ████

story that two of their personnel had been killed on assignment in Baghdad in an engagement with US Forces (Exhibit S).

7. The Document Exploitation Team at FOB RUSTIMYAH conducted an examination of the media cards in the cameras and extracted hundreds of photos from each. Of significance are photos of MG Lynch taken at a press conference on 24 June, 2007, indicating that the photographer had press credentials in order to gain access to the Coalition Press Information Center (CPIC), in Baghdad's Green Zone (Exhibit R). Additional photos from one of the Canon digital cameras recovered on site (see Exhibit Q) show a male who appears to be Namir Noor-Eldeen based on the fact he is wearing an identical shirt to the one shown in the Reuters article (Exhibit S).

8. Conclusions.

a. I have nothing which conclusively identifies the bodies of the two Reuters affiliates. The ground forces were still receiving small arms fire and did not have sufficient time or personnel to photograph or search the bodies for identification. Once Iraqi Security Forces arrived, that tasked was assumed by the Iraqi Police.

b. I know that two military-aged males are seen carrying cameras which match the description of the CANON EOS cameras carried by Mr. Noor-Aldeen. Those cameras were recovered at the scene by soldiers from Bravo Company 2-16 IN, and the images recovered from their media cards showed images consistent with professional photographers and images which appear to be of Mr. Noor Aldeen himself.

c. I conclude that the two Reuters affiliates were in the company of the armed insurgents who had been firing on members of Bravo Company, 2-16 Infantry, at the time of the engagement, as Bravo Company and Iraqi Security Forces attempted to clear Zone 30 as part of OPERATION ILAAJ on the morning of 12 July, 2007. The preponderance of the evidence leads me to conclude that Mr. Namir Noor-Eldeen and Mr. Saeed Chmagh were killed on 12 July during the engagement by Apache helicopters.

d. I conclude that the presence of the Reuters employees was not known to any of the US Forces operating in the area that morning. The cameramen made no effort to visibly display their status as press or media representatives and their familiar behavior with, and close proximity to, the armed insurgents and their furtive attempts to photograph the Coalition Ground Forces made them appear as hostile combatants to the Apaches that engaged them. Furthermore, the mere fact that two individuals carried cameras instead of weapons would not indicate that they were noncombatants as the enemy commonly employ cameramen to film and photograph their attacks on Coalition Forces.

9. As to the presence of the children in the black van, it is obvious from the radio transmissions on the gun-camera tapes that the Apache pilots thought the van was to be used as a means of escape for the wounded insurgents. The van arrives as if on cue, and is immediately joined by two military-aged males who appear from the nearby courtyard. The children are never seen, while the driver slides open a door and then retakes his seat while two other males attempt to

4

load the first insurgent into the vehicle. It is unknown what, if any, connection the van had to the insurgent activity.

10. Recommendations. My recommendations to reduce the likelihood of similar casualties in the future are as follows:

(b)(5)

11. POC for this investigation is the undersigned at VOIP phone (b)(2)High or SIPR email (b)(2)High

(b)(6), (b)(3)

MAJ, IO
Investigating Officer

5

2-2 ID_Civ Death in Cbt Ops (Reuters Employees) 12JUL07 IO MAJ (6), (b)

061937Z

A

Possible Cameras with telephoto lens

2-2 ID_Civ Death in Cbt Ops (Reuters Empl

7 IO MAJ

EX A

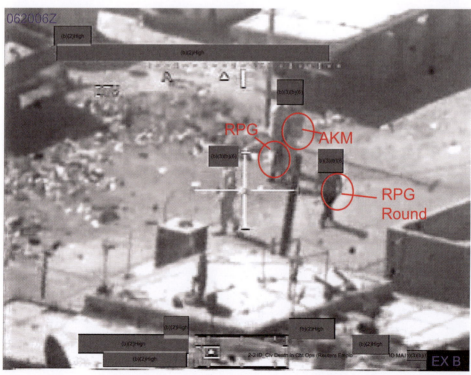

062006Z

RPG

AKM

RPG Round

2-2 ID_Civ Death in Cbt Ops (Reuters Emplo

IO MAJ

EX B

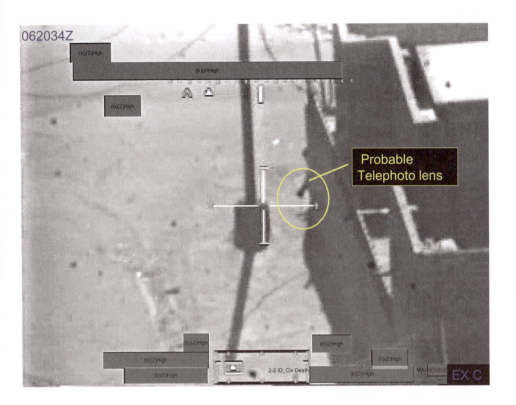

062034Z

(b)(2)High
(b)(2)High
(b)(2)High

Probable
Telephoto lens

2-2 ID_Civ Death

(b)(2)High
(b)(2)High
(b)(2)High
(b)(2)High
(b)(2)High
(b)(2)High
MAJ (b)(3)(b)(6)

EX C

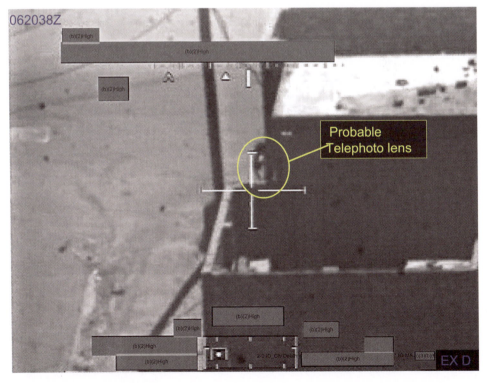

062038Z

(b)(2)High
(b)(2)High
(b)(2)High

Probable
Telephoto lens

(b)(2)High
(b)(2)High
(b)(2)High
(b)(2)High
(b)(2)High
2-2 ID_Civ Death
(b)(2)High
IO MAJ (b)(3)(b)(6)

EX D

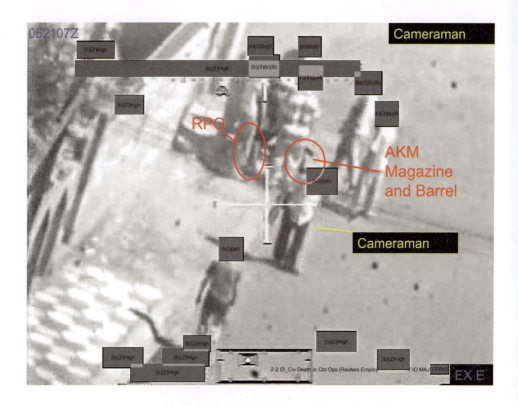

062107Z

(b)(2)High

(b)(3)(b)(6)   (b3)(b6)

(b)(2)High   (b)(3)(b)(6)

Cameraman

(b)(3)(b)(6)

(b)(3)(b)(6)

(b)(2)High

(b)(3)(b)(6)

RPG

AKM
Magazine
and Barrel

(b)(b6)

(b3)(b6)

Cameraman

(b)(2)High

(b)(2)High   (b)(2)High

(b)(2)High   (b)(2)High

(b)(2)High

2-2 ID_Civ Death in Cbt Ops (Reuters Employ   IO MAJ (3)(b)

EX E

062603Z

(b)(2)High

(b)(2)High

3 Military Aged Males,
including Driver

(b6)   (b6)

(b6)

(b)(3)(b)6

(3)(b)

(b)(3)(b6)

(b)(2)High

(b)(2)High

(b)(2)High   (b)(2)High

(b)(2)High

2-2 ID_Civ Death   IO MAJ (3)(b)

EX F

063153Z

(b)(2)High

First Bradley on scene

(b)(2)High

(b)(2)High

(b)(2)High

2-2 ID_Civ Death in Cbt Ops (Reuters Employ

EX G

063944Z

Soldier Carrying wounded Girl

(b)(2)High

(b)(2)High

(3)(b)

(3)(b)(

(b)(3)(b6)

(b)(3)(b)(6)

(b)(3)(b)6

(b)(2)High

(b)(2)High

(b)(2)High

(b)(2)High

(b)(2)High

2-2 ID_Civ Death in Cbt Ops (Reuters Empl

7 IO MA (x3)(b)6

EX H

SWORN STATEMENT

For use of this form, see AR 190-45; the proponent agency is PMG.

PRIVACY ACT STATEMENT

1. LOCATION	2. DATE *(YYYYMMDD)*	3. TIME	4. FILE NUMBER
AL AMIN , Baghdad, Ira	20070714	1103	

5. LAST NAME, FIRST NAME, MIDDLE NAME	6. SSN	7. GRADE/STATUS
(b)(6), (b)(3)	(b)(6), (b)(3)	O-3 /CPT

8. ORGANIZATION OR ADDRESS

B C 2-16 Id

9.

I, _____ (b)(6), (b)(3) _____ , WANT TO MAKE THE FOLLOWING STATEMENT UNDER OATH:

Question 1: What was your mission/orders on the morning of 12 July 2007? CLEAR AL AMIN OF AIF IN ZONE ASSIGNED IN ORDER TO ALLOW FREEDOM OF MANEUVER FOR CF.

Question 2: When you arrived at the scene of the Apache/van engagement ((b)(2)High), what did you observe? I observed multiple casualties, 11 total to include 2 wounded children and 2 wounded adults. THE FIRST 3 KIA were against the wall of a home with an RPG launcher, a wounded AIF had a RPG Round underneath him. Another was located in the road while another approximately 25 ft away was located in the trash pile. One individual was in the drivers seat of the van, both kids were in

Question 3: During what time period were you present at this location? the van, two other KIA were to the east of the van. A KIA and a wounded individuals were located in the courtyard of a home
At approximately 0930 until 1030/1100.

Question 4: What actions did you take while at this location? While at this objective I ensured that security on the roof tops were maintained at 360°. WE DID A BRIEF SSE AT THE SITE DUE TO THE FACT THAT ONE AIF MEMBER WAS LYING ON A RPG ROUND AND ALL INDIVIDUALS WERE ON THEIR STOMACHS. THE RISK OF BEING BOOBY TRAPPED WAS THE REASON FOR NOT TOUCHING THE BODIES. THOSE WHO WERE BREATHING I HAD MY MEDICS RENDER AID AND WE EVAC'D THE

Question 5: What significant events (if any) occurred at this location while you were present? CHILDREN IN THE BRADLEYS ATTACHED WHILE ON SITE WE WERE UNDER CONSTANT SMALL ARMS FIRE AND THE TWO ADULT MALES WERE EVAC'D FROM THE EAST. MEDICAL TREATMENT WAS RENDERED TO INJURED AIF. EOD BY MY COMPANY WHO TURNED THEM OVER BLEW UP RPG LAUNCHERS, RPG Rockets and AK47s. TO MP ON RTE PLUTES.

Question 6: Did you observe anyone (dead or wounded), that you believed to be a noncombatant? Why?
I observed the 2 children and believed them to be noncombatants. Ages of children were the reason why I believe this, they appear to be around 4 and 6 years of age.

(b)(6)

10. EXHIBIT	11. INITIALS OF PERSON MAKING STATEMENT	
J	(b)(6)	PAGE 1 OF 2 PAGES

ADDITIONAL PAGES MUST CONTAIN THE HEADING "STATEMENT OF _____ TAKEN AT _____ DATED _____

THE BOTTOM OF EACH ADDITIONAL PAGE MUST BEAR THE INITIALS OF THE PERSON MAKING THE STATEMENT, AND PAGE NUMBER MUST BE INDICATED.

DA FORM 2823, NOV 2006   DA FORM 2823, DEC 1998, IS OBSOLETE   APD PE v1.00

2-2 ID_Civ Death in Cbt Ops (Reuters Employees) 12JUL07 IO MAJ(b)(6), (b)(

9. STATEMENT   *(Continued)*

(b)(6)

Nothing Follows

AFFIDAVIT

I, _____ (b)(6), (b)(3) _____ , HAVE READ OR HAVE HAD READ TO ME THIS STATEMENT
WHICH BEGINS ON PAGE 1, AND ENDS ON PAGE __2__ . I FULLY UNDERSTAND THE CONTENTS OF THE ENTIRE STATEMENT MADE
BY ME. THE STATEMENT IS TRUE. I HAVE INITIALED ALL CORRECTIONS AND HAVE INITIALED THE BOTTOM OF EACH PAGE
CONTAINING THE STATEMENT. I HAVE MADE THIS STATEMENT FREELY WITHOUT HOPE OF BENEFIT OR REWARD, WITHOUT
THREAT OF PUNISHMENT, AND WITHOUT COERCION, UNLAWFUL INFLUENCE, OR UNLAWFUL INDUCEMENT.

(b)(6), (b)(3)   nt)

WITNESSES:)(6), (b)(scribed and sworn to before me, a person authorized by law to
                                    administer oaths, this __14__ day of _July_ . _2007_
_____   at _Buchland Iraq_
_____   (b)(6), (b)(3)
ORGANIZATION OR ADDRESS   _____ (Signature of Person Administering Oath)
_____   (b)(6), (b)(3)
_____   3)((Typed Name of Person Administering Oath)
ORGANIZATION OR ADDRESS   _UCMJ_
                                    (Authority To Administer Oaths)

INITIALS OF PERSON MAKING STATEMENT
         (b)(6)   PAGE 2 OF 2 PAGES

2-2 ID_Civ Death in Cbt Ops (Reuters Employees) 12JUL07 IO MAJ)(6), (b)(

1. LOCATION		2. DATE *(YYYYMMDD)*	3. TIME	4. FILE NUMBER
COP Bushmaster, Baghdad, Ir:		20070714	1030	

5. LAST NAME, FIRST NAME, MIDDLE NAME	6. SSN	7. GRADE/STATUS
(b)(6), (b)(3)	(b)(6), (b)(3)	1LT / O-2

8. ORGANIZATION OR ADDRESS

B Co 2-16 IN

9.

I, _____ (b)(6), (b)(3) _____, WANT TO MAKE THE FOLLOWING STATEMENT UNDER OATH:

Question 1: What was your mission/orders on the morning of 12 July 2007?

Clear OBJ Bronc and Silver North in order to allow freedom of maneuver for BN main effort.

Question 2: When you arrived at the scene of the Apache/van engagement ((b)(2)High), what did you observe?

my Plt arrived about 10 minutes after the Apache engaged. We saw 11 military aged males and two kids in the van. There where 3 males grouped together about 15 m north of the van. Near them was an RPG and two AK-47s.

Question 3: During what time period were you present at this location?

0950 - 1100

Question 4: What actions did you take while at this location?

Initially we cleared through the objective in order to secure it. When we moved by the van I saw the little girl and called my medic SPC (b)(6), (b)(3) to treat her. When we moved back through dismounted we saw the boy, who we initially thought was dead move and began to treat him. Both were moved into the BFV.

Question 5: What significant events (if any) occurred at this location while you were present?

Why 3-4 truck engaged one AIF carrying an RPG south of the OBJ. It is undetermined whether he hit the target, we also heard small arms to the east where Crazy Horse also engaged targets.

Question 6: Did you observe anyone (dead or wounded), that you believed to be a noncombatant? Why?

All of the males on the objective were all similarly dressed. All were wearing western style pants and shirts. I could not distinguish any of them specifically as a noncombatant when we arrived on the obj. The only non combatants were the two kids that we evacuated to FOB Loyalty for medical treatment.

(b)(6)

(b)(6)

(b)(6)

(b)(6)

10. EXHIBIT	11. INITIALS OF PERSON MAKING STATEMENT		
	(b)(6)	PAGE 1 OF 3 PAGES	

ADDITIONAL PAGES MUST CONTAIN THE HEADING "STATEMENT OF _____ TAKEN AT _____ DATED _____

THE BOTTOM OF EACH ADDITIONAL PAGE MUST BEAR THE INITIALS OF THE PERSON MAKING THE STATEMENT, AND PAGE NUMBER MUST BE INDICATED.

DA FORM 2823, NOV 2006   DA FORM 2823, DEC 1998, IS OBSOLETE   APD PE v1.00

2-2 ID_Civ Death in Cbt Ops (Reuters Employees) 12JUL07 IO MAJ b)(6), (b)(3

STATEMENT OF ___ILT___ (b)(6), (b)(3) ___ TAKEN AT _COP Bushmaster_ DATED _14 JUL 07_

9. STATEMENT *(Continued)*

Question 2: Person 1 was south of the of the van. Person two was near a courtyard where the 11th man (not pictured was). Person 3 was the group of 3 individuals. Person 4 was about 5m east of person 3 lying on top of an RPG round. Near him was the black and tan camera. Person 5 was about 10 meters north east of the van. Person 6 was in an open area w/ trash in the center of the courtyard. Person 7 was also near the center of the courtyard. The two kids were still in the van on the passenger side of the cab. The driver of the van was dead and slumped over in his seat.

Question 4: I also picked up the black and tan camera by person 4 and secured it in the LMTV. The all black camera was secured by my soldiers, which was near the 11th man in the courtyard. Once the rest of the company arrived on the OBJ we secured it until the NPs came to secure all of the bodies.

——— nothing follows ———

(b)(6)

INITIALS OF PERSON MAKING STATEMENT

(b)(6)

PAGE 2 OF 3 PAGES

DA FORM 2823, NOV 2006

APD PE v1.00

2-2 ID_Civ Death in Cbt Ops (Reuters Employees) 12JUL07 IO MAJ)(6), (b)(

STATEMENT OF __1LT__ (b)(6), (b)(3) ___ TAKEN AT _COP Bushmaster_ DATED 14JUL07

9. STATEMENT (Continued)

(b)(6)

AFFIDAVIT

I, __1LT__ (b)(6), (b)(3) _____, HAVE READ OR HAVE HAD READ TO ME THIS STATEMENT
WHICH BEGINS ON PAGE 1, AND ENDS ON PAGE __3__ . I FULLY UNDERSTAND THE CONTENTS OF THE ENTIRE STATEMENT MADE
BY ME. THE STATEMENT IS TRUE. I HAVE INITIALED ALL CORRECTIONS AND HAVE INITIALED THE BOTTOM OF EACH PAGE
CONTAINING THE STATEMENT. I HAVE MADE THIS STATEMENT FREELY WITHOUT HOPE OF BENEFIT OR REWARD, WITHOUT
THREAT OF PUNISHMENT, AND WITHOUT COERCION, UNLAWFUL INFLUENCE, OR UNLAWFUL INDUCEMENT.

(b)(6), (b)(3)

(b)(3)(b6)   (Signature of Person Making Statement)

WITNESSES: Subscribed and sworn to before me, a person authorized by law to
administer oaths, this __14th__ day of __July__ , __2007__
_____   at _COP Bushmaster_ _____

(b)(6), (b)(3)

ORGANIZATION OR ADDRESS   b3)(b6   (Signature of Person Administering Oath)

(b)(6), (b)(3)

(Typed Name of Person Administering Oath)

ORGANIZATION OR ADDRESS   (Authority To Administer Oaths)

INITIALS OF PERSON MAKING STATEMENT
(b)(6)   PAGE 3 OF 3 PAGES

DA FORM 2823, NOV 2006   APD PE v1.00

2-2 ID_Civ Death in Cbt Ops (Reuters Employees) 12JUL07 IO MA (b)(6), (b)(3

SWORN STATEMENT

For use of this form, see AR 190-45; the proponent agency is PMG.

PRIVACY ACT STATEMENT

AUTHORITY: Title 10, USC Section 301; Title 5, USC Section 2951; E.O. 9397 Social Security Number (SSN).

PRINCIPAL PURPOSE: To document potential criminal activity involving the U.S. Army, and to allow Army officials to maintain discipline, law and order through investigation of complaints and incidents.

ROUTINE USES: Information provided may be further disclosed to federal, state, local, and foreign government law enforcement agencies, prosecutors, courts, child protective services, victims, witnesses, the Department of Veterans Affairs, and the Office of Personnel Management. Information provided may be used for determinations regarding judicial or non-judicial punishment, other administrative disciplinary actions, security clearances, recruitment, retention, placement, and other personnel actions.

DISCLOSURE: Disclosure of your SSN and other information is voluntary.

1. LOCATION FOB Rustamiyah, Baghdad, Ir	2. DATE *(YYYYMMDD)* 2007 07 14	3. TIME 1530	4. FILE NUMBER

5. LAST NAME, FIRST NAME, MIDDLE NAME (b)(6), (b)(3)	6. SSN (b)(6), (b)(3)	7. GRADE/STATUS O-2

8. ORGANIZATION OR ADDRESS
HHC / 2-16 IN

9.

I, _____ (b)(6) _____, WANT TO MAKE THE FOLLOWING STATEMENT UNDER OATH:

Question 1: What was your mission/orders on the morning of 12 July 2007?
The mortar platoon was tasked to contain/isolate the eastern side of the Battalion Objective in order to prevent any local nationals from entering or exiting the area.

Question 2: When you arrived at the scene of the Apache/van engagement ((b)(6)), what did you observe?
Upon arrival at the scene of the Apache/van engagement I observed approximately eight military aged males dead vicinity the North west corner. There was Bushmaster elements already on scene and a Bradley which was being used as the CASEVAC platform.

Question 3: During what time period were you present at this location?
I was present on scene from approximately 121230JUL07 to 121400JUL07

Question 4: What actions did you take while at this location?
While on scene I moved my platoon to the north east corner where we secured that side of the objective.

Question 5: What significant events (if any) occurred at this location while you were present?
While on scene Crazy Horse (the Apaches) engaged a house to the east where people with weapons were observed going in. There was also an RPG round blown in place by EOD.

Question 6: Did you observe anyone (dead or wounded), that you believed to be a noncombatant? Why?
No I personally did not see any dead or wounded who were not military aged males.

(b)(6)

10. EXHIBIT	11. INITIALS OF PERSON MAKING STATEMENT (b)(6)	PAGE 1 OF 2 PAGES

ADDITIONAL PAGES MUST CONTAIN THE HEADING "STATEMENT OF _____ TAKEN AT _____ DATED _____

THE BOTTOM OF EACH ADDITIONAL PAGE MUST BEAR THE INITIALS OF THE PERSON MAKING THE STATEMENT, AND PAGE NUMBER MUST BE INDICATED.

DA FORM 2823, NOV 2006   DA FORM 2823, DEC 1998, IS OBSOLETE   APD PE v1.00

2-2 ID_Civ Death in Cbt Ops (Reuters Employees) 12JUL07 IO MAJ (b)(6), (b)(

9. STATEMENT   *(Continued)*

(b)(6)

AFFIDAVIT

I,   (b)(6), (b)(3)   , HAVE READ OR HAVE HAD READ TO ME THIS STATEMENT WHICH BEGINS ON PAGE 1, AND ENDS ON PAGE ___2___ . I FULLY UNDERSTAND THE CONTENTS OF THE ENTIRE STATEMENT MADE BY ME. THE STATEMENT IS TRUE. I HAVE INITIALED ALL CORRECTIONS AND HAVE INITIALED THE BOTTOM OF EACH PAGE CONTAINING THE STATEMENT. I HAVE MADE THIS STATEMENT FREELY WITHOUT HOPE OF BENEFIT OR REWARD, WITHOUT THREAT OF PUNISHMENT, AND WITHOUT COERCION, UNLAWFUL INF (b)(6), (b)(3)

(b)(6), (b)(3)

(Signature of Person M (b)(6), (b)(3) 3)(b)

WITNESSES:

(b)(6), (b)(3)

Subscribed and sworn to before me, a person authorized by law to administer oaths, this _14_ day of _July_ , _2007_

at _FOB Rustamiyah, IRAQ_

HHC 2-16 IN

ORGANIZATION OR ADDRESS

(b)(6), (b)(3)

(b)(3)(b6) *(Signature of Person Administering Oath)*

(b)(6), (b)(3)

_1 LT_ *(Typed Name of Person Administering Oath)*

ORGANIZATION OR ADDRESS

(Authority To Administer Oaths)

INITIALS OF PERSON MAKING STATEMENT

(b)(6)

PAGE _2_ OF _2_ PAGES

2-2 ID_Civ Death in Cbt Ops (Reuters Employees) 12JUL07 IO MAJ (b)(6), (b)

1. LOCATION		2. DATE (YYYYMMDD)	3. TIME	4. FILE NUMBER
COP Busamaster , Baghdad, Iraq		20070712		

5. LAST NAME, FIRST NAME, MIDDLE NAME	6. SSN	7. GRADE/STATUS
(b)(6), (b)(3)	(b)(6), (b)(3)	E-4

8. ORGANIZATION OR ADDRESS

B CO 2-16 In 4SBCt 1stID

9.

I, _____(b)(6), (b)(3)_____ , WANT TO MAKE THE FOLLOWING STATEMENT UNDER OATH:

Question 1: What was your mission/orders on the morning of 12 July 2007?

To cordon/clear objectives bronze and silver

Question 2: When you arrived at the scene of the Apache/van engagement (b)(2)High , what did you observe?

what appeared to be three bodies in the street, 3-4 bodies that were piled near the east wall, 1 body inside, and 1 WIA still alive inside the courtyard. I did not inspect the van, or see if there were any bodies near the van

Question 3: During what time period were you present at this location?

Approx 1000 - 1130

Question 4: What actions did you take while at this location?

Initially I started treatment of the military age male in the courtyard. he had shrapnel damage to both lower extremities, and his (R) arm. I applied a tourniquet to the three main affected limbs and proceded to cut his clothes off to check for further injury. I found 2 superficial wounds along (cont.)

Question 5: What significant events (if any) occurred at this location while you were present?

The military age male that was pulled off the RPG and initially believed to be dead was found to be breathing. Both wounded males were evacuated.

Question 6: Did you observe anyone (dead or wounded), that you believed to be a noncombatant? Why?

I did not see any evidence that any of the dead or injured were non-combatants. All were in the vicinity of weapons (AK-47's/RPgs) and there were no visible press passes, or other indicators that they were noncombatants

10. EXHIBIT	11. INITIALS OF PERSON MAKING STATEMENT		
M	(b)(6)	PAGE 1 OF 3 PAGES

2-2 ID_Civ Death in Cbt Ops (Reuters Employees) 12JUL07 IO MAJ (6), (b)

(b)(6)

STATEMENT OF SPc ⬛⬛⬛ (b)(6), (b)(3) ⬛⬛⬛ TAKEN AT COP Bashmaster DATED 20070714

9. STATEMENT   (Continued)

continuing question 4: the lateral portion of his (R) chest with one deep penitrating wound to his abdomen. He continuously made the sign for drinking, and asked for water (which made me suspect abdominal injury/poss internal bleeding) I denied him water based on medical findings. I also found what appeared to be scars on his back that looked recent, though I can not ascertain what they were from. I bandaged this male as much as possible before I was alerted to a second survivor.
this male was in the street, and had been pulled off the RPG that EOD later destroyed in place. He was breathing, but bleeding, with a large amount of shrapnel damage to lower extremities. I applied 1 CAT to his (R) Leg, and 1 Israeli bandage to his (L) calf. I did not notice any other injuries and the priority became transport. We transported them to the checkpoint on RtE Pluto, where, there we transfered them to Iraqi EMS.

———————— Nothing follows ————————

(b)(6)

9. STATEMENT   *(Continued)*

(b)(6)

AFFIDAVIT

I, __SPC__ (b)(6), (b)(3) _____, HAVE READ OR HAVE HAD READ TO ME THIS STATEMENT
WHICH BEGINS ON PAGE 1, AND ENDS ON PAGE _____. I FULLY UNDERSTAND THE CONTENTS OF THE ENTIRE STATEMENT MADE
BY ME. THE STATEMENT IS TRUE. I HAVE INITIALED ALL CORRECTIONS AND HAVE INITIALED THE BOTTOM OF EACH PAGE
CONTAINING THE STATEMENT. I HAVE MADE THIS STATEMENT FREELY WITHOUT HOPE OF BENEFIT OR REWARD, WITHOUT
THREAT OF PUNISHMENT, AND WITHOUT COERCION, UNLAWFUL INFLUENCE, OR UNLAWFUL INDUCEMENT.

(b)(6), (b)(3)

(Signature of Person Making Statement)

WITNESSES:

Subscribed and sworn to before me, a person authorized by law to
administer oaths, this __14__ day of __July__, __2007__
at _____ (b), (b)

(b)(6), (b)(3)

_____
ORGANIZATION OR ADDRESS

(Signature of Person Administering Oath)

(b)(6), (b)(3)

(Typed Name of Person Administering Oath)

_____
ORGANIZATION OR ADDRESS

(Authority To Administer Oaths)

INITIALS OF PERSON MAKING STATEMENT

(b)(6)

PAGE 3 OF 5 PAGES

DA FORM 2823, NOV 2006

APD PE v1.00

2-2 ID_Civ Death in Cbt Ops (Reuters Employees) 12JUL07 IO MAJ (6), (b)

SWORN STATEMENT

For use of this form, see AR 190-45; the proponent agency is PMG.

PRIVACY ACT STATEMENT

1. LOCATION COP Bushmaster , Baghdad, Ir	2. DATE (YYYYMMDD) 20070714	3. TIME 1030	4. FILE NUMBER

5. LAST NAME, FIRST NAME, MIDDLE NAME (b)(6), (b)(3)	6. SSN (b)(6), (b)(3)	7. GRADE/STATUS O-2

8. ORGANIZATION OR ADDRESS
2ND PLT B Co 2-16 IN 1ID

9. I, (b)(6), (b)(3) , WANT TO MAKE THE FOLLOWING STATEMENT UNDER OATH:

Question 1: What was your mission/orders on the morning of 12 July 2007?
To Clear OBJ Bronze + Silver South BCT facilitate the BN ME and allow freedom of Maneuver for fellow Rangers.

Question 2: When you arrived at the scene of the Apache/van engagement ((b)(2)High what did you observe?
My PLT was 3rd in ODM and arrived at the OBJ at app 1000. When we arrived I observed 3rd plt establishing security as well as multiple male bodies and weapons scattered among the scene.

Question 3: During what time period were you present at this location?
I was present on location from 1000-1130.

Question 4: What actions did you take while at this location?
My plt task on the OBJ was to secure EOD while they destroyed the ordinance as well as the N + W cordon of the OBJective.

Question 5: What significant events (if any) occurred at this location while you were present?
When I arrived on scene I noticed soldiers from 2-16 + 1-8 CAV evacing 2 small children from the scene. During clearing of the scene we came across 1 male still alive but badly injured where my medic (b)(6), (b)(3) immediately begoun working on to help save.

Question 6: Did you observe anyone (dead or wounded), that you believed to be a noncombatant? Why? on to help save.
No I believe all were involved. There were 2 rpg launchers, multiple rounds for them and an AK-47 on scene. Some of the males were describe by Hotel 2-6 as the ones taking pop shots at his PLT all day. All males were found within 20 meter radios to the wpn on the ground. Between the radio traffic from Crazy Horse before and during the engagement as well as what I took note of on scene. I believe that all males involved were not in any way non combatants.

10. EXHIBIT (b)(5) N	11. INITIALS OF PERSON MAKING STATEMENT (b)(6)	PAGE 1 OF 3 PAGES

ADDITIONAL PAGES MUST CONTAIN THE HEADING "STATEMENT OF _____ TAKEN AT _____ DATED _____

THE BOTTOM OF EACH ADDITIONAL PAGE MUST BEAR THE INITIALS OF THE PERSON MAKING THE STATEMENT, AND PAGE NUMBER MUST BE INDICATED.

DA FORM 2823, NOV 2006   DA FORM 2823, DEC 1998, IS OBSOLETE   APD PE v1.00

2-2 ID_Civ Death in Cbt Ops (Reuters Employees) 12JUL07 IO MAJ (6), (b)

STATEMENT OF ▮▮▮ (b)(6) ▮▮▮ TAKEN AT _Cop Bushmaske_ DATED _2007 07 14_

9. STATEMENT *(Continued)*

Body 1 was located about 5 meters from the van on the south side.

Body 2 was located on the inside courtyard from the RPG launcher, about a meter away

Body 3,5,6 - were huddled together with 1 AK-47 and RPG launcher about 5 meters north of the van.

Body 4 - was laying in the middle of the street w/ 1 RPG round under his body about 1 meter from bodies 5,4,6.

Body 7 - located across the street from bodies 3-5 about 5 metes

Body 8 - located in trash pile about 5-10 meters from body 7

Body 9 - located about 1 meter from body 5. Nothing Follows. ▮(b)(6)▮

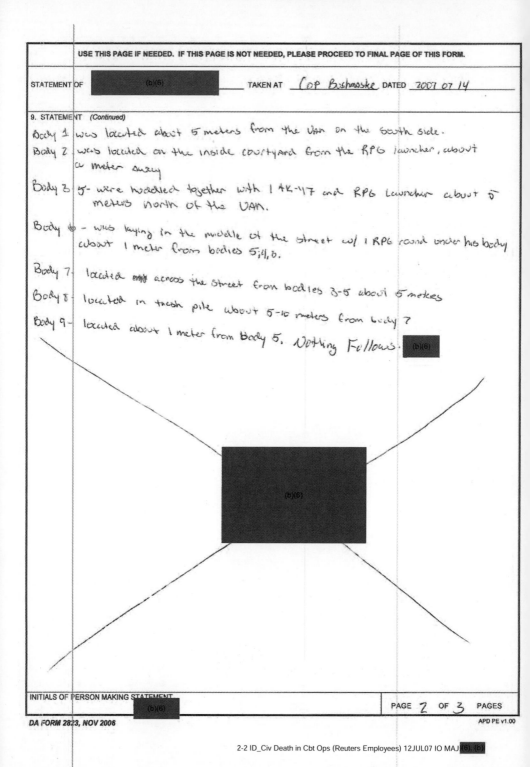

INITIALS OF PERSON MAKING STATEMENT ▮(b)(6)▮   PAGE 2 OF 3 PAGES

DA FORM 2823, NOV 2006   APD PE v1.00

STATEMENT OF ▮(b)(6)▮ TAKEN AT Cop Bushmaster DATED 20070714

9. STATEMENT *(Continued)*

AFFIDAVIT

I, ▮(b)(6)▮ , HAVE READ OR HAVE HAD READ TO ME THIS STATEMENT
WHICH BEGINS ON PAGE 1, AND ENDS ON PAGE 3 . I FULLY UNDERSTAND THE CONTENTS OF THE ENTIRE STATEMENT MADE
BY ME. THE STATEMENT IS TRUE. I HAVE INITIALED ALL CORRECTIONS AND HAVE INITIALED THE BOTTOM OF EACH PAGE
CONTAINING THE STATEMENT. I HAVE MADE THIS STATEMENT FREELY WITHOUT HOPE OF BENEFIT OR REWARD, WITHOUT
THREAT OF PUNISHMENT, AND WITHOUT COERCION, UNLAWFUL INFLUENCE ▮(b)(6)▮

▮(b)(6)▮
(Signature of Person Making Statement)

WITNESSES:

Subscribed and sworn to before me, a person authorized by law to
administer oaths, this 14 day of July , 2007
at COP Bushmaster Baghdad, Iraq

_____

ORGANIZATION OR ADDRESS

▮(b)(6)▮
(Signature of Person Administering Oath)

▮(b)(6)▮
(Typed Name of Person Administering Oath)

_____
ORGANIZATION OR ADDRESS

UC, MF
(Authority To Administer Oaths)

INITIALS OF PERSON MAKING STATEMENT
▮(b)(6)▮

PAGE 3 OF 3 PAGES

DA FORM 2823, NOV 2006

APD PE v1.00

2-2 ID_Civ Death in Cbt Ops (Reuters Employees) 12JUL07 IO MAJ ▮(6), (b)▮

Photos

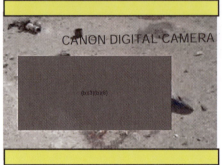

Exhibit O

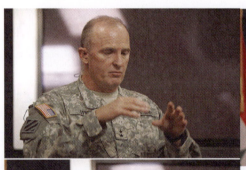

MG Lynch Press Conference at
Coalition Press Information Center,
International Zone, Baghdad, Iraq.

24 JUNE, 2007 1437 Hours

HIBIT P

Possibly Mr (b)(6)

11 JULY, 2007 1038 Hours

IBIT Q

Bravo Company, 2-16 IN HMMWV

12 JULY, 2007 1026 Hours

HIBIT R

Reuters employees killed in Iraq

Thu Jul 12, 2007 6:08PM BST

Email This Article | Print This Article | RSS

-Text+LONDON (Reuters) - An Iraqi photographer and driver working for Reuters in Iraq were killed in Baghdad on Thursday in what police said was American military action and witnesses described as a helicopter attack.

Photographer Namir Noor-Eldeen, 22, and driver Saeed Chmagh, 40, were killed in eastern Baghdad, the international news and information company said.

The U.S. military said it was looking into the reports but had no immediate statement.

A preliminary police report obtained by Reuters said Noor-Eldeen and Chmagh had been killed by a "random American bombardment" that killed nine other people.

The report was issued by the al-Rashad police station, the closest station to the scene. Reuters obtained a photocopy of the report. It was based upon witness accounts of the incident and signed by a lieutenant-colonel, the head of the station.

Noor-Eldeen had called a Reuters colleague to say he was taking photographs of a damaged building.

Witnesses interviewed by Reuters in the al-Amin al-Thaniyah neighbourhood said Noor-Eldeen and Chmagh, who also worked as a cameraman's assistant, were near the building around the time a U.S. helicopter fired on a minivan.

"The aircraft began striking randomly and people were wounded. A Kia (minivan) arrived to take them away. They hit the Kia and killed ... the two journalists," said one witness, Karim Shindakh.

Shindakh and three other witnesses said U.S. soldiers came and took Noor-Eldeen's camera equipment, which has not been recovered

A witness has returned Noor-Eldeen's press cards to Reuters.

TV footage showed the front of the minivan had been badly mangled. There was a large hole in the roof. A pool of blood lay near the curb, while shrapnel marks pocked the wall of a house.

The deaths take to six the number of Reuters employees killed in Iraq since U.S.-led forces invaded the country in 2003 to topple Saddam Hussein.

"Once again we are left mourning colleagues who have met an untimely death while doing their job in Iraq," said Reuters chief executive Tom Glocer.

2-2 ID_Civ Death in Cbt Ops (Reuters Employees) 12JUL07 IO MAJ (6), (b)

"Our sympathies and thoughts are with their families, friends and colleagues today," added Glocer.

"Noor-Eldeen and Chmagh's outstanding contribution to reporting on the unfolding events in Iraq has been vital. They stand alongside other colleagues in Reuters who have died doing a job that they believe in."

Reuters Editor-in-Chief David Schlesinger said the deaths were a tragic reminder of the risks journalists face in covering the war in Iraq.

"The job our reporters do is a critical one - telling the world what is happening on the streets of Iraq on a daily basis," said Schlesinger.

"Reuters will continue to do all it can to protect journalists who must work in dangerous and difficult conditions but still have a right to do their jobs."

Noor-Eldeen was single. Chmagh was married with four children.

GLOSSARY

Unfortunately, when dealing with the military there are hundreds of abbreviations and phrases used to mean different things. Most, if not all, are not obvious in their meanings, so I have attempted to aid the reader who is unfamiliar with this by explaining some of them for you here.

AIF: Anti-Iraqi Forces. The catchall term used to describe bad guys who were shooting at us. Since it was difficult to determine exactly what sect or organization someone belonged to from the aircraft, anyone hostile that we engaged were typically called AIF.

air assault: An air assault is the process of inserting a unit (as small as a squad of ten or as large as a battalion of four hundred) of soldiers on an objective/target by helicopter. Is also used as an all-purpose phrase at Fort Rucker, Alabama (the home of Army aviation), or at least it was when I attended flight school. It was used as a greeting of the day and as an acknowledgment of some piece of information being passed along by a fellow soldier. For example, "Go over there and paint that trash can, Candidate McClinton." "Air assault, Sir!" For some it's the "Hooah" of Army aviation.

AMPS: Aviation Mission Planning System. A hardened computer designed to be a portable mission-planning station for aviation operations in austere environments. Loaded with special software, it can be used to develop flight routes and to plan and rehearse aviation missions. For operations with AH-64Ds, it is used primarily to load information onto a computer data card (the size of a credit card; also known as a PCMICA) that is inserted into the aircraft, which transfers mission data to the aircraft computer.

AQI: Al Qaeda Iraq

AWT: Attack weapons team (usually 2 × AH-64s). Prior to 9/11, US Army attack helicopter battalions trained to fight formations of enemy armor as company (six to eight ships) or battalion (up to twenty-four aircraft) elements. The nature of the enemy we were facing in Afghanistan and Iraq caused a change in tactics; part of that was operating in two-ship formations called attack weapons teams.

battle captain: The battle captain is the commander's representative in the tactical operations center or command post. They are there to make day-to-day decisions involving the battalion's aircraft, pass information to the AWTs, and interact with the units we support.

BDE: Brigade. An aviation brigade at that time (2006–2007) usually consisted of two battalions of attack-recon aircraft (AH-64s or OH-58Ds) and two battalions of lift and medevac assets (UH-60s and CH-47s) and an aviation intermediate maintenance battalion (AVIM). During OIF 06-08, the 1st Air Cavalry Brigade (1 ACB) had the following units assigned to it: 1st and 4th BN, 227th Aviation Regiment, which were equipped with AH-64D Longbow Apaches; 2nd and 3rd BN, 227th Aviation Regiment, which were equipped UH-60s for lift and medevac and CH-47D Chinooks and the 615th Forward Support Battalion (FSB), which provided additional aviation maintenance support.

BFT: Blue Force Tracker was a transponder system that was installed on aircraft and ground vehicles; linked to the moving map display in the cockpit of an AH-64, it allowed the crew to quickly locate the position of friendly forces on the battlefield. We would also use its text-messaging capabilities to send messages to our command post.

BHO: Battle handover. A process by which one attack weapons team would hand over an operation that was in progress to another team. We utilized a checklist giving us specific items to be briefed in a certain order, so everyone knew what to expect.

BN: Battalion. A battalion is an organization of around four hundred soldiers. Aviation battalions usually have six companies, Alpha through Echo, and Headquarters and Headquarters Company, also called HHC.

CAS: Close air support. A term usually used in reference to USAF USN or USMC attack or fighter aircraft being used to drop ordnance in support of ground operations. The most common CAS platforms in theater were the F-16, F/A18, and A-10.

CH-47: Medium cargo helicopter used by the US Army. Also called a Chinook, Shit-hook, Nonessential Bus (look, he made an electrical joke!), the School Bus, Two Palm Trees Humping a Dumpster, or just Hook. During OIF 06-08 they flew almost exclusively at night.

CO: When used in a sentence and pronounced "See Oh," it refers to the commander or commanding officer. It can also be a written abbreviation for a unit of organization called a company. Confusing, I know, but that's the kind of people we are. A flight aviation company usually numbered between thirty and forty personnel. It was not uncommon for maintenance and support companies have over a hundred soldiers assigned.

COP: Combat outpost. The concept of the COP came into full bloom during the surge period of 2007–2008. During that time, units moved off the larger forward operating bases (FOB) such as Camp Taji and moved into small, defended areas among the populace.

CSM: Command sergeant major. The CSM is the senior ranking noncommissioned officer in a unit (BN and above). In a lot of aviation units, the CSM seemed to go out of their way to start fights with the warrant officers. I never quite understood that attitude. The buffoons who played that game were, for the most part, ineffectual oxygen thieves who were living examples of the "Peter principle."

CW2: The most common warrant officer rank in the US Army. Historically, it was the rank where you start to know something about what it is you are supposed to be doing as an aviator. This is the part where I lose it and go on a rant about how the US Army ruined flight school when they made all the warrant officer candidates WO1s when they started flight school. Back when I went to flight school (when it was hard), a warrant officer candidate (WOC) remained a WOC until the day before you received your wings at graduation. The day before you graduated flight school, you were appointed a warrant officer 1 in the United States Army. The purpose behind this was to remind you that you were an officer first, aviator second. You then went forth to your unit as a brand-new WO1, which you remained for two years until you were promoted to CW2. Now a flight school student is a WO1 for however long it takes to graduate from flight school and attend follow-on courses before arriving at their assigned unit. We would get pilots who were promoted to CW2 almost as soon as they arrived, and in some rare cases received some aviators who were promoted to CW2 while in flight school. The end result is that while in the old days seeing a CW2 usually meant something, now it's anyone's guess about the person's experience level.

CW4: Chief warrant officer 4. This was at one time the highest warrant officer grade, but somebody somewhere decided they needed another rank, and for our sins we got CW5s. A CW4 is the highest-ranking warrant officer assigned at the BN level.

CW5: There are many exceptions to this rule now, but when I first encountered CW5s, I couldn't think of a position that was more useless in Army aviation. CW5s were guys who hid out at BDE and came down to the BN on occasion to harass the junior warrant officers and generally make a nuisance of themselves; that is, when they weren't kissing the BDE commander's ass. That has changed a lot in the last several years, and we now have many people who are doing good things, although there is always that minority who are hanging around breathing everyone's oxygen and keeping the trees alive.

DIV: Division. In First Attack's case, we were assigned to the 1st Cavalry Division, normally based at Fort Hood, Texas. The division owns four ground maneuver brigades and the 1st Air Cavalry Brigade. A division usually has between ten thousand and sixteen thousand soldiers assigned to it.

FARP: Forward arming and refueling point. An area designated for helicopters to land and refuel and, if needed, rearm. Camp Taji had a FARP conveniently located east of the runway.

fast mover: A term used to describe fighter or attack aircraft, or any fixed-wing aircraft, for that matter

FLIR: Forward-looking infrared radar. It is a device that allows the viewer to see images produced by the heat of objects in the infrared light spectrum. On the AH-64D Longbow helicopter, a FLIR is integrated into the TADS. Threat identification through the FLIR system can be extremely difficult. Although the AH-64 crew can easily find the heat signature of a vehicle, it may not be able to determine friend or foe. Forward-looking infrared detects the difference in the emission of heat in objects. On a hot day, the ground may reflect or emit more heat than the suspected target. In this case, the environment will be "hot" and the target will be "cool." As the air cools at night, the target may lose or emit heat at a lower rate than the surrounding environment. At some point the emission of heat both from the target and the surrounding environment may be equal. This phenomenon is called IR crossover, and it makes target acquisition/detection difficult to impossible. IR crossover occurs most often when there is high humidity, or the environment is wet. This is because the water in the air creates a buffer in the emissivity of objects. This limitation is present in all systems that use FLIR for target acquisition. As technology has advanced, this has become less and less of an issue, but during OIF 06-08 it was a major factor on occasion.

FOB: Forward operating base (pronounced like Bob, but with an F sound at the beginning). A FOB was a little slice of America in Iraq. Huge sprawling bases that over time held just about anything a base back home had, with the added attraction of incoming mortar and rocket fire. The FOB that 1-227th ARB operated out of was a former Iraqi military base known as Camp Taji, which at one time was also known as Camp Cooke. People who live on FOBs but never go outside the wire on missions are called FOBBITs.

HDU: Helmet display unit. See IHADSS for more info.

HESCO basket: The HESCO basket is used for flood control and military fortification. It is made of a collapsible wire mesh container and heavy-duty fabric liner and used as a temporary to semipermanent dike or barrier against blasts or small arms. It has seen considerable use in Iraq and Afghanistan. The name comes from the British company that developed it in the 1980s. Assembling the HESCO basket involves unfolding it and filling it with sand, dirt, or gravel. It's so simple a caveman could do it.

Hooah: Hooah (pronounced "WHO-ah") is a catchall phrase that was originally meant to be a sign of enthusiasm. Its abuse over the years has led to use of the word in a cynical or sarcastic manner and even brought about the establishment of "Hooah-free zones." Today most people who use this word are either clueless or sycophants hoping to impress the boss. Personally, I avoided the use of this word at all costs. To me, hooah is the sound a mind makes when it slams shut.

HVT: High-value target. Somebody at Multi-National Division–Baghdad (MND-B) kept a most-wanted list; the people on it were considered high-value targets. The 1-227th assisted on missions whose goal was the capture HVTs, but often this most-wanted list didn't mean too much to the average crew.

IHADSS: AH-64 aviators use the Integrated Helmet and Display Sighting System (IHADSS). The IHADSS helmet, at the time of its development, was lighter in weight and provided improved impact protection over the then-current SPH-4-series helmet. The IHADSS was the only helmet approved for the AH-64 and has been in use for over twenty years. A unique feature of the IHADSS helmet is that it serves as a platform for a helmet-mounted display (HMD, a.k.a. HDU). The HMD provides pilotage and fire control imagery and flight symbology. In order to view the HMD imagery, the helmet/HMD must be fitted such that the exit pupil of the HMD is properly aligned with the aviator's eye each time it is donned. This makes the fit and stability of the IHADSS helmet critical considerations. Achieving a proper fit of the IHADSS helmet is complicated by its intricate system of straps and pads. A proper, customized, repeatable fit is required in order to maintain the exit pupil position and optimize the resulting full field of view (FOV). Fitting of the IHADSS helmet typically takes several hours to complete. This fitting process must be repeated every time aviators are transferred to a new duty station, since they cannot take the IHADSS helmet with them. It is part of the AH-64 aircraft system and is unit property and a pain in the rear.

medevac: Medical evacuation, usually provided by an HH or UH-60 helicopter. Not to be confused with a CASEVAC, which is causality evacuation and uses any means of transportation available.

NVG: Night vision goggles. The Aviator Night Vision Imaging System (ANVIS) goggles are about the size of a small pair of binoculars, weigh about 20 ounces, and are mounted on the front of the pilot's flight helmet by means of a mounting and quick-disconnect assembly. An automatic gain control maintains uniform phosphor brightness to compensate for varying levels of infrared energy. Visual acuity for the unaided person at night is equal to having 20/200 vision. Current NVGs allow a person to see with the equivalent of 20/40 vision. The main drawback to the NVGs is the limited field of view, which requires constant scanning. Also, sometimes they are just referred to as "goggles," as in "I flew goggles last night."

OIF: Operation Iraqi Freedom. Each phase of OIF had a number. Initially OIF was referred to as OIF 1, 2, and 3, but eventually, as the war went on, OIF rotations were designated by the physical year they occurred in. The time span covered in this book was generally referred to as OIF 06-08.

PNVS: Pilot Night Vision System. To fly at night, the pilot of an AH-64 utilizes the PNVS. Mounted above the TADS on the nose of the aircraft, the PNVS contains an infrared camera slaved to the head movements of the pilot. The PNVS can rotate ±90 degrees in azimuth and +20/−45 degrees in elevation. The PNVS has a high rate of movement (120° per second) to enable it to accurately match the pilot's head movement. The images generated by the PNVS are directed to the HDU, which is mounted on the pilot's helmet and is also known as the Integrated Helmet and Display Sighting System (IHADSS).

REDCON: Readiness level. There are various readiness levels that apply toward getting an aircraft ready to fly. REDCON 1 means the aircraft is ready to take off. It is also sometimes shortened to RED 1. Each readiness level has a different meaning and time associated with it. For instance, RECON 2 meant that you are running on the APU and could depart within five minutes. We had an SOP that gave us the meanings of all these things, which I never could remember.

RLO: Real live officers. It's a phrase that some warrant officers use to describe commissioned officers. The fact is, warrant officers ARE commissioned officers when they reach the rank of CW2. The trouble is, more than a few commissioned officers treat warrant officers as an officer only when it suits them (when they need someone to do an officer job that they don't want to do); hence the term "RLO."

ROE: Rules of engagement are a constantly evolving set of rules that explain in excruciating detail when and where we are able to engage the enemy.

S1: The personnel section of a unit. It can also be used to describe the BN adjutant. Some people, to avoid confusion, also use the phrase "S1 actual," to ensure we are talking about the person and not the section.

S2: The intelligence section of a unit is often referred to as the S2. It can also be used to describe the BN intelligence officer.

S3: The operations section of a unit is often referred to as the S3. It can also be used to describe the BN operations officer. The S3 runs the TOC (*see below*) and produces operations orders that give the commanders intent and direct the BN.

S4: The supply section of a unit is referred to as the S4.

S6: The unit communications section

SIGACT: Significant action. This is usually related to combat, although it could mean anything that was considered 'significant." Pronounced "SIG-act."

SIPRNET: Secret Internet Protocol Routing Network. In other words, an internet connection capable of handling SECRET information. Also called "sipper," as in "I need to get on the sipper."

SOP: Standard operating procedure

spur ride: A "spur ride" is a technique where a downed aviator will attach himself to the outside of his wingman's aircraft and then be flown to safety. This is done by attaching a D ring that is on the aviator's survival vest and a strap to one of several hardpoints on the exterior of the aircraft. By all accounts, this was first done with AH-1 Cobras during the Vietnam War, and the practice has continued to this day, as has been seen in this book. The name "spur ride" comes from the practice that was used during the horse cavalry days to retrieve a rider who had lost his horse.

TACP: Tactical air control party is a small team of Air Force personnel who provide airspace deconfliction and terminal control of close air support. In simplified terms, they give approval for aircraft to drop bombs on or shoot at a specific target. While they belong to the Air Force, they are attached to various ground units across the battlefield. Pronounced: "TACK-pee."

TADS: Target Acquisition and Designation System. A complex device mounted on the nose of an AH-64, it consists of a FLIR, day television, and laser designator, which allows the crew (primarily the CPG) to locate, identify, and engage targets at distances outside the effective range of the enemy's weapon systems.

TIC: Troops in contact. Pronounced "tick." TIC had the second priority of any mission we flew; medical evacuation (medevac) was first. A TIC meant that friendly forces were in contact with the enemy and had requested air support. We would normally move at our fastest available speed to the friendly location once a TIC was received. Additionally, most TICs became TWICs (troops were in contact) once the enemy heard the approaching aircraft. If they were still there when we arrived, they were either deaf, highly motivated, crazy, or a combination of all of the above.

TOC: Tactical operations center. The TOC was the command post, which was in the headquarters building. The battle captain works there, and aircrews receive their mission briefing there. During OIF 06-08, First Attack's TOC was a large room with about ten to twenty computers (all with SIPRNET access), several radios, and a Blue Force Tracker console. Pronounced "tock."

TOT: Time on target

UH-60: A troop transport helicopter acquired by the Army in the 1980s to attempt to replace the irreplaceable, the UH-1 Huey. Known as the Black Hawk, Shit-hawk, or Sixties, or sometimes shortened to just Hawk. We called the pilots lift guys, hawk drivers, leaf eaters, or herbivores, depending on how big of jerks they or we were being at the time.

warrant officer: Warrant officers in the United States are technical leaders and specialists. Chief warrant officers are commissioned by the president of the United States and take the same oath as regular commissioned officers. They may be technical experts, with long service as enlisted personnel, or direct entrants, notably for US Army helicopter pilots. Warrant officer aviators are notable for their striking good looks, incredible bravery, good humor, and modesty.

Winchester: Code word for out of ammunition

ENDNOTES

Chapter 4

1. Pamala Hess, "Analysis: Black Hawk Down Heroes," UPI, February 16, 2007, https://www.upi.com/Defense-News/2007/02/16/ Analysis-Black-Hawk-down-heroes/27701171638229/.

Chapter 5

1. Lorianne Woodrow Moss, "Unsung Heroes: The Army Scout Who Swam through a River and Cut through an Electric Fence," Task and Purpose, May 28, 2015, https://taskandpurpose.com/community/ unsung-heroes-the-army-scout-who-swam-through-a-river-and-cut-through-an-electric-fence/.

2. "GIs Return to Their War Zone and Find It Peaceful," NBC News, January 10, 2010, https://www.nbcnews.com/id/wbna34790128.

3. Michael Hutson, "I Didn't Know Screen Doors Could Fly," *Knowledge* (US Army Safety Center), August 2011, 6–9.

Chapter 7

1. Robert Gates, speech regarding "the Surge," April 11, 2007, http://www.defense.gov/transcripts/transcript.aspx?transcriptid=3928.

2. Christopher Walach, e-message to the battalion staff, April 16, 2007.

3. Ann Scott Tyson, "Pilots Shot Down in Iraq Tell of Dramatic Escape," *Washington Post*, July 4, 2007.

4. Nathan Hoskins, "1st Air Cav Pilots Recognized for Daring Rescue," 1st Air Cavalry Brigade Public Affairs Office, July 27, 2007.

5. Greg Jaffe, "At Lonely Outpost, GIs Stay as Hope Fades," *Wall Street Journal*, May 3, 2007.

6. Ernesto Londono and Amit R Paley, "In Iraq, a Surge in US Airstrikes; Military Says Attacks Save Troops' Lives, but Civilian Casualties Elicit Criticism," *Washington Post*, May 23, 2008.

INDEX

A

AGM-114, 18, 200

AIF, 23–25, 49, 54, 69, 73, 79, 81, 96–98, 124, 133–134, 162–163, 172, 178, 188, 198

Air Medal, 140

An Najaf, 12, 72–73, 78

AQI, 60, 79, 160

Attack Weapons Team, 15, 160–161, 165, 212

Awards, 87, 140, 148

AWT, 15, 20, 23, 32–33, 52, 58, 63, 68–69, 72, 74–75, 78–79, 96–101, 118, 124, 133–134, 141–143, 150, 153, 160–163, 165–166, 175, 178, 180, 187, 197–198, 212

B

Baghdad, 17, 24, 26, 36, 46, 48, 52–54, 59, 62–64, 66–68, 72, 82, 88, 112, 116–117, 120, 122, 131–133, 135-137, 140–141, 148–149, 153–154, 160-161, 163–164, 167–169, 171, 175, 181, 211–214

Baghdad International Airport, 24

Balad, 24, 66, 97, 101, 105–106, 123, 133, 135, 207

BIAP, 24, 112, 131–133, 142, 181

C

D

E

F